Walking London's River

The Thames from Hampton Court

to Woolwich

By the same authors:

INDIA Travellers Survival Kit
SRI LANKA Travellers Survival Kit

Walking London's River

The Thames from Hampton Court

to Woolwich

John Leak

Colette Leak

"I love walking in London.
Really it's better than walking in the country."
Mrs Dalloway, Virginia Woolf, 1925.

Point One Publishing

Walking London's River
The Thames from Hampton Court to Woolwich

ISBN-13 9798326231239

Published by:
Point One Publishing
5 Hoselaw Farm Cottages
Kelso
TD5 8BP
thamesbook@outlook.com

Contents

Wanderings among the walks

3. Practical Stuff

4. Sources

5. And finally…

1. Background

THE RIVER THAMES

The River Thames, at 215 miles (346km), is the longest river flowing entirely through England. The Thames rises at Thames Head seasonal springs near Cirencester in Gloucestershire; this is 109m (356ft) above sea level. The river is held to end at The Nore sandbank near the Isle of Sheppey in the estuary. The River Severn is slightly longer at 220 miles (354km), and has a much greater flow than the Thames, but rises in Wales and flows through Wales before crossing the border into England.

The origin of the name Thames is obscure. The Romans called it Tamesis, presumably adapting an already existing name. The French Thamise and the German Themse follow the theme. Between its source and where it is joined by the River Thame the river is often referred to as the Isis, especially around Oxford. The origin of Isis is equally obscure. It was recorded as Isa in ca1360 and as Isis in 1577. The idea that Thame and Isis combined to form Tamesis does not hold water. The tidal reach below Teddington Lock is known as as the Tideway.

Forty-five locks control river levels and allow navigation. The only ones we walk past are at Teddington (which is also the largest) and Richmond. Until fifty years ago, these locks were busy with barges carrying coal, timber and other bulk cargo upstream.

During the 17th century the Thames was still clean enough for its fish to be a good part of Londoners' diet. The stories that a clause in the indentures of London apprentices limited the number of times a week they could be fed salmon appear to be apocryphal; and are told in several other parts of the world.

Not long after that, the Thames became London's sewer. Pepys remarked on 'houses of office', or latrines, built over the river and its tributaries. Because the river is tidal, this detritus does not simply flow out to sea. Things became worse in the 19th century with population growth and industrial pollution. Oxygen was absent from the water and nothing could live in it. In later years, a docker or waterman who fell in was taken straight to hospital for a stomach pump and a typhoid shot.

Before the mid-19th century, much of London's drinking water came from the river and was the cause of many epidemics. Polluted water also seeped into wells some distance from the river. Cholera had arrived in London in 1832, probably by a ship from India. An outbreak in 1854 led Dr John Snow to

1

determine it was water-borne. He chained up the pump that was the source; it can still be seen in Broadwick Street in Soho. Nothing more was done until things came to a head 1858.

The Great Stink was the result of a hot summer and new sewers that flowed into the river. The smell was so bad that curtains soaked in bleaching powder (a nasty chemical made by treating slaked lime with chlorine gas) had to be hung over the windows of the Houses of Parliament. The politicians were forced to act, and Joseph Bazalgette (1819-1891) was commissioned to build a proper system leading to remote treatment plants. Drinking water was brought in from safer sources out to the West, and you pass one of these on the walk from Hampton Court Bridge to Kingston.

Problems persisted as heavy rain could overwhelm Bazalgette's system and cause raw sewage to flow into the river; as, for the moment, it still can. John remembers in the early 1960s travelling in a friend's speedboat from Putney Bridge to the Prospect of Whitby pub and encountering great masses of fermenting sewage floating on the surface. Never was a pint more welcome.

A new super-sewer under the river is due for completion in 2025 and should finally prevent any raw sewage form entering the river.

We refer to the North and South Banks. They can equally well be described as the Left and Right Banks as you look downstream. You may even hear the terms Middlesex and Surrey Banks after the old counties. Middlesex, swallowed up as London expanded, lives on in its cricket team. The -sex suffix, as in Middlesex, Essex and so on, comes from the same root as seaxe, a type of sword (as depicted on Kew Bridge). It means, simply, a place inhabited by Saxons.

LONDON

London was a Roman foundation, and is where it is because of the river. Whether there was a township here before the Romans settled it in AD43 is debatable. The Romans chose it because they could bring their ships this far up the river; it is also the lowest point at the river can forded or readily bridged. The Romans had built their first timber bridge by around AD60, probably nearer to Westminster than the present London Bridge, and the city grew around the two ends of it. The Romans built a walled city north of the river, and parts of this wall can be seen near Tower Hill tube station and at The Barbican.

The city prospered, growing to a population of 24,000 or so. Fragments come to light when the foundations for a new building are dug. This all came to an end in AD410 when Rome recalled the legions to deal with problems closer to home. The Roman city was left to fall apart and, despite reoccupation by Alfred the Great (871-899), that was it until William the Conqueror arrived on the scene in 1066.

The Normans restored order and, for the first time since the Romans, ruled a united England, plus southern Wales. Trade, mainly in textiles and wine, flourished, and the population grew steadily. There were perhaps 75,000 Londoners in 1500 at the beginning of the century that saw England emerge as a worldwide trading nation. By the end of the century the population was 200,000, and it doubled in the next fifty years. In the 16th century, it is reckoned that a quarter of London's population earned its living directly from the river.

By 1700, Britain had a well-developed international banking system, largely due to Dutch and Jewish know-how. The Jews had been excluded from England since 1290 until Oliver Cromwell invited them back in 1656 to help him finance his wars with Holland and Spain. Cromwell's godly Protestants and the Jews themselves believed that the move would hasten the return of their respective Messiahs. It certainly aided the growth of prosperity and, in due course, the professions and the arts.

Britain's colonisers were unashamedly bourgeois. Trade followed the flag, and strife was bad for business. By 1750, Great Britain was the largest trading nation in the world, and London the busiest port.

This and the availability of capital set the scene for the Industrial Revolution between 1760 and 1840. Most things that had been done by hand could now be done by machines. The advent of steam power also revolutionised transport, previously dependent on horse power and the wind. Contrary to the popular belief that this was a thing of the north of England and Clydeside in Scotland, London had its fair share of 'dark satanic mills'. Little was made elsewhere that was not also made in London.

London was the largest city in the world from 1831 to 1925 succeeding Pekin (as Beijing was then called) and handing over to New York in 1925. The actual figures were around 1,350,000 in 1831 and 7,750,000 in 1925.

Visitors used only to the centre of London will be pleasantly surprised at the countryside – not to mention peace and quiet – just a short train ride away.

THE NORTH BANK WALK

This walk follows the north or left bank as you face downstream, from Hampton Court to Trinity Buoy Wharf at the mouth of the River Lea. The total distance is 36½ miles/58.4km, though this is easily broken down into shorter distances using public transport. The directions assume that you start walking from the west towards Central London. Historically, this was often referred to as the Middlesex Bank from the ancient county of that name.

THE SOUTH BANK WALK

The full path runs from Teddington Lock through Richmond, Kew, and the centre of London to the River Darent. It is 33½ miles (54km) from Teddington Lock to the Woolwich Free Ferry (1½ miles (2.4km) past the Thames Barrier) and an extra 10 miles (16km) to the River Darent on the border between Outer London and Kent.

This South Bank Walk is part of the 185 miles (298km) Thames Path, one of Britain's long-distance footpaths, from the source of the river in Gloucestershire to the Woolwich foot tunnel. The South Bank Walk is generally freer from traffic noise and road walking than the North Bank.

THE ARMCHAIR THAMES

When the rain looks as if it will never stop, or you have a touch of man-flu, you can always enjoy the river from the comfort of your sitting room. All you need is this book, internet access, and an adequate supply of the beverage of choice.

www.panoramaofthethames.com will lead you to two panoramas of the Thames. The older is the Samuel Leigh Panorama of 1829. The original consisted of 45 hand-coloured prints, bound together in concertina form, and 60ft (18.3m) long. The panorama runs the 15 miles (24km) from Westminster to Richmond.

Its modern equivalent was shot mainly in 2014, and it is surprising how much has changed already.

Used with Open Street Map (www.openstreetmap.org) and, where traffic is allowed, Google Streetview, you can have a riverside stroll with the minimum of exertion.

2. The Walks

1. BUSHY PARK AND HAMPTON COURT

It may seem odd to start this walk with a place not even on the river. Bushy Park, however, is tied historically to Hampton Court Palace, and you can make a delightful circular walk from Kingston station through the park to the palace and back along the river. On the other hand, if you are tired of the hustle and bustle of London, the park is the perfect place to escape to the country.

When Henry VIII acquired Hampton Court Palace in 1526, he enclosed the park as his hunting reserve. There are still herds of wild deer in the park and, more recent interlopers, flocks of green parakeets, "live emeralds," as Edward Lear described them.

For the circular walk, cross Kingston Bridge, bear left, and turn right into Church Grove. Enter the park by Church Grove Passage opposite the Church of St John the Baptist. Past Hampton Wick Royal Cricket Club, you can continue straight to the Diana Fountain or branch right at roughly 45° between the copses to the SHAEF memorial. You may encounter a pond or two, but keep heading in the general direction.

During the Second World War, in the run-up to D-Day, **General Eisenhower** had his Supreme Headquarters Allied Expeditionary Forces (SHAEF) in the northern part of the park. There is a memorial to that effect and another to the United States Eighth Army Air Force (as it was until 1947), whose headquarters, Camp Griffiss, had been here since 1942. From here, it is an easy walk to Chestnut Avenue and on to the Diana Fountain.

Continuing on the direct path, behind the wall on your left are the stables and paddocks where shire horses are kept and bred. These are real working horses; they mow, do the haymaking, and haul the tourist wagons you may see. Note all the mistletoe in the trees approaching the Diana Fountain.

The **Chestnut Avenue** was laid out by Sir Christopher Wren in 1713 on the orders of William III as an approach to the palace. The **Diana Fountain** and its basin were part of this scheme. Diana is the Roman goddess of hunting, the countryside, and the moon, Artemis being her Greek equivalent. The French sculptor Hubert Le Sueur (ca1580-1658) made the statue and charged £200 for his efforts. This is a well-travelled statue; it was installed first in the gardens of Somerset House in central London during the reign of Charles I (1625-1649) and moved to the Privy Garden of Hampton Court Palace in 1656 during the Commonwealth.

Turn left at the fountain, and you come to the **Hampton Court Gate** of the park. Opposite is the **Lion Gate** of Hampton Court Palace; the lion couchant is of Coade stone and was modelled by Thomas Hardwicke in 1821. Looking through the gates, you can just see the end of the maze. Lion Gate is now permanently closed, so you can no longer walk through to the palace forecourt. Instead, walk past the King's Arms Hotel and follow the road around to the left. A couple of days before Christmas, a cherry tree was in blossom.

King's Arms Hotel, 2 Lion Gate, Hampton Court Road KT8 9DD. Attractive 17th century building. Real ale, but really more of a hotel/restaurant these days. Recent interior refurbishment draws much criticism.

Pretty much up until the 20th century, London was, by modern standards, a crowded, noisy, and filthy place. Just about anyone who could afford it wanted a place in the country. Given the poor roads and primitive carriages, the obvious place to build was along the river, where boats provided a reasonably safe and comfortable means of travel. (Re-reading this paragraph before publication, one can't help feeling that history is repeating itself).

Hampton Court Palace was first built from 1514 onwards by Thomas Wolsey, Lord Chancellor of England. Later, as Cardinal, Wolsey unwittingly loosed the Reformation in England by failing to get Vatican approval for the annulment of Henry VIII's marriage to Catherine of Aragon, the first of his six wives. Henry VIII acquired the palace after Wolsey fell from royal favour, and he expanded and improved it, as did following monarchs. The Great Hall is the oldest surviving Elizabethan theatre in England, and in the time of Elizabeth I (1558-1603), a German visitor described the place as the grandest palace in Europe.

Oliver Cromwell lived here with his family during the Commonwealth (1649-1660), England's brief period as a republic. Charles II commissioned Sir Christopher Wren to build a 'new Versailles', but that plan foundered on a lack of money. The last significant phase of building started in the reign of William & Mary (1688-1702) and continued through to the time of George II (1727-1760), after which the palace was rarely used. The palace was opened to the public by Queen Victoria in 1838, the year after her accession.

The palace is well worth visiting, as much for the fine art collection as the splendid apartments and gardens. It also houses one of only fifty or so real (i.e. royal) tennis courts spread around England, Scotland, Eire, France, Australia, and the USA.

The gardens include 60 acres (24ha) of recently restored formal gardens and 750 acres (304ha) of parkland. There is also the Great Vine, planted in 1769, and still producing a large crop of grapes. Entrance charges to palace and gardens are high and justified only for a thorough visit rather than a quick look.

When you reach the palace forecourt, you see over the road a famous old hostelry and an excellent newcomer:

6

The Mitre Hotel, Hampton Court Road KT8 9BN. Tel: 020 8979 9988. Built in 1666 by Andrew Snape, the King's Sergeant Farrier, to cater for visitors to the palace. Snape's son (also Andrew) became a renowned academic and cleric, later headmaster of Eton. After a spell as a private house, The Mitre reverted to being an inn in 1840 and was a popular social centre for local people. It has been renovated as a boutique hotel with facilities including a riverside terrace brasserie.

The Mute Swan, 3 Palace Gate, Hampton Court KT8 9BN. Tel: 020 8941 5959 Brunning & Price. Free house, real ale and good food. Busy, so best to book a table.

Walking around the corner from Gardenarium takes you to **The Old Court House**, home for a time of Sir Christopher Wren. Queen Anne gave Wren a fifty-year lease on this house in lieu of pay for work on St Paul's Cathedral.

Hampton Court Bridge, dating from 1933, is a reinforced concrete structure faced in brick and stone to match the local architecture. Its predecessors include an iron bridge (1865) and what has been described as the largest timber chinoiserie bridge ever built. Plaques on the left end of each side list the people involved, including Sir Edwin Lutyens as architect.

Getting there. Overground train from Waterloo to Hampton Court station. Alternatively, train to Kingston station and then bus 111 to Hampton Court. It is, in fact, a pleasant walk of 2 miles (3km) from Kingston station through Bushy Park to the palace, which would make a round walk of about 5 miles (8km).

Walking. Hampton Court Bridge to Kingston Bridge is 2¾ miles (4.5km), no refreshments in between.

2. HAMPTON COURT BRIDGE TO KINGSTON BRIDGE

The bridge gives access to the riverside Barge Walk, so-called as it was the towpath for horses (and teams of men) hauling barges. For most of the way, there is a made-up path higher up, useful when the Barge Walk is muddy.

From the start of the path, you look across the river to Cigarette Island Park, named after the houseboat *Cigarette* once moored there. The platforms of Hampton Court Station extend over the combined mouth of the **Rivers Mole and Ember**. The Mole rises near Horsham in East Sussex and flows 50 miles/80km to here. Once heavily polluted, it now supports many fish including brown trout. The name is possibly from the Latin *mola*, a mill, but more likely a back-formation from Molesey just upstream. The Ember is very short, really just another channel of the Mole.

Turks Hampton Court Pier. Turks Thames Cruises run a boat service from here to Kingston (35 minutes) and perhaps on to Richmond, usually Easter to October only; details here: https://www.turks.co.uk.

Walking down to Turks Pier, you can see the entrance (probably shrouded by ivy) to a **tunnel** used to carry goods from the riverside to the palace cellars.

Another pier a little further on offers boat services into central London (Easter to October), curtailed at present by repairs to Hammersmith Bridge.

The battlemented building adjacent to the wall is the **Banqueting House**, a misnomer as it was built around 1700 for informal meals. Later used as a playroom for the royal children, it is now available as a wedding venue.

The view through the railings is of the recently restored formal Baroque **Privy Garden** of William III, and the **South Front** of the palace as redesigned by Wren. The railings were built by the ironworker Jean Tipou, a Huguenot refugee from France. These are currently being restored; note the national emblems of the four countries making up the United Kingdom.

Further on, the gate to the left in red brick and stone pillars, leads into the **Home Park** and affords distant views of the palace.

Until Teddington and Richmond Locks were built, the Thames here was tidal and regularly submerged **Thames Ditton Island** and the smaller Swan Island and Boyle Farm Island. In the 20th century, it became fashionable to have a camping shack on the island despite the lack of any amenities. Building the footbridge in 1939 meant that water, electricity, and sewage could be laid on. Proper houses were then built, but flooding can still see the island submerged by several feet of water.

Opposite the island, a section of the Barge Walk is cobbled; one wonders if it was all like that. The attractive house nearby is **The Pavilion**, designed by Wren as a summer house for William III. The house achieved notoriety in the 1960s for its tenant Cecil King, publisher of the *Daily Mirror*, and his supposed plans for a coup d'état against the Labour government of the time.

An ugly circular structure appears to be a vent for waterworks. At the time of writing, one of the classic Oxford college barges was moored just over the river.

The square building over the river at **Seething Wells** was a pumping station of the Lambeth Waterworks Company that provided clean water to London. Seething is a corruption of Siden Wells, considered medicinal springs. The high walls downstream contain the deep filter beds. Plans to develop this area were foiled by local opposition, and the beds have become a wildlife sanctuary.

The buildings on **Raven's Ait** stem from its previous use as a training base for sailing and boat handling. It is now a conference and wedding venue. There are many more *aits* and *eyots* in the Thames; the word derives from the Old English *ig* or *ieg* = island + *-eth* = small. Rarely used in conversation, the word has appealed to numerous authors.

By the southern end of Raven's Ait, a footpath leads into Home Park. From here you can look down **The Long Water** to the fountain and east front of the palace. Also here is **Rick Pond**, used at weekends by model yacht racers.

The prominent church on the other bank is the Catholic **Church of St Raphael**. It was built in 1846, shortly after the Catholic Emancipation Act became law, as the private chapel of a Catholic Armenian previously resident in India.

The **Hogsmill River** joins the Thames 300m before Kingston Bridge. Rising near Ewell in Surrey, it is only 6 miles/10km long, but powered many mills. Gunpowder mills supplied the British army during the Napoleonic Wars and anyone who would pay during the American Civil War. Millais pictured *Ophelia* (in Tate Britain) in the Hogsmill, and Holman Hunt set the dalliance of his *Hireling Shepherd* (in Manchester Art Gallery) on its meadows.

The last part of the walk is under spreading horse chestnut trees. As you walk up the incline to the bridge, note the three salmon emblem of Kingston cast into the fence posts.

Kingston Bridge. There has been a bridge here since the 12th or 13th century, and for many years, it was the first bridge upstream of London Bridge. The present bridge, of brick faced with stone, was finished in 1828 and widened on the upstream side in 1914. Below the bridge is a cluster of interesting old boats.

Getting there. Kingston overground station, trains from Waterloo.

Walking. Kingston Bridge to Teddington Lock along the south bank (only) is 2 miles (3km).

3. KINGSTON-UPON-THAMES

Kingston-upon-Thames is the oldest (AD925) of the three traditional Royal Boroughs, the others being Leamington Spa and Kensington & Chelsea. The upon-Thames suffix distinguishes it from Kingston-upon-Hull in the East Riding of Yorkshire, though that is usually referred to simply as Hull. It has always been an important market town, with its oldest charter granted by King John in AD1200, and is still the county town of Surrey.

Despite modern development, the core of the town around the marketplace retains its medieval layout and many historic buildings.

All Saints Church, Market Place, KT1 1JP, is close to the bridge. The church is mainly 15th century, with a brick tower added in the 18th century. Lots of history here, but despite a fine new organ, the interior has been mutilated by modernisers.

The **Market House,** in Italianate style, dates from 1838. The iron columns and beams were cast locally. The gilded statue of **Queen Anne** (1702-1714) over the entrance came from the previous market house of 1505. The thriving market operates seven days a week and has good inexpensive street food stalls. You can reflect that the buskers are following in the footsteps of Eric Clapton.

Druid's Head, 3 Market Place, KT1 1JT. Tel: 020 8546 0723 Greene King. Real ale and food. Partly early 16th century, how do they get away with those windows?

The **Henry Shrubsole** memorial is nearby. Shrubsole was a local man who made good, three times mayor, and with a reputation for improving the lot of ordinary people.k

From the bottom end of the Market Place, turn right onto High Street, and you soon come to the imposing neo-Georgian **Guildhall**. Replacing the Market Hall as town hall this was completed in 1935, and has been extended since. The three salmon on a shield reflect their former abundance in the river and the importance of fishing to Kingston.

The **Coronation stone**, to the right of the Guildhall, is said to have been used at the crowning of nine Saxon kings from Edward the Elder in AD900 to Æthelred the Unready in 979. Coins of each of these kings were inset around the plinth.

From here, you can follow the Hogsmill River to the **Clattern Bridge;** built around 1175 and twice widened since, it is probably the oldest bridge in Britain still in use. The name, recorded in 1293 as Clateryngbrugge, is said to derive from the sound of horses' hooves. A ducking stool for nagging wives was in use nearby up to 1745. The centre arch was one of the goals in a riotous game of mass football played every Shrove Tuesday. Carry on along the Hogsmill River until you reach the Thames, and follow the promenade to Kingston Bridge. You can rent a self-drive electric boat (capacity eight people) by the bridge: https://goboat.co.uk/kingston/ for details.

At the junction of Old London Road and Wheatfield Way is *Out of Order*, a sculpture by David Mach of twelve red phone boxes arranged like falling dominoes.

Kingston Heritage Centre (formerly Museum), Wheatfield Way, KT1 2PS. Tel: 020 8547 6440. Has a lot on local history and an art gallery (frequent changing exhibitions) on the upper floor. Photographers and cinema enthusiasts will find the section on Eadweard Muybridge (1830-1904) interesting. The building (1904) was funded by Dale Carnegie. At much the same time, radical Battersea refused Carnegie's money as coming from a strikebreaker.

4. KINGSTON BRIDGE TO TEDDINGTON LOCK

Because the left bank below Kingston Bridge is so built up, we need to cross over and follow the south bank to Teddington Lock. Access to the riverside path is from the upstream side of the bridge.

Remains of an old bridge are incorporated in the wall of the John Lewis store, though this was behind hoardings when we passed. Walk past **Turks Pier** and slipway; Turks runs excursion boats to Hampton Court and Richmond.

Kingston railway bridge dates from 1907 and replaces an earlier bridge of 1863. The dock on the left, which appears to have been partly filled in, was for **Kingston Power Station**, a coal-fired unit that operated from 1893 to 1980; it was behind the gardens, its site now occupied by flats. The wharf past the dock still has a large windlass and mooring bollards. **Canbury Gardens** was laid out in 1890 on the site of old gravel pits and common grazing land. The **Secret Cafe** was once public bogs. The **bandstand** still sees concerts on Sunday afternoons in summer.

The Boaters' Inn, Canbury Gardens, Lower Ham Road, KT2 5AU. Tel: 0208 541 4672. Metropolitan Pub Co. Real ale and food. Modern building right on the river.

The **Rosie Mitchell** memorial commemorates a 15-year-old who collapsed and died whilst rowing on the river.

Past the pub and Kingston Rowing Club is the **Millennium Red Oak**, over by the road. *Quercus rubra* is a native of North America and faster-growing than native species, named for its bright red foliage in autumn. This is assuming we were looking at the right oak tree as some yobbo had destroyed its plaque.

In the river are **Steven's Eyots,** named after a local waterman. The larger island, shown on old maps as Tathim's Island, is the base of the Small Boat Club, a members' club for motor boat enthusiasts, and the only people allowed access to this conservation area. Membership is open to non-boat owners.

Albany Boathouse, dating from ca1900, appears now to be business premises. The **Half-mile tree** stands where the riverside path diverges from Lower Ham Road. The original 500-year-old elm was cut down in 1951 as dangerous and replaced the following year. The name is a bit of a mystery as it is certainly more than a half-mile from Kingston Bridge.

The **Hawker Centre** is named after the Sopwith/Hawker aircraft company, whose most famous products were the Sopwith Camel, the Hawker Hurricane, and the Harrier jump-jet. They used the river to test their World War I vintage float planes, their original factory being nearby in Kingston. A couple of the roads nearby are named after their aircraft – would you want to live on Camel Grove? – and others after Battle of Britain airfields.

Opposite the Hawker Centre is **Trowlock Island**, said to take its name from the trow, a kind of barge, which seems unlikely as trows were used solely on the River Severn and in the West Country. There are bungalows (originally meaning a single-storey house in the Bengali style) on the island, and it is also the base of the Royal Canoe Club. Access is by a hand-hauled chain ferry from Broom Road on the other bank.

Approaching Teddington Lock, two locks once led to the extensive gravel workings, though nothing remains now. As you pass the moorings for the lock, an apple tree was almost ready for scrumping in late September, and there are evergreen oaks.

11

The **Teddington Lock** and weir system dates from the middle of the 19th century. Teddington Lock is the highest point that tides reach. The **Teddington Lock Footbridge** was completed in 1889; a cantilever span crosses the navigable channel, and a suspension bridge the weir race. The first provides a bird's-eye view of the system. Note the three locks for boats of different sizes: the barge lock, launch lock, skiff lock, (this cheerfully known as the coffin lock), and a boat skid. It is hoped to use the weir for a hydroelectric plant.

The blocks of flats visible from the suspension bridge stand on the site of **Teddington Studios**. Many feature films and, latterly, popular television shows were made here between 1910 and 2014. Between 1931 and 1958, the studios were owned by Warner Brothers and used to make 'quota-quickies', British-made films that entitled the big American studios to release their main output in Britain. The studios were severely damaged by a V2 missile in 1944.

In late 1940, a German bomb badly damaged the sluices beside the weir, and the river drained all the way up to Molesey Lock at Hampton Court Bridge. This disrupted barge traffic carrying coal and other goods to Oxford and prevented boats built at Thornycroft's Hampton works from moving downstream. It is said that not a word of this ever appeared in the papers. It also meant that local people could supplement their rations with the fish killed by the blast. Repairs took seven weeks.

Pleasure boating has been popular on the Thames since at least the early 19th century. Many small boatyards on the river produced everything from rowing skiffs and punts to (more recently) powerful sea-going cruisers. During both world wars, these small yards built patrol boats, motor torpedo boats, and the like for the Royal Navy. **Tough Brothers** was one of the more downstream of these businesses. Their boathouse was on Ferry Road, and yard on Manor Road. They built over twenty boats for the Navy and five air-sea rescue launches for the Royal Air Force.

Angler's Arms, 3 Broom Road, TW11 9NR. Tel: 020 8977 7475. Fullers. Real ale and pub food. Outdoor seating by the river. The main entrance is on Broom Road, but there is access from the end of the footbridge.

Tide End Cottage, 8 Ferry Road, TW11 9NN. Tel: 020 8977 7762. Greene King. Real ale and food. Beer garden. Note the sign in the forecourt rescued from Tough's Boatyard.

Getting there. For Teddington station (trains to Waterloo), walk straight ahead up Ferry Road, then High Street, until you reach Station Road (about 15 minutes).

The large (and never quite finished) former church to the left at the crossroads is now the **Landmark Arts Centre**, Ferry Road, TW11 9NN.

Over the road from that is the **Church of St Mary with St Alban**, a red brick building dating in parts to the 13th century. Attractive glass and interesting memorials; scientists will be interested in that to Stephen Hales. The St Alban in the name refers to the Arts Centre building, which was intended to supplant it as the parish church.

Further up on the right, at 163-167, is a plaque to the actress **Peg Woffington** (1720-1760), who built these cottages as almshouses. She was the mistress of **David Garrick** (1717-1779), the actor and impresario. He was of Huguenot stock, his family having escaped religious persecution in France. His friend Samuel Johnson said, "His profession made him rich, and he made his profession respectable." He lent his name to a club, a theatre, and a street in The City. He lived, just outside the scope of this book, a mile from Hampton Court, where he built a temple to Shakespeare.

Walking. Teddington Lock Footbridge to Richmond Bridge is 3¼ miles (5.25km) on the north bank and 2¾ miles (4.5km) on the south bank. Teddington Lock to Twickenham station (via the north bank) is 2 miles (3.25km). The railway station in Twickenham is 300m from the river.

5. TEDDINGTON LOCK TO RICHMOND BRIDGE

From here, and all the way past Greenwich, you have the choice of walking either bank.

North bank

Walk around the back of the Boat Shop (past the entrance to the Boathouse Design Studio), and follow the riverside path to **Manor Road Recreation Ground** with seating overlooking the river. Walk away from the river to the old drinking fountain and turn right to access:

The Wharf Restaurant & Bar, 22 Manor Road, Teddington TW11 8BG. Tel: 020 8977 6333. Set in Tough Brothers' old factory. Drinks (no real ale) and affordable snacks in the attractive bar. Fine dining in a glass-fronted room overlooking the river. Live (not rock) music.

The **Royal National Lifeboat Institution** is the main life-saving organisation around Britain's coasts. This is the highest upriver of their four Thames stations, behind Fairmile House, 30 Twickenham Road, TW11 8AB. For the significance of the Fairmile name, see Lockhart Marine under Brentford.

From here, it is 15 minutes of tedious and shadeless road walking along Twickenham Road and Strawberry Vale. Hop on a R68 bus to the Michelham Gardens stop, and you won't miss anything. To the right past Ruy Motors and an off-licence is:

Jawbone Brewing, Unit C, 1 Strawberry Vale, Twickenham, TW1 4RY. Craft brewery. Their tap room is now open, so you can have a drink on the premises. Check the website for opening hours: www.jawbonebrewing.com.

Past the brewery is **Swan Island.** Originally known as Milham's Ait after Harry Milham, who built it up using clay from the excavation of the London Underground. Still privately owned and not exactly of public access, it is occupied

13

mainly by the large family-owned Newman's Shipyard and some forty houseboats. Part of the island is visible from Radnor Gardens.

At the roundabout, Waldegrave Road (blue plaque to Noel Coward at №131) leads to **Strawberry Hill House**. This Gothic fantasy was built from 1745 onwards by Horace Walpole (1717-1797); the house and gardens have been restored recently. Walpole's father Robert was the first man to be titled Prime Minister; he it was who said, 'The way to ensure summer in England is to have it framed and glazed in a comfortable room'. Access to the gardens is free; check here for tickets to the house: https://www.strawberryhillhouse.org.uk/visit-us/

Radnor Gardens was the gardens of three houses over the road. It takes its name from the Earl of Radnor, who owned one of the houses; long after his ownership, a German bomb destroyed it in 1940. Once an island, the gardens are now firmly attached to the mainland, though you can see the remains of the steps down to the river. Café and toilets at the entrance. The 1921 **war memorial** depicts an unusually joyous soldier; plaques on the plinth show women of the auxiliary services, RFC pilots, and Royal Navy personnel. The **bowling green** here, like all in the south of England, is flat; oop north they have crown greens, gently humped in the centre. Lawn bowls was the game played by Sir Francis Drake before he set sail to sort out the Spanish Armada in 1588.

Alexander Pope Hotel, Cross Deep, Twickenham, TW1 4RB. Tel: 020 8892 3050. Youngs. Real ale and food (Sunday roast). Post-war building replacing a pub destroyed by a V1 flying bomb in 1944. Now vastly expanded as a hotel. Pleasant enough, but the Barmy Arms and the White Swan are not that far away and not on a busy road.

The famous **Pope's Villa** and grotto were built by Alexander Pope (1688-1744), the poet, satirist, and art critic. He is second only to Shakespeare for entries in *The Oxford Dictionary of Quotations*. Probably his best-known coining is 'damning with faint praise'. The house and grotto were pretty much destroyed by a later owner fed up with sightseers. The location is indicated by a plaque on the wall of Radnor House School.

High up on the wall of the school building, presumably so no one can get at it, is a **blue plaque** to Henry Labouchère (1831-1912), described as a radical MP and journalist. What it does not tell you is that Labouchère, a fierce homophobe, was responsible in 1885 for making any form of sexual contact between men illegal. It was his amendment to an unrelated bill that did for Oscar Wilde, Alan Turing, and many others. Labouchère also invented a roulette system, which makes him very popular with casino owners. If you do fancy your chances at the wheel, get six people together and try the reverse Labouchère.

At a "villa in Twickenham" (thought to be in Saville Road, off Heath Road). **Lady Mary Wortley Montagu** (1689-1762) experimented with variolation to confer immunity to smallpox. This and Jenner's subsequent development of vaccination led to the eventual elimination of this dreadful disease from the world.

Entering Twickenham town, bear right at the traffic lights and right again down Wharf Lane to the river. The elevated **Diamond Jubilee Gardens** give a view across to Eel Pie Island, also a café and toilets here.

Twickenham Museum, 25 The Embankment, TW1 3DU (entrance on Church Lane). Tel: 020 8408 0070. Free. Saturday 1300-1500hrs, Sunday 1400-1600hrs. http://www.twickenham-museum.org.uk

The footbridge leads to **Eel Pie Island,** a favourite picnic place in the 19th century. Steamers ran from central London, as mentioned by Charles Dickens in *Nicholas Nickleby*. The name derives from the hotel on the island, famous for its eel pies. Before burning down in 1971, it had become popular as a jazz and rock venue; bands who performed here included the jazzers Acker Bilk and George Melly, The Rolling Stones, Pink Floyd, and many more. The tradition lives on at the rhythm and blues Eel Pie Club in The Cabbage Patch pub on nearby London Road, Cabbage Patch being the nickname of the Rugby Football Union's Twickenham stadium a short walk away. Otherwise, the island was largely occupied by boatbuilding works (two remain), and there are about fifty houses. William Hartnell, the original *Doctor Who*, lived here during the 1960s. First proposed in 1889, the footbridge was eventually put in place in 1957.

Barmy Arms, The Embankment, Twickenham, TW1 3DU. Tel: 020 8892 0863. Greene King. Real ale and food. Charming place with friendly staff. Riverside seating. Barm is a brewing term for the froth on beer as it ferments, and barmy is English slang for crazy.

The **Church of St Mary the Virgin** is quite a mixture, having a 15th century tower with an 18th century neoclassical nave attached. This resulted from the collapse in 1713 of the earlier nave, which was older than the tower. It is said that the collapse was foreseen by the parish priest who preached in the open air. Some memorials of the old church were salvaged and reinstalled. A window commemorates the Berkeley brothers, who were pre-revolutionary governors of American colonies. Alexander Pope is under a slab marked simply with the letter P. Oldest is the brass to Richard Burton, cook to King Henry VI, dated 1443. One of the eight bells in the tower dates from the early 16th century. A memorial to Thomas Twining (1675-1741), the tea merchant, stands in the churchyard. Note the flood stone in a wall near the church, and don't park your car in an unauthorised space!

Eel Pie Island Museum, 1-3 Richmond Road, Twickenham TW1 3AB, tells the story of Eel Pie Island and the characters associated with it. Full details: https://www.eelpiemuseum.co.uk Walk straight up Church Street from St Mary's Church. A stroll the other way along **Church Street** is fun if you have time to spare in Twickenham.

Champion's Wharf, Riverside TW1 3DT. Play beach complete with Viking longship, perfect for children. Also of interest are the artworks and **quotations** from Pope, who is honoured by a memorial urn. Charming riverside gardens named after William Champion, who operated the Twickenham Ferry.

York House was built in the late 17th century by the Yorkes, a family long associated with Twickenham. The house became council offices in 1923, its external appearance unspoiled. Its last private owner was Sir Ratan Tata (1871-1918) of the Parsee industrial dynasty. He developed the gardens and, in 1909, acquired a job lot of Italian statuary that he formed into a decorative **fountain**, and thereby hangs a tale. The previous owner of the statues was Whitaker Wright (1846-1904), promoter of dodgy companies and seller of even dodgier bonds. His extravagance ran to a glass smoking room under the lake on his estate. After his conviction for fraud at the Royal Courts of Justice, he committed suicide there by taking cyanide.

York House Gardens extend well behind the fountain, and you can cross the footbridge to see the main part of the gardens on the other side of Riverside road. In the far corner of the gardens, near the tennis courts, is a real curiosity, one of London's few remaining *pissoirs*. It's green, cast iron, has four stalls, and is in full working order. Like its Parisian contemporaries, there is neither provision for ladies nor a wash basin. Cast into the metal is the injunction, once common, for gentlemen to 'Please adjust your dress before leaving'.

Behind the pissoir is **Gokhale Walk**. Gopal Krishna Gokhale (1866-1915) was a mathematics professor and early leader in India's struggle to free itself from the British Raj. A social reformer, he counselled both Mahatma Gandhi and Mohammed Ali Jinnah (founder and later Governor-General of Pakistan). Sir Ratan Tata financed Gokhale's Servants of India Society and took an interest in its work. The Tata family has long been known for its social conscience and business integrity. Leave the gardens and follow Riverside (road) to:

The White Swan, Riverside. Twickenham, TW1 3DN. Tel: 020 8744 2951. Free house. Real ale and food. Garden right on the river, which sometimes floods the road outside – and even the gents' bogs in the basement. One of the best pubs along the river, or in England for that matter. The wooded ground opposite is the eastern end of Eel Pie Island.

Following Riverside again, you reach Orleans House Gardens and **Orleans House Gallery,** Orleans Rd, Twickenham TW1 3BL. Tel: 020 8831 6000. Orleans House was a fine Palladian villa dating from 1710; it gained its present name when the Duc d'Orleans stayed there from 1813-1815. The main part of the house was demolished in 1926, leaving a splendid later addition, a domed octagonal baroque room now the nucleus of the art gallery. There is a permanent collection of 17/18th century art and frequently changing exhibitions. Note the watercolour of the Lass of Richmond Hill pub in Richmond. Café. Well worth a quick look. Free.

Rejoin the riverside path to **Hammerton's Ferry**. In 1909, Walter Hammerton started to run a ferry from here to the south bank adjacent to Ham House. Lord Dysart, the landowner on the other bank, and William Champion, who operated the Twickenham Ferry by Eel Pie Island, resented this enterprise. The case dragged on until 1916, and eventually, Hammerton obtained a royal warrant for his service. This warrant is said to be in the hands of his grandson, Phil Collins. Twickenham Ferry is long gone, but Hammerton's still operates from March to October 1000-1800hrs. You can also hire rowing boats. Hammerton's original rowing skiff is in the Museum of London Docklands.

Marble Hill House, Richmond Road, Twickenham TW1 2NL. Tel: 020 8892 5115. English Heritage. Wednesday to Saturday, April to October. Free. The best preserved of all the grand villas along this stretch of the river was built by Henrietta Howard (1689-1767), the mistress of King George II. She had the help of many friends in realising the project, including Alexander Pope, who laid out the gardens. The house and grounds have been extensively restored recently.

Between Marble Hill House and the river is an **Eastern black walnut tree**, thought to be the largest in Britain and probably 300 years old.

It's a bit away from the river, but there is a blue plaque to **J.M.W. Turner** at 40 Sandycombe Road, TW1 2LR, the country house that he designed for himself. This is behind Marble Hill Park at the junction with St Margaret's Road.

From Hammerton's Ferry, it is a straightforward walk along the riverbank to Richmond Bridge. **Glover's Island** was called Petersham Ait until 1875 when it was bought for £70 by one Glover. Some years later, he tried to sell the island to Richmond Corporation, then the local authority, for £6000 (about £600,000 today). As an inducement, he threatened to erect a large billboard, thus spoiling the view from posh Richmond Hill. He eventually settled for a lot less, and the island became public property with the proviso that it should never be built on.

Shortly before the bridge, you enter **Cambridge Gardens**. Café and toilets here. When the Germans invaded Belgium at the start of the First World War in 1914, many Belgians found refuge elsewhere. Among the refugees who came to England was **Charles Pelabon** (1881-1958), a French engineer who took over a roller-skating rink close to Cambridge Gardens and started to produce shell casings (to be filled elsewhere) for the Allied armies. The business expanded and employed 2,000 people, mostly Belgian; indeed, the area became known as *une cité belge sur la Tamise*. After the war, the main building became an ice rink, the largest in Europe. Ribbentrop, Nazi Germany's foreign minister, had a house nearby when ambassador to Britain and was a keen patron. Later, and more pleasingly, Torville and Dean trained there.

South bank

Teddington Lock Footbridge replaced the ferry here in 1889. The first element is a suspension bridge that crosses the river downstream of the weir to a narrow man-made island: English Heritage calls this Creweyte or Swan Ait, though the latter conflicts with Swan Island a little downstream. Paths run north and south along the island, though these have been blocked in the past due to anti-social behaviour. A girder bridge crosses the Lock Cut and provides a good view of **Teddington Lock**, which dates from the middle of the 19th century. Note the three locks for boats of different sizes: the barge lock, launch lock, skiff lock, the last cheerfully known as the coffin lock, and a boat skid. The barge lock has intermediate gates to save water when not full.

Teddington Lock is the highest point that tides reach. From the lock, it is 152 miles (243km) upstream to the river's source and 129 miles (206km) to Lechlade, the highest navigable point. Restoration, hopefully, of the Thames and Severn Canal, which joins the river near Lechlade, would restore a link between Bristol and London and reopen some pleasant cruising for small boats.

Pleasure boating has been popular on the Thames since at least the early 19th century. Many small boatyards on the river produced everything from rowing skiffs and punts to (more recently) powerful sea-going cruisers. During both world wars, these small yards built patrol boats, motor torpedo boats, and the like for the Royal Navy. **Tough Brothers** was one of the more downstream of these businesses. During the Second World War, they built over twenty boats for the Royal Navy and five air-sea rescue launches for the Royal Air Force.

Several plaques on the lock-keeper's office tell the history of the lock and the people involved with the river. In 1940, Douglas Tough collected over 100 boats from the Upper Thames to be used to evacuate the British Army from Dunkirk, known as **Operation Dynamo**. The memorial, formerly at Tough's boatyard, is further down the beautifully kept garden. A nice place for a picnic with seating and shade, and a toilet in the lock-keeper's building. On a lighter note, Monty Python filmed their Fish-slapping Dance here. Plans to use the weir for a hydroelectric plant, common enough on continental navigable rivers, arouse controversy.

An **obelisk** 360 yards (320m) below the lock on the Surrey side marks the jurisdiction of the Port of London Authority downstream and the Thames Conservancy upstream, a division introduced in 1909. The PLA still exists, but the Thames Conservancy disappeared into the all-enveloping maw of the Environment Agency in 1996.

Due to tree growth, you see little of the opposite bank from Teddington Lock to the far end of Eel Pie Island. An industrial light railway owned by the Ham River Grit Company ran along the towpath from Teddington Lock to the wharf at the Thames Young Mariners site.

Thames Young Mariners is an activity centre for youngsters to learn canoeing and sailing. The 10-acre (4ha) lagoon is the sole survivor of extensive gravel pits. The pits here were mostly filled in with rubble cleared from London after the Blitz. The lock from the river was installed so barges could load the gravel at any state of the tide. On a high tide, they could transport it up or downstream. Angling in the lagoon is strictly controlled, but you can expect to catch anything from brown trout to zander.

The attractive Art Deco **Thames Eyot flats** on the opposite bank were built in 1933 on the site of Poulett Lodge. An 18th-century loggia and small shell grotto stand in the south of the grounds, and a boathouse and wet dock to the north.

Over to the right, the woodland and open space is the **Ham Lands Nature Reserve**. This section of the river opposite Twickenham is known as Cross Deep. From the far end of Eel Pie Island, you look across to the White Swan pub. A little further on where the moorings start on the other side, a gap in the trees to the right gives a glimpse of:

Ham House, Ham Street, Ham, TW10 7RS. The National Trust reckons this is the most perfectly preserved 17th-century house in Europe. The rich interiors date from the time of the Duke and Duchess of Lauderdale ca1670. Charles II was a visitor. The formal gardens in the French style are in their original state, having escaped the 18th century fashion for landscaping. The statue of Father Thames in front of the house is of Coade stone, made by John Bacon (1740-1799); a twin is in the Terrace Garden further on.

Hammerton's Ferry, in the middle of the moorings, provides a crossing from March to October 1000-1800hrs. Full story in the North Bank section.

Benches along here commemorate, amongst others, Marcus Hewitt, who was a prisoner of war from 1942 to 1945 in Manchuria (part of north-eastern China conquered by Japan in 1932), and Count Steven Ouvaroff, who John remembers as an Australian racing driver in the late 50s and early 60s.

You have a view of **Marble Hill House** at the end of the moorings on the other bank. From the slipway at the end of River Lane, you get your first view of the **Star and Garter** building and, to its left, the Gothic-styled **Petersham Hotel**.

River Lane leads into **Petersham**, still a pleasant village that has escaped suburbanisation. The **Church of St Peter**, Church Lane, is an interesting Georgian church that has grown out of a medieval chapel. Among the chest tombs in the churchyard is that of George Vancouver, the Royal Navy officer who surveyed the Pacific coast from Washington state right up to Alaska in 1791-95. His grave is against the wall to the southeast of the church, and there is a tablet inside.

Glover's Island was called Petersham Ait until 1875, when it was bought for £70 by a man of that name. Some years later, he tried to sell the island to Richmond Corporation, then the local authority, for £6000 (about £600,000 today). As an inducement, he threatened to erect a huge billboard, thus spoiling the view from posh Richmond Hill. He eventually settled for a lot less, and the island became public property with the proviso it should never be built on.

Ignoring the shortcut at the kissing gate on the left, you come to **Eileen's Café** and a public toilet.

Buccleuch Gardens and **Terrace Gardens**, the other side of the main road, were the grounds of three grand 19th century houses, two of them once owned by the Duke of Buccleuch, a title in the Scottish Borders near Melrose founded in 1663. One of the houses came into the Buccleuch estate by marriage in 1790. An 18th century tunnel called Grotto Gate connects the two gardens. The houses are long gone, but the layout of their gardens remains and became a public park in 1881.

In the upper garden is a Coade stone Father Thames figure, a twin of the one at Ham House. This garden goes up to Richmond Hill road; there is also a café. In the 17th century, this was a busy place turning local clay into bricks and tiles for shipping along the river.

The **Gothic Gardens** were the gardens of Gothic House (not the one on The Green), which was demolished in 1938. The house had been built in 1792 for a wealthy lawyer's widow; the structure was stuccoed brick with the usual crenellated roofline. The house was let out for much of the 19th century, with Madame de Stael staying there with her daughter in 1813. Beside it is **Stein's Restaurant**, a Bavarian beer garden.

Thames River Boats runs services to Westminster and Hampton Court from the bank here. Details: https://www.thamesriverboats.co.uk/

Just before the bridge is **Bridge House Gardens**. A bust of Bernardo O'Higgins (1778-1842) stands here. O'Higgins was a man of Irish-Spanish ancestry who, after many setbacks, led Chile to independence from Spain. His link to Richmond is educational. The Armada de Chile (the Chilean Navy), which he founded, usually has a ship named for him, currently an attack submarine. Many of their other ships are named after men of British or Irish heritage, obviously a people not ashamed of their history. O'Higgins has a blue plaque at Clarence House, 2 The Vineyard TW10 6AQ, where he stayed.

Richmond Bridge

The bridge was completed in 1777 and widened in 1937. It is the oldest surviving bridge over the river in Greater London. The tall milestone at the town end of the bridge warns against vandalism for which the penalty was 'Transportation to one of His Majesty's colonies for seven years'. Seating replaced the tollbooths when the tontine scheme that had funded construction expired in 1859.

Getting there. Richmond overground and tube stations combined, trains from Waterloo and the tube network. Turn left out of the station and follow The Quadrant and Hill Street round to the river.

Walking. Richmond Bridge to Kew Bridge on the north bank is 4 miles (6.5km), and 3 miles (5km) on the south bank.

Swans

The story of England's swans starts with a gift from the Queen of Cyprus to Richard I (the Lionheart) who reigned 1189-1199. Swans were regarded as royal birds and have always enjoyed protection. The theft of an egg could lead to a year's imprisonment. Apart from the Crown, only two of the City's livery companies, the Dyers and the Vintners, are allowed to own swans on the Thames.

Even today, there is a Keeper of the King's Swans responsible for all the swans on the river. Accompanied by the Marker of the Swans, he presides over the ceremony of Swan Upping, an annual round-up and marking of the year's cygnets. The Dyers' birds get one nick on the beak and the Vintners' two. The Crown's birds are left unmarked, acknowledging their ownership of all unmarked birds. This is not, as you may have suspected, one of our little jokes.

---

6. RICHMOND

Before he took the throne from Richard III, Henry VII (1485-1509) was the Earl of Richmond in Yorkshire. When he rebuilt the royal manor house here, formerly known as Shene, he renamed it Rychemonde, and the town grew around it. Destroyed by fire in 1499, Henry rebuilt the palace on a much grander scale as **Richmond Palace**. Anne of Cleves lived here after her divorce from Henry VIII, but thereafter the palace was little used. Queen Elizabeth I liked the palace and died there in 1603. Not, however, before she had installed a flush toilet, possibly the first recorded since Roman times. After the execution of Charles I in 1649 the palace was left to fall apart.

The Green is an attractive urban open space. Once used for jousting and archery, the gentler game of cricket took over in 1666 and is still played regularly.

The Cricketers, The Green, Richmond, TW9 1LX. Tel: 020 8940 4372. Metropolitan Pub Company. Real ale and food. One of the oldest pubs in Richmond, dating from 1770.

The **Prince's Head**, 28 The Green, Richmond, TW9 1LX.Tel: 020 8940 1572. Fullers. Real ale and food. In the early part of the 20th century the pub lost its licence for allowing 'disorderly women' on the premises. The new landlord fixed that by banning all women, a stipulation since relaxed. Both these pubs support cricket teams.

Off the south-western side of The Green, The Wardrobe (road) leads through the **gatehouse**, built in 1501, to the scant remains of the palace. The arms are those of Henry VII. The gatehouse is still owned by the Crown Estate and let on a long lease. It leads to the fine, but later, houses of Old Palace Yard and on to **Old Palace Lane** which runs down to the river.

The White Swan, 26 Old Palace Lane, TW9 1PG. Tel: 020 8940 0959. Real ale and food. Charming country pub. Gastro pub but affordable light bites at lunchtime.

Asgill House, the Palladian house at the bottom of the lane, was built on the site of the palace's brewery.

Richmond Hill. The highest part of Richmond has grand views, notably of Richmond Park, a royal hunting reserve up to the time of George II. As with other towns and villages along the river, the wealthy built fine houses here away from the city's disease, filth, and hubbub. This Richmond disputes with the one in

Yorkshire the origin of the folk song *Sweet Lass of Richmond Hill*, though the evidence does point north.

Walk up Richmond Hill (road) from the bridge. At №46 is a blue plaque to **Celia Johnson**, the actress (*In Which We Serve* and *Brief Encounter*) and wife of Peter Fleming, Ian's brother. **Mick Jagger** lived for a time at №116 Downe House, and Jerry Hall does now.

The Roebuck, 130 Richmond Hill, TW10 6RN. Tel: 020 8948 2329. Greene King. Real ale and food. Famous old pub. Outdoor seating and a tremendous view.

The former **Royal Star and Garter Home** stands at the top of Richmond Hill. This is the building that dominates the skyline as you walk towards Richmond on either side of the river. The story starts in the late 18th century with a tavern called the Star and Garter. Lord Dysart, the landowner, was a Knight of the Garter, the most senior order of knighthood in Great Britain founded in 1348. In the 19th century the business expanded rapidly, with the enlarged tavern becoming a social centre for wealthy locals and Londoners. By 1860 the tavern had been replaced by a huge neo-French château hotel. The various ructions in 19th century France saw both Louis-Philippe and Napoleon III staying here. By 1906, the hotel was empty, and in 1914 it was commandeered as a hospital for First World War casualties. After the war it became accommodation for disabled ex-servicemen, and in 1922 was replaced by the present building. This continued in use until 2013, when it became uneconomic for the charity to update the building; they decided to support four separate, more manageable homes and sold the building for conversion to flats.

Lass of Richmond Hill, 8 Queens Road, TW10 6JJ. Tel: 0208 940 1306. Young's. Real ale and food. Garden.

Turner painted the view from Richmond Hill looking upstream: *England: Richmond Hill on the Prince Regent's Birthday*. The painting is currently on loan to the Museum of Fine Arts in Boston, but can be seen here: https://www.tate.org.uk/art/artworks/turner-england-richmond-hill-on-the-prince-regents-birthday-n00502. Turner also sketched Richmond Bridge, viewing by appointment at Tate Britain. It is said that Byrd likened the view of the James River in Virginia to that from Richmond Hill, and so named his new township Richmond.

In the pavement directly outside Richmond station is a plaque to Lt/Col. **Bernard Freyberg** who won the Victoria Cross in France on 13th/14th November 1916; he later became the youngest general in the British Army during that war. In the Second World War he commanded the New Zealand forces in Crete and North Africa, including the defence of Maleme airfield in Crete. He was governor-general of New Zealand from 1946 to 1952 and died in Windsor Castle, where he was Constable, in 1963. A blue plaque marks his birthplace at 8 Dynevor Road TW10 6PF nearby.

7. RICHMOND BRIDGE TO KEW BRIDGE

North bank

From the bridge approach, walk along Willoughby Road and Ducks Walk to **Twickenham Rail Bridge**, where you rejoin the river. The bridge was built in 1846 and rebuilt on the original piers in 1908.

Midway between the two bridges, look left, and you will see a small red brick building with a pointed roof, a witch's house, Colette thought. Its twin is over the river but hidden by trees. These were the two access points to a **tunnel** under the river built by the Metropolitan Water Company sometime between the building of the two bridges. Reports vary on whether this was intended as a pedestrian way or a conduit for water mains. It is said to be possible to crawl through, but you certainly are not encouraged to find out for yourself.

Twickenham Road Bridge was built in 1933 to relieve traffic congestion in Richmond.

Follow Ranelagh Drive to **Richmond Lock**. The removal of the many piers of the old London Bridge in 1861 caused the river to flow a lot faster, so, at low tide, the river through Richmond and Twickenham became a narrow stream between mud banks. The answer was to install the present sluice system to hold back water as the tide ebbed. Each sluice gate weighs 32 tons, and the supporting structure is disguised as the two footbridges. One old penny (1/240th of a pound) was the toll to cross, and now it's free.

Isleworth is recorded in the Domesday Book of 1086 as the Manor of Gristlesworde. The Domesday Book was compiled at the behest of William I (1066-1087) to assess his new kingdom for taxation. Centuries later, ships brought coal from Newcastle and timber from the Baltic to the wharves, and now there are houseboats.

Follow the riverside path as far as Thistleworth Marina. Thistleworth appears to be a 16th century variation of Isleworth. The signed path to Charleville Mews leads to where the muddy River Crane joins the Thames but is a dead-end, so continue to the main road. Cross the Crane and rejoin the path through an unsigned opening in the yellow London brick wall. The first part of this path was the site of Isleworth Pottery. Over to the left is a modern housing development based on **Isleworth House**, which was built for George III's chaplain and was later a convent. Over to the right is **Isleworth Ait**, a valuable nature reserve and home to the Thames door snail. In the backwater is a large floating workshop and a floating dock.

Town Wharf, Swan St, Old Isleworth TW7 6RJ. Tel: 020 8847 2287. A Samuel Smith pub in, unusually for them, a modern building. Real ale and food. Nicely fitted out. The path traverses their ground-floor terrace.

The **Duke of Northumberland's River** is actually a canal built to power water mills. Walk up the canal and turn right into Church Street.

London Apprentice, 62 Church Street, TW7 6BG. Greene King. Real ale and food. A 15th century building with an 18th century façade. One of the great riverside pubs, it takes its name from the apprentices who used to row up here on their day off. Dog friendly since 1731. A black swan was on the river, and a tame wee corbie noisily begged for crumbs.

The house before the church, The Rectory, once housed a painting known as the *Isleworth Mona Lisa*. Brought to England in the 18th century, it is currently in a bank vault in Switzerland whilst the great and the good of the art world argue just how much of it was actually painted by Leonardo da Vinci.

All Saints Parish Church, 63 Church St, Isleworth TW7 6BE. Like Syon Ferry House, the church was gutted by fire in 1943. One account says that this was caused by incendiary bombs, another arson. All that remains of the original building is the 14th century ragstone tower. The nails that make up the cross came from the old roof and were salvaged after the fire. Now mounted on the East Chapel, the unusual sundial of 1707 is graduated to tell the time in Isleworth, Jamaica, Jerusalem, and Moscow. Jamaica because the benefactor had been governor there, but Moscow? Under the yew tree is a plague pit containing 149 victims of the Great Plague of 1665. A ferry operated from near the church up until 1960.

The Pavilion. This late 18th century building was the upper part of the Syon Park boathouse. The ground in front has been raised and now conceals the wet docks under each wing. In 1805, Turner rented **Syon Ferry House** for a year and used it as a base to enrich his already wide knowledge of the river. Both are hidden behind the estate wall and visible only from the opposite bank.

Brentford was recorded as Breguntford as early as AD704. The place takes its name from the River Brent, which means high or holy river. Here, we need to make a hefty detour inland because the entire riverfront of Syon Park remains in its original undrained and unembanked state. The only way to see this is from the opposite bank or, better, a boat.

Syon House, then a building in Italian Renaissance style, came into the ownership of the Percy family, the Dukes of Northumberland, in 1594. It has been held by the family ever since; a family habit perhaps, the Percys acquired their seat at Alnwick Castle in the 13th century and still live there. Robert Adam altered the house extensively in the 1760s, the interiors are spectacular, whilst Capability Brown went to work on the grounds.

The East Front is surmounted by a splendid lion, better seen from the other bank. The lion was taken from the dukes' London town house when it was demolished to create Northumberland Avenue, linking the river and Trafalgar Square. Many parts of the house and grounds have been used as film locations, often for music videos. The house and grounds are open to the public: https://www.syonpark.co.uk. Syon and Sion are variants of Zion, the biblical term for Jerusalem and Israel as a whole. The name comes from an abbey on the site now occupied by the house.

You can fish for trout (fly only) very reasonably: https://alburyestate fisheries.co.uk. Straight on past the Garden Centre, the glass dome of the Great Conservatory is visible from the path. The modern hotel may seem jarring, but the upkeep of a place like this is very expensive. Follow the lane to London Road (A315), turn right. Cross the River Brent, noting the locks to the north.

The **River Brent** and the **Grand Union Canal** meet the Thames in Brentford, and the dock was a major transshipment point between the river, the inland waterways, and the railway. The Grand Union and Regents Canals loop right around the north of London, connecting Brentford to Limehouse Basin. This is a walkable 31½ miles (50.5km).

The signed path beside the River Brent from the bridge is very uneven and of little interest. Better, turn into The Ham and walk down to the former railway bridge that brought the tracks into the dock. This is where the other path joins The Ham. Under the bridge, go straight on up steps where the road bends left. This brings you to a footbridge over the river; at the end, go sharp left down concrete steps to the riverside. This narrow and muddy path is unusable for wheelchairs; users should go straight on from the end of the footbridge to Augustus Close and turn left to pick up Dock Road. Others can follow the path to the double lock. Steps go up to Dock Road that leads to Brentford High Street. Alternatively, take the footbridge over the lock, backtrack along the lock, and cross two footbridges to:

Brewery Tap, 47 Catherine Wheel Road, Brentford, TW8 8BD. Tel: 0208 568 6006. Fullers. A true old-fashioned locals' pub. Garden.

Nearby is **Johnson Island Artists** and Gallery. Beside the lock is a large barge aground as a residence.

The cobbled Dock Road gives a good view of the shipbuilding and repair yard; note the use of floating docks. Several historic vessels, written off for scrap, are being restored here. At Brentford High Street, turn right. Over the road, on the corner of Alexandra Road, is the **Brentford Memorial**. This records the two Battles of Brentford fought in the grounds of Syon House. In 1016, Edmund Ironside defeated the Dane Canute, and in 1642 Royalist cavalry under Prince Rupert routed two battalions of Parliamentarian infantry. In neither case did the victor gain much advantage. Also mentioned are Cassivellaunus, who tried to stop Julius Caesar crossing the river in 54BC and Offa, King of the Mercians, who held a church council in AD780.

From Brentford High Street, turn right down Timber Wharf Walk before the Heidelberg building. Follow the path past the shipyard, more good views here, and along to the mouth. Double back and walk right around Soaphouse Creek to join Ferry Wharf. You look across to the **Liquidity** sculpture (Simon Packard 2004) engraved with fish and mermaids; this caused controversy when installed as it blocked the view from the new flats.

Alfred Lockhart Marine Ltd, Ferry Lane, were timber merchants and boat builders. They were pioneers of mass-production methods in yacht building. When the Fairmile design bureau was organising production of motor torpedo boats and armed patrol boats before the Second World War, they consulted Lockhart Marine. Eventually, Lockhart produced the prefabricated wooden kits to build 883 of these and other boats in small yards all over the country, not a few on the Thames.

Continue past Team Keane Watersports to **Dahlia Bridge**. This leads to **Lot's Ait** and its reactivated boatyard. The island was once known as Barbel Island because of the species of fish caught there. We've never had the chance to try barbel, but it sounds no more appetising than pike, and the liver and roe are poisonous. Many of the steel lighters used to transport goods between London Docks and Brentford were built here; for the moment, a revival of boatbuilding has held off the apartment builders. It has been said that scenes of Bogart and Hepburn in the water for *The African Queen* were shot here; it seems more likely that they were shot at the nearby Isleworth Studios.

When you reach a dead-end, turn inland and then right through the car park of the arts centre, and right again to the river. There are steps here unsuitable for wheelchairs that will have to go up to the High Street and turn right.. At the top of the steps is a good view of the boatyard and across the river to Kew Palace.

Waterman's Art Centre, 40 High St, Brentford TW8 0DS. Tel: 020 8232 1010. Galleries, theatre, and cinema.

Past the Art Centre, wheelchairs can rejoin the path through Waterman's Park. The long island is Brentford Ait, which will appear to be two separate islands at high tide. This path brings you back to Brentford High Street which, with its extension Kew Bridge Road, is home to two of London's more esoteric museums:

The **Musical Museum**, 399 High St, Brentford TW8 0DU. Tel: 020 8560 8108. A museum of mechanical music, from tiny music boxes to a mighty Wurlitzer. Founded in an old church nearby, the museum moved to its bespoke new home in 2009. Frequent concerts and tea dances: www.musical-museum.co.uk/

London Museum of Water and Steam, Green Dragon Lane, Brentford TW8 0EN. Tel: 020 8568 4757. A 200m walk from the Musical Museum. Formerly Kew Bridge Steam Museum. Part of London's water supply system since 1838. Anyone interested in old machinery will love this. The star exhibit (among many) is the 250 ton 90-inch beam engine; one stroke lifts 472 gallons (2142l) of water. The 100" engine is even larger but no longer in working order. Also a narrow gauge (2 feet) railway. The prominent tower is not a chimney, it contains pipe systems to regulate pressure. Generally open only at weekends. Details: waterandsteam.org.uk/

Somewhere along here was **Brentford Gas Works**. In the days before natural gas from the North Sea, a gasworks opened in 1820 on the river bank. Coal was distilled to make town gas, a flammable gas consisting mainly of hydrogen, methane, and poisonous carbon monoxide. This was a smokey, smelly business producing some nasty toxins; as children, we always held our noses when being driven past. Despite moving much of the capacity to a larger site in Southall (still on the Grand Union Canal), production continued here until the 1950s.

A sign points down steep steps to **The Hollows**. This leads to a narrow riverside path. You can't see much, but at least it gets you away from the traffic.

One over the Ait, 8 Kew Bridge Rd, Brentford TW8 0FJ. Tel: 020 3581 5700. Fuller's pub in an old warehouse. Real ale and food. Verandah and terrace overlooking the river (reserved for diners, we were told). The name is a play on the old expression "one over the eight", meaning too much to drink, thus assuring us that eight pints of beer is a perfectly reasonable intake. Our brief impression was of unfriendly staff.

South Bank

Richmond Riverside, best seen from the bridge or the opposite bank, is a pleasing leisure and retail development opened in 1988. The architect Quinlan Terry preserved the facades of houses dating back to the early 18th century. The **war memorial** is in the far corner of the gardens

Boathouses are adjacent to the bridge. You can hire a traditional Thames rowing skiff by the hour: http://richmondboathire.co.uk

Museum of Richmond, Second Floor, Old Town Hall, Whittaker Avenue, TW9 1TP. Tel: 020 8332 1141. info@museumofrichmond.com. Local history and changing exhibitions. Free.

The White Cross, Riverside (off Water Lane) Richmond TW9 1TH. Tel: 020 8940 6844. Young's. Real ale and food. Founded in 1740 and rebuilt in 1838. An interesting place to be at high tide.

The large wooded island is **Corporation Island,** and the two smaller ones **Flowerpot Islands.** Corporation Island was the setting for one of the last photographs taken of The Beatles as a group.

The riverside path here is **Cholmondeley Walk**, named after the Earl of Cholmondeley, who had a house here in the 18th century. His ancestors trace their line to the 12th century, and his descendants (as marquesses) still hold Cholmondeley Castle in Cheshire. Cholmondeley is, and apparently always has been, pronounced as Chumlee.

Twickenham Rail Bridge was built in 1846 and rebuilt on the original piers in 1908, as evidenced by the maker's plate on the downstream side.

Midway between the rail and road bridges, look right and, obscured by trees, you will see a small red brick building with a pointed roof. Turn and look over the river to see its twin. These are the two access points to a **tunnel** under the river built by the Metropolitan Water Company sometime between the building of the two bridges. Reports vary as to whether this was intended as a pedestrian way or a conduit for water mains. It is said to be possible to crawl through, but you certainly are not encouraged to find out for yourself.

Twickenham Bridge was built in 1933 to relieve traffic congestion in Richmond. Note the Egyptian detailing above the cutwaters and elsewhere. Unfortunately, this and the rail bridge cut off the Old Deer Park from the town. The water channels beside the path are for flood relief.

After this bridge, the stainless steel **Meridian marker** is due south of the King's Observatory (see below). Line up the row of slates in the path with the notch in the top of the marker, and you'll see the observatory in a break in the trees. This is, of course, not the prime meridian that runs through Greenwich. Nor is it unique; the two southern stone obelisks lined up with different rooms and pieces of equipment in the observatory. A northern obelisk has become visible as tree clearance has opened up the old vistas planned by Capability Brown.

Richmond Lock. The removal of the many piers of the old London Bridge in 1831 caused the river to flow a lot faster, so at low tide the river through Richmond and Twickenham became a narrow stream between mud banks. The answer was to install the present sluice system to hold back water as the tide ebbed. Each sluice gate weighs 32 tons, and the supporting structure is disguised as the two footbridges. A toll was charged for the footbridges (one old penny, 1/240th of a pound). At the time of our visit only the upstream footbridge was open.

The grey building downstream of Richmond Lock on the north side was built in the 1960s as a boathouse. It later became Pete Townshend's **Eel Pie Recording Studios**. This was a commercial undertaking, and The Who, Siouxsie and The Banshees, and Thin Lizzie all recorded here. Townshend used to commute by boat when temporarily deprived of his driving licence. Townshend sold the property in 2008, and it is now a private residence.

The **Old Deer Park** was the garden and grounds of Richmond Palace. Still owned by the Crown Estates, part is leased to the Royal Surrey Golf Club, and the rest is playing fields. Richmond, London Scottish, and London Irish are among the rugby clubs based here, as is the Richmond Cricket Club.

George III founded the **King's Observatory** in 1769 for his own use and the education of his sons. The architect was Sir William Chambers, who also designed the Pagoda nearby in Kew Gardens. The observatory was used until 1840, when many of the instruments were taken to the Science Museum. Latterly, it has been used for meteorological observations, and is now a private residence. Pre-booked visits are possible: www.kingsobservatory.co.uk. You get a closer view of the observatory further on.

After Thistleworth Marina, the view of the opposite bank is cut off by Isleworth Ait, a nature reserve. The relief channel on the right of the path is worth watching for the wildlife. Past Isleworth Ait, a clearing of the bankside trees allows a panorama from the London Apprentice pub to **The Pavilion**. This late 18th century building is the upper part of the Syon Park boathouse. The ground in front has been raised and now conceals the wet docks under each wing. In 1805 Turner rented the fine **Syon Ferry House** (to the left of The Pavilion) for a year and used it as a base to enrich his already wide knowledge of the river. Both these buildings are hidden behind the estate wall and visible only from this side of the river.

From the **northern obelisk** and its stainless steel marker, you get a slightly better view of the King's Observatory. Just past the obelisk, you start to get your first glimpses of Syon House. Along here the waterway gives way to a **ha-ha** (a sunken wall) marking the boundary of Kew Gardens. A drawbridge over the ha-ha, now disused, once gave access to the gardens. Note also the opposite bank in its original undrained state.

The **Royal Botanical Gardens**, popularly known simply as **Kew Gardens,** started life as the pleasure garden of a Jacobean palace, the Dutch House, a favourite of George II. During the mid-18th century the grounds were developed as a botanical garden by Augusta (1719-1772), widow of George II's son Frederick Prince of Wales, and mother of George III. Apart from the glasshouses, the grounds boast several follies, a 163ft (50m) high pagoda, and Kew Palace. Over the years, variously acquired seeds or cuttings of tea, cinchona (quinine), and rubber trees have been propagated here for commercial exploitation in what were then British India, Ceylon (Sri Lanka), and Malaya. Serious research continues. Kew Gardens is not the place for a quick look around; you could easily spend a day there.

Partly because of the gardens and the royal presence, Kew attracted naturalists, artists, and thinkers, not to mention refugees from the French Revolution in 1789 and later upheavals on the Continent. Zoffany lived over the river, and Pissaro painted in Kew Gardens.

The view of the east front of **Syon House** opens up, surmounted by the lion moved here from Northumberland House in Central London. Look to the right of the path for a view through an avenue of trees to the **Palm House**, one of the several large glasshouses in Kew Gardens. In late April, a profusion of daisies in the grass gave the impression of a snowstorm.

A little further on, you see the entrance to **Brentford Dock Marina**. Then comes the main entrance to the docks where the Grand Union Canal joins the river. The stainless steel sculpture *Liquidity* marks the entrance to Soaphouse Creek. Abreast of the car park is **Lot's Ait**, with its boatbuilding works and moored houseboats.

Inland waterways

By 1840, Britain had an inland waterway system a little short of 4000 miles (6400km). There were few navigable rivers, and primarily, the system relied on canals dug by manpower. It was possible to travel from London to Skipton in Yorkshire. Other routes stretched as far as Bristol in the west and down to the south coast. Early and rapid development of the railways meant that there was no incentive to develop broader and higher capacity canals, as happened on the continent. The existing canals are limited to boats either 7ft (2.1m and, commonly referred to as narrow boats) or 14ft (4.3m) wide; there is no connection from south to north for boats wider than 7ft.

A horse could shift a canal boat weighing 30 tons, compared with maybe a 1¼ ton cart on the indifferent roads of the time. The canals are little deeper than a laden boat, and apparently this aids hydrodynamic efficiency.

Part of the canal system loops right through northern London from Brentford Dock in the west to Limehouse Basin in the east, and the **London Canal Museum** is located on the Regent's Canal at 12/13 New Wharf Road, King's Cross, London N1 9RT. Tel: 020 7713 0836. Closed Monday/Tuesday. A mid-19th century warehouse shows Victorian canal operations and the lives of canal workers. King's Cross or Pentonville Road tube stations.

Another interesting access point to the canal is at Camden Lock and its associated market. See www.camdenmarket.com. Water buses operate from here to London Zoo and Little Venice.

Overlapping Lot's Ait is **Brentford Ait**, in two parts separated by Hog Hole. To the right of the path is the North Front of the **Dutch House**, the sole remaining fragment of the various buildings that constituted Kew Palace. This Jacobean house, built in 1631 for a Flemish merchant, was the home of George III in childhood and his preferred abode in summer. The house is open to the public as part of Kew Gardens.

Carry straight on for Kew Bridge, or make a detour into some of Kew's history. Follow Ferry Lane as it turns away from the river, and you come to Kew Green (which is a road); go straight ahead along the wooded Love Lane, and just to the right of where you rejoin Kew Green (road) is:

Hooker House, 49 Kew Green TW9 3AA. A blue plaque tells that this was the home of Sir William Hooker (1785-1865), an intrepid traveller and plant collector. He became the first director of Kew Gardens and was succeeded by his son Joseph.

The house with the portico over the pavement is **Cambridge Cottage,** one time home of the Duke of Cambridge, son of George III.

King's Cottage, at №33, was owned by the Earl of Bute, an advisor to George III. There are, in effect, two houses, the later one of four bays built in front of the earlier. Only an aristo, and a wealthy one at that, could refer to this rather fine house as a cottage.

The royal family's presence in the several residences in Kew Gardens required a suitable church. The **Church of St Anne** on the Green was built in 1710-14 by Queen Anne and later enlarged by George III. The portico, bell tower, and octagon are all 19th century additions. The Hookers father and son are buried here, as are the artists Gainsborough and Zoffany.

On the far side of the Green is the **Cricket Club** pavilion, and behind that **The Cricketers**, 79 Kew Green, TW9 3AH. Tel: 020 8940 6904. Free house. Real ale and food. Mock Tudor gastropub. Terrace overlooking The Green, and beer garden. Looming over The Green to the north is the tower of Brentford pumping station, now the London Museum of Water and Steam.

Over the other side of the fearsome South Circular Road from the church is the **Coach and Horses**, 8 Kew Green, TW9 3BH. Tel: 020 8940 1208 Youngs. Real ale and food. Rooms. Old Georgian coaching inn, though heavily modernised.

The parade of shops by the Coach and Horses includes: **Andrew Davis**, 6 Mortlake Terrace, TW9 3DT. Tel: 020 8948 4911. Paintings and other Thames-related stock.

Lloyds of Kew, 9 Mortlake Terrace, TW9 3DT. Tel: 020 8948 2556. Traditional and well-stocked second-hand bookshop.

Walking towards Kew Bridge from the Coach and Horses, you cross Gloucester Road. **Camille Pissarro** rented №1 in 1892, as marked by a blue plaque, and painted both the church and The Green. A little further on you see a blue plaque to **Arthur Hughes** (1832-1915) at 22 Kew Green. He was an illustrator and artist in the Pre-Raphaelite style.

Kew Pond was an inlet from the river and is still topped up on a high tide. Pass the **Greyhound** gastropub on your back to the bridge.

Staying on the riverside path, and just before the bridge, is **Kreisel Walk** (off Bush Road). Kreisel is German for a gyro, and the term is also used for a twisty bit of a bobsleigh run. Since this is straight and level, we suppose it may refer to the Austrian philosopher-mathematician Georg Kreisel (1923-2015), who lived most of his life in Britain.

Kew Bridge.

The first bridge was a timber affair of seven arches built in 1759. That was replaced by a stone bridge in 1789. The present bridge, officially the King Edward VII bridge, with a much wider roadway, was completed in 1903. This is an elegant wide-arched bridge designed by Sir John Wolfe Barry, who was also involved with Tower Bridge (but not Southend Pier). Between the arches are the arms of the ancient counties of Surrey and Middlesex (three seaxes, a Saxon sword). A plaque in the bridge's centre on the downstream side tells its story.

Getting there. Kew Bridge overground station is just over the road from the north end of Kew Bridge. Kew Gardens tube station is a mile away. The 65 bus runs between Kew Bridge and Richmond station. Kew Pier is on the south bank near the bridge.

Walking. Kew Bridge to Chiswick Bridge is 1¾ miles (2.75km) on the north bank and 1¼ miles (2km) on the south bank. Barnes Footbridge is a further 1 mile (1.5km).

8. KEW BRIDGE TO CHISWICK BRIDGE

North bank

A pleasant stroll after the mayhem of Brentford High Street. **Strand-on-the-Green** is the most westerly of the four villages that formed Old Chiswick. Despite the infill building of the last two centuries, it has retained much of its village charm. At a time when salmon and other fish were plentiful in the river, this was a fishing village. The Strand element of the name comes from Old English meaning a shore, as it does in modern English. The Strand, a street in central London, comes from the same source. Chiswick itself is recorded as Chesewye in 1230; the name may mean cheese farm, though there are other interpretations. Chiswick occupies all the land in one of the river's many ox-bows.

Paddle board hire and tuition under the arches of Kew Bridge: www.active360.co.uk/

The Steam Packet, 85 Strand-On-The-Green, W4 3PU. Tel: 0203 994 8140. Brunning & Price. Real ale and food. A new pub in an old building. Restaurant and outdoor tables overlooking the river. Live music on Fridays. The adjacent building is now the head office of Fuller, Smith, and Turner, from where they manage their 380 or so pubs.

Bell and Crown, 11-13 Thames Rd, Strand on the Green, W4 3PL. Tel: 020 8994 4164. Fuller's. Real ale and food. An 18th century pub and safer for tall customers than the Bull's Head.

The fine 18th century houses here attracted many distinguished residents over the years. **Johann Zoffany** (1733-1810), the artist, lived at №65. He specialised in informal portraits ("conversation pieces") and large pictorial canvases. Like other European artists, he spent time in India working for both Indian and British clients. *The Last Supper* altarpiece in St John's Cathedral, Calcutta is his work, and there is another, rather closer, in St Paul's Church in Brentford. Several more of his works are in Tate Britain. Carla Lane, the scriptwriter *(Liver Birds)*, was a later resident.

At №46 & 47 is a former malthouse, though the characteristic pyramidal roofs behind are only really visible from the other bank. This was later a workshop of Ailsa Craig Engines, marine engineers and pioneers of outboard motors.

Dylan Thomas (1914-1953), the rumbustious and hard-drinking Welsh poet, lived for a time at Ship House Cottage (among many other places). His finest work was *Under Milk Wood*, but most people remember the titles *Do Not Go Gentle Into That Good Night*, and *And Death Shall Have No Dominion*, if little more. Strong stuff and well worth reading.

Oliver's Island was called Strand Ayt until the mid-18th century, which makes it unlikely that its name derives from Oliver Cromwell having taken refuge there. And even more unlikely that he got there via a secret tunnel. It is known that there was a smithy on the island, and that barge building and repair was carried out. The City of London (then the navigation authority) collected tolls from a barge moored by the island, and that is how the City Barge pub got its name. Fuller's brew a light bitter (3.8% ABV) called Oliver's Island. Well worth a try

№29 the **Post House** was once a post office. №28 is **Tunnel Cottage**, so-called as it is built over Post Office Alley, an old right of way. The cottage was rebuilt in 1752. The riverside path floods at high tide, and you may find yourself beating a retreat through the tunnel to Thames Road.

City Barge, 27 Strand-on-the-Green, W4 3PH. Tel: 0208 994 2148. Metropolitan Pub Co. Real ale and food. A 14th century pub that was badly damaged by a parachute mine in 1940 and heavily rebuilt. Must be 50 (and a bit!) years since I first had a pint here. And for the first time in many years, I have just been offered the choice between a straight glass, known in some parts of the country as a sleever or a slip-handled glass, and a dimple jug.

Kew Railway Bridge was built in 1869 of wrought iron lattice girders on cast iron piers to carry trains to Richmond. It is unusual in carrying both overground and tube trains. The arched abutments are red brick with stone detailing. The bridge features in *The Dalek Invasion of Earth*, an early episode of *Doctor Who*. Strand-on-the-Green Sailing Club is based in the arch.

Bull's Head, 15 Strand-on-the-Green W4 3PQ. Tel: 020 8994 1204. Chef and Brewer (Greene King). Real ale and food. Another winner. Oldest licensed of the pubs along here (1722).

№11 has a blue plaque to **Donald Pleasence** (1919-1995). He was an English stage and film actor who started his career as a railway clerk. Best known for his many parts in horror films, he also appeared as Blofeld in *You Only Live Twice* and in *The Great Escape*. This latter was fitting as he completed sixty bombing sorties as a radio operator in Bomber Command before being shot down and made a prisoner-of-war.

Hopkin Morris Cottages is a row of three almshouses along Grove Row. The name dates from 1933, though the foundation is perhaps as far back as the mid-16th century. Three plaques on the end wall facing the river tell the story of renovations over the years. Note the chimney pots.

The path meets Grove Park Road by a pink granite **drinking fountain**, one of 109 endowed by the Reardon Memorial Trust and put up by the Metropolitan Drinking Fountain and Cattle Trough Association. Miss Ellen Reardon also endowed accommodation for homeless women and help for indigent solicitors and their widows. Wonder of wonders, the fountain still works providing water for humans and dogs. Nearby are the remains of Grove Park Drawdock and Pier. Follow Grove Park Road to a mini roundabout, then bear right into Hartington Road. A path signed to the river is a dead-end.

St Paul's Church (1872) was endowed by the Duke of Devonshire and designed by his architect Henry Currey. The church grounds and the vicarage next door are popular film locations, and *Tinker, Tailor, Soldier, Spy* and *The Theory of Everything* set scenes here. And those British television favourites *Grantchester*,

Lewis, and *Endeavour* have all used St Paul's as a substitute for Cambridgeshire or Oxford. Dylan Thomas lived for a short time at The Vicarage.

Opposite the church is **Hartington Court**, a fine 1930s Art Deco apartment block. **Thames Village** was built in the 1950s (and looks it) on the site of a gravel pit. Note the roads called **Chiswick Staithe**. Staithe is a word from the Norse *stoth* meaning a landing stage, common enough in Norfolk but very rare down here. There is a former fishing village in North Yorkshire called Staithes, but locals pronounce that more like Steeas. Finally, turn down Chiswick Quay (road) to reach the river and the marina.

Chiswick Quay Marina started life as the rather grandiosely named Port of Chiswick when the ornamental lake of Grove House was connected to the river. Cubitt's built concrete barges here using gravel from the nearby pit. As the demand for barges dried up, the dock became Cubitt's Yacht Basin. Developers wanted to fill this in but settled for a rather pleasing scheme with Mediterranean influences.

Cross the lock gates at the entrance to the marina and follow the path around the back of the boat clubs. This brings you to the bridge.

South bank

There is a pedestrian passage under Kew Bridge. If you are starting from Kew station, you need to walk the full length of the bridge on the downstream side and then double back towards the river.

Westerly Ware is ancient common land, once more extensive, and cattle still grazed here in 1920. 'Ware' is a variant of weir and thought to relate to local fishermen who once used this space to dry and repair their nets. Today, it is a public park with tennis courts and attractive war memorial gardens.

Kew mortuary, just outside the war memorial gates, was for bodies retrieved from the river when the local parish was obliged to deal with them; built in 1870 or so, it is now used as a tool shed by Kew Gardens Rotary.

Kew Gardens Pier is on the Thames River Boats route from Westminster Pier to Richmond; full details: https://www.thamesriverboats.co.uk/

Oliver's Island was called Strand Ayt until the mid-18th century, which makes it unlikely that its name derives from Oliver Cromwell having taken refuge there. And even more unlikely that he got there via a secret tunnel. It is known that there was a smithy on the island, and that barge building and repair was carried out. The City of London (then the navigation authority) collected tolls from a barge moored by the island, and that is how the City Barge pub got its name.

Opposite the island are **Short Lots**. Allotments are small parcels of land, typically 300 square yards (250m^2), made available to local residents for their cultivation. The Inclosure Acts (mainly in the 18th century) assigned ownership of previously common or waste land, and the provision of allotments was intended to relieve hardship among the 'labouring classes'.

Kew Railway Bridge was built in 1869 of wrought iron lattice girders on cast iron piers to carry trains to Richmond. It is unusual in carrying both overground and tube trains. The arched abutments are red brick with stone detailing. The bridge features in *The Dalek Invasion of Earth*, an early episode of *Doctor Who*.

Snail reserve. The rare two-lipped door snail or Thames door snail (*Alinda biplicata*) is found here and on (the inaccessible) Isleworth Ait. It has a spiral shell and a clausilium or door to close the opening in the shell. It is generally only seen in daytime after rain when it comes out to graze on algae and lichen.

The National Archives, TW9 4DU. The Public Record Office, the main repository of government and legal records dating back to the Norman Conquest (1066), is in Chancery Lane in the City. Lack of space led to the building of this new facility in 1977. The original Domesday Book (1086) is kept here, and there are readers' facilities for the millions of documents. Special exhibitions and lectures take place regularly. Little is visible from the path because of new building.

Look across the river to where there is no riverside path to see London University Boat Club and Hartington Court flats.

Kew Biothane Plant is redundant, and planning consent has been sought for old people's housing. When I saw biothane on the map, I expected some sort of green gas production or the like. Biothane turned out to be a trade name for non-allergenic strapping coated with PVC or TPU.

Chiswick Bridge

The bridge opened in 1933 as part of the same traffic relief scheme as Twickenham Bridge. The structure is of reinforced concrete faced with Portland stone.

Getting there. Buses do run over Chiswick Bridge, but walking on to Barnes Footbridge and getting a train there is easier.

Walking. Chiswick Bridge to Barnes Footbridge is 1 mile (1.5km), or 2¾ miles (5.25km) to Hammersmith Bridge.

9. CHISWICK BRIDGE TO BARNES BRIDGE

North bank

Walk under Chiswick Bridge, behind **Tideway Scullers School,** which is in fact a rowing club founded in 1957. The clubhouse was built in 1984, and the club is notable for training young rowers.

There are two forms of competitive rowing: sculling and sweep rowing. Sculling is where the oarsman (or woman) has two oars, one in each hand, as opposed to sweep rowing where the person has both hands on one oar. You will

35

see examples of both on the river. Sculls are generally for one, two, or four rowers. We have seen a sculled eight on the river, apparently used for training rather than racing. Sculling can also refer to the technique of propelling a dinghy with a single oar over the stern; rarely seen these days, but the reason many rowing dinghies have a notch in the centre of the transom.

The black and white **finishing post** of the University Boat Race is just downstream of the clubhouse. Look across the river for the corresponding **University Stone**. Over to your left is Duke's Meadow Golf Club and, behind that, Chiswick Rugby Football Club, though invisible from the river bank.

The massive Mortlake Brewery, now disused, and The Ship pub are on the other bank.

Dan Mason Drive, running parallel to the footpath, is named after one of the two brothers who ran a soap company in Chiswick from the late 19th century. Well-known brands included Mansion House red floor polish and Cherry Blossom boot polish. Cherry Blossom's great rival Kiwi, as any old-time squaddie will tell you, is better for spit and polish. Kiwi is an Australian brand, named after the New Zealand flightless bird because the wife of one of the inventors came from there. Progressive employers, Dan and Charles Mason gifted the playing fields to their employees. Dandy Nichols, who played Alf Garnett's long-suffering wife Else in *Till Death Do Us Part*, worked for the company before taking to the stage.

Thames Tradesmen's Rowing Club, based in the Chiswick Boathouse, was founded in 1897. Its name derives from a very English bit of snobbery; most rowing clubs were for men (only men in those days) in 'non-physical work'. The TTRC was open to all-comers.

The path continues under the railway bridge on a new footbridge. Alternatively, follow the old route along Dan Mason Drive parallel to the railway line, which gives access to **Duke's Hollow Nature Reserve**, a bosky ravine. At the end of the road is a footpath under the line.

South bank

Mortlake is mentioned in the Domesday Book as such. The origin of the name is obscure but, unlike Aigues-Mortes in southern France, apparently nothing to do with either dead or water.

Parliament Mews was built on the site of Cromwell House, which took its name from Thomas Cromwell, Lord Great Chamberlain to Henry VIII, not to be confused with Cromwell *père et fils* of the Civil War and Commonwealth a hundred years later.

The **University Stone** marks the finish of the University Boat Race course (the start is in Putney); a corresponding black and white post stands on the other bank. The **Head of the River Race** is run over the same course as the University Boat Race, but downstream and on an ebb tide. This event takes place during March and is a time trial, with boats being sent off at ten-second intervals. The popularity of rowing as a competitive sport is evidenced by entries having to be limited to 420 boats. The race was founded in 1925 by Steve Fairbairn whose memorial is further downstream. He insisted, tongue firmly in cheek, that it was not really a race, just a means of getting crews to exercise over a longer distance.

Over to the right from the marker is an interesting enclave of old houses. Behind its 18th century stucco **Leyden House** is a 15th century timber-framed structure. Its front wall bears the portcullis fire mark of the Westminster Insurance Company.

The Ship, 10 Thames Bank, SW14 7QR. Tel: 020 8876 1439. Greene King. Real ale and food. Famous old pub (formerly Taylor Walker) that dates from 1781 and has a fine Act of Parliament clock over the fireplace. Good view of the river.

Next door to the pub is the huge former **Mortlake Brewery**. There had been a brewery on this site since the 15th century, a monastic foundation. The present one became known as the Stag Brewery only after the demolition of the original Stag Brewery in Pimlico in 1959. In the 19th century, it was taken over by Watney, latterly the brewer of so disgusting keg beers that they inspired the formation of the Campaign For Real Ale (CAMRA). After passing through the hands of various international fizzy lager conglomerates it was sold to a developer in 2015. Proposals to develop the site are currently held up by the usual planning argy-bargy. For the moment, it has found a new use as a film location.

You cross an old **slipway-cum-drawdock** in front of Boat Race House. The path here is very rough; you can only avoid this by walking 200m inland to Low Richmond Road and turning left.

The Limes, 123 Mortlake High Street, SW14 8SN was built in the 1720s for the Countess of Strafford. The Georgian facade and Tuscan porch are later. The house became Mortlake Town Hall in 1895, but after bomb damage in 1940 was converted to offices, then flats. Turner painted two views from the house, though both are now in the USA.

Sir Richard Burton (1821-1890) was a soldier, scholar, and explorer, but probably best remembered today as translator of the *1001 Nights* and the *Kama Sutra*. He died in Trieste, and his widow Isabel brought his body to the Catholic burial ground in South Worple Way for burial, though he was more atheist than Roman Catholic. She designed his memorial in the style of a bedouin tent and joined him there on her death in 1896. The interior is visible through a window at the rear. A collection relating to Burton is on show at Orleans House in Twickenham.

Barnes, like Mortlake, is mentioned (as *Berne*) in the Domesday Book. Unlike Mortlake, the origin of the name is simple: it means just that, barns. The canons of St Paul's Cathedral held the manor up until the Dissolution, and the Dean and Chapter still have the right to appoint the vicar.

The riverfront road is **The Terrace**, with a number of fine houses. Outside №27 or №28, the Comte d'Antraigues and his wife were murdered in 1812 by an

Italian former servant who then shot himself. The couple had spied for and upset just about every side in the convoluted politics of the Napoleonic Wars.

Ye White Hart, The Terrace, SW13 0NR. Tel: 020 8876 5177. Young's. Real ale and food. A fine Victorian pub overlooking the river. The pub was once headquarters of Barnes Football Club. The club is known to have existed in 1862, and the following year, it became a founder member of the Football Association. In the years before the rules were formulated, the game could be extremely rough, more like rugby. The club took part (against Richmond) in the first game to be played under the new rules, and was first to play a match in competition for the FA Cup in 1871/2. The club has recently been reformed.

Barnes Bridge

The first railway bridge, a cast iron structure, was opened in 1849. Following the Tay Bridge disaster in 1879, and the collapse of another cast iron bridge on the Brighton line, thoughts turned to a replacement. This was built in the 1890s alongside the existing bridge to a wrought iron (looked more like steel to us) bowstring girder design; the pedestrian walkway was added at the same time. The spans of the earlier bridge were left in place, best seen from underneath; it is proposed to turn it into a garden bridge.

Getting there. Trains to Barnes Bridge station from Waterloo (do not confuse with Barnes station, and note that not all Barnes trains go to Barnes Bridge). A footbridge to the north bank is attached to the rail bridge.

Walking. Barnes Bridge to Hammersmith Bridge is 2 miles (3.25km) on the north bank and 1¾ miles (3km) on the south bank.

10. BARNES BRIDGE TO HAMMERSMITH BRIDGE

North bank

From the end of the footbridge from Barnes Bridge station, follow the path past a bandstand and two shelters. Inland is **Duke's Meadow**, a large open space with many sports fields. Two gaily decorated pylons mark the limit of Duke's Meadow as you reach the developments around Chiswick Pier.

Chiswick Pier is a mooring for houseboats, mostly Dutch-built and with interesting histories. The exception is *Reliance*, a Humber barge built in Knottingly, Yorkshire in 1933. Also there is a **Royal National Lifeboat Institution station**, and their orange rescue boat is usually moored at the northern end of the pier.

Inland from the pier (up Corney Road) is **Chiswick House & Gardens**, Burlington Lane, Chiswick W4 2RP. Lord Burlington designed this fine Palladian house in the 1720s to display his art collection; appropriately, his townhouse on

Piccadilly is now the Royal Academy. After mixed fortunes, including time as a lunatic asylum, the house has recently been restored. The landscaped gardens with follies and statues are an early example of their kind. Entry free to English Heritage members. Continue along the path to the slipway and:

Church of St Nicholas, Church Street. The tower dates from 1446, and the rest was rebuilt (rather nicely) in the 19th century. The church is open on Sunday afternoons. Note the flood plaque low down by the entrance gate. **Hogarth**, the cartoonist and artist who lived nearby, is commemorated (epitaph by David Garrick the actor) adjacent to the church. Also here are Frederick Hitch (monument with helmet), who won the Victoria Cross at Rorke's Drift, and Henry Joy, the bugler who sounded the charge for the Light Brigade at Balaclava. Whistler too, but finding any of them in this large and rather unkempt area is another matter.

Over the road from the church is the tower of the **Lamb Brewery**, a contemporary of Fuller's but closed since 1920.

You can walk up Church Street and brave the underpasses of the Hogarth Roundabout on the Great West Road (A4) to reach **Hogarth's House**, where prints of his work are on display. Open 1200-1700 except Monday, entry free.

Between 1864 and 1909, Church Wharf was the base of **Thornycroft Shipbuilding**. The business began when the young Joseph Thornycroft, son of the sculptor Thomas (*Boudicca* by Westminster Bridge), built a fast steam launch. The yard soon expanded and eventually completed over 250 vessels, providing work for 1700 people. Many of these vessels were torpedo boats, precursors of the destroyer; customers included most European navies and also Imperial Japan and South American navies. The largest ship built at Chiswick was *HMS Speedy*, a 74m (242ft) long torpedo boat of 810 tons. Later boats were capable of up to 30 knots (35mph or 56km/hr). By this time, Hammersmith Bridge had become an obstacle, with masts and funnels having to be dismantled. As a result, major shipbuilding moved to Southampton and small vessels upriver to Platt's Eyot at Hampton. A separate Thornycroft company produced first steam and then petrol-engined commercial vehicles and, before the First World War, high quality cars.

We now follow **Chiswick Mall** with its display of fine vernacular architecture. Many of these houses have a riverside garden over the road. **Bedford House** was the home of the actor Sir Michael Redgrave (1908-1985) and his talented family. **Red Lion House** was once a pub of that name and is next door to the Griffin Brewery.

Chiswick Eyot is on the right. The green pole at the southern end is roughly half distance on the boat race course. Osiers, thin willow offshoots were grown here for basket making.

Griffin Brewery, Chiswick Lane, W4 2QB. There has been a brewery on this site since the 16th century. Different brewers operated here until, in 1848, the business evolved into Fuller, Smith & Turner. Following Young's of Wandsworth selling off its brewing business in 2006, this was the last major brewery in

London. Now, it is owned by Asahi, the Japanese drinks conglomerate. Guided tours if you think it's worth touring what is now a multinational's premises. In a further sign of the times, Fullers used the so-called Covid pandemic as an excuse to close and sell the Mawson's Arms, in effect the brewery tap. At least the beer shop up Chiswick Lane South is still open.

Real ale

Real ale is traditional British beer. The fundamental difference from other beers is that it is still alive and fermenting when put into the delivery container, traditionally an oak cask, more often stainless steel these days. Real ale needs careful handling and attention to keeping the dispense lines and hand pumps clean. Failure to do this results in a flat and sour drink. This is why the big brewers, from the 1960s onwards, turned to producing pasteurised, pressurised keg beers. Pasteurising the beer destroys the natural carbon dioxide; the gas that has to be added dissolves into the beer and makes it bright or fizzy. Real ale should be served at cellar temperature, say 10-12°C; any colder spoils the flavour.

The Campaign for Real Ale (CAMRA) was founded in 1971; it has been one of the real successes of consumerism in the United Kingdom in forcing the big brewers to continue making real ale and opening the market to newcomers.

Walpole House, named after Horace Walpole's nephew Thomas, was once a school where Thackeray was a boarder; it is said to have inspired Miss Pinkerton's Academy in *Vanity Fair*. Daniel O'Connell (1775-1847), the Irish nationalist who founded the National Bank of Ireland, lodged here whilst studying law in London.

Mari Deli Dining, 1a Eyot Gardens, W6 9TN. Tel: 0207 041 9251. Amazing place, anything from a sandwich to Dover sole or lobster linguini, and all done on the premises. Tiny inside, so booking essential if you want a meal. https://maridelidining.com

Around Mulberry Place, Chiswick Mall becomes Hammersmith Terrace, a reflection of old borough boundaries. The houses on the right face the river; what we see are the back doors. Three houses have blue plaques:

№12. **A.P. Herbert** (1890-1971). Lawyer, sailor, soldier, humorous writer (*Punch* and *Misleading Cases*), and Independent MP for Oxford University. He was instrumental in reform of the divorce laws and was the only non-commissioned officer to attend the House of Commons in uniform. He loved the Thames and commuted to the House in his boat *Water Gipsy*. Quite a character.

№7. **Sir Emery Walker** (1851-1933) was an artist, engraver, and printer involved in the Arts and Crafts Movement. This is one of very few houses still to have original William Morris wallpaper in most rooms. Guided tours and full information: https://www.emerywalker.org.uk

№3. **Edward Johnston** (1872-1944). Typographer and calligrapher. You'll have seen his work; he designed the roundel motif and clear sans-serif typeface for the London Underground. Note that this plaque is in a sans-serif style rather than the usual serif one – compare it with the other two nearby.

The Black Lion, 2 South Black Lion Lane, W6 9TJ. Tel: 0208 748 2639. Free house. Real ale and food (more interesting than most). 18th century building with a skittle alley. Bills itself as a country pub, and that's just how it feels. Portrait of A.P. Herbert (see above) over 'his' table. Outside seating and steps down to river.

Church of St Peter, Black Lion Lane. Built 1827-29 in Grecian style. The statue *Draped Woman* outside by the Czech sculptor Karel Vogel was installed in 1959. The church and sculpture are the other side of the Great West Road; take the subway at the end of Black Lion Lane.

The Old Ship, 25 Upper Mall, W6 9TD. Tel: 020 8748 2593. Youngs. Real ale and food. Covered riverside terrace and more outside seating. Mixture of old and new, and very stylish. Dog friendly.

London Corinthian Sailing Club, Linden House, 60 Upper Mall, W6 9TA. Tel: 020 8748 3280. An old established club (1894), based here since 1963, offers sail training and dinghy racing. Fine Georgian building from around 1730.

48 Upper Mall bears on its side wall a blue plaque to **Eric Ravilious** (1903-1942); best known as a war artist, he went missing flying on an air-sea rescue mission from Iceland. Weltje Road, incidentally, is named after a chef of the Prince Regent (later George IV) who lived here in retirement.

Rivercourt House dates from around 1800 and is now part of Latymer Upper School, founded in 1624.

Kelmscott House, 26 Upper Mall. This house, built in about 1780, has two claims to fame. In 1816, Sir Francis Ronalds invented the electric telegraph in the back garden, only to be told by the Admiralty that the idea had no future in peacetime; telegraph at that time meant mechanical semaphore towers. There is a small white plaque on the front of the building. William Morris (1834-1896), one of the founders of the Arts and Crafts Movement, took the lease in 1879 and named it after Kelmscott Manor, his country house upriver in Oxfordshire. The house is now privately owned, but the William Morris Society has a museum in the basement and puts on frequent events. Details: https://williammorris-society.org/. Note the trees in front of the next two houses.

The Dove, 19 Upper Mall, W6 9TA. Tel: 020 8748 9474. Fullers. Real ale and food. Cashless. James Thomson is said to have written *Rule Britannia* here in 1740; Thomas Arne composed the music later the same year. Riverside terrace. The front bar is said to be the smallest in England. The longest, by tradition, though oft disputed, is that of the Cittie of Yorke on High Holborn. Another pub associated with A.P. Herbert, and other literary greats.

Just past The Dove is a blue plaque to **T.J Cobden-Sanderson** (1840-1922), an artist and bookbinder friend of William Morris who invented the Arts and Crafts tag.

The path enters **Furnivall Gardens** and becomes the Lower Mall; this built-up area was heavily bombed and later cleared to create the gardens. Dr Frederick Furnivall, a controversial character, was a co-founder and editor of the Oxford English Dictionary. In 1896, he founded the Furnivall Sculling Club which, by 1907, had active female members. The club still exists, and its boathouse is beside the path.

Hammersmith Creek used to flow through the gardens, providing moorings and boatbuilders' yards, sometimes referred to as 'Little Wapping'. Redundant by 1936, it was covered over, though the eagle-eyed may spot the outfall.

Rutland Arms, 15 Lower Mall, W6 9DJ. Tel: 0208 748 5586. Greene King. Real ale and food. Traditional pub where you can get a snack lunch that doesn't cost the earth. Rutland was for centuries the smallest county in England.

Blue Anchor, 13 Lower Mall, W6 9DJ. Tel: 020 3951 0580. Hippo Inns. Real ale and food (good but gastropub prices). Outdoor seating. First licensed in 1722. Holst is said to have composed his *Hammersmith Suite* here, though pedants will tell you there is no such piece of music. This is hair-splitting; the piece titled *Hammersmith* is a prelude and scherzo, and, for good measure, there are *Brook Green* and *St Paul's Suites*. The pub is glimpsed in the closing credits of *Minder*.

South bank

The road along the riverside is The Terrace. Blue plaques tell that Ninette de Valois lived at №14 and Gustav Holst at №10. de Valois (1898-2001) was a dancer, ballet teacher, and founder of the Royal Ballet who has the distinction of having lived right through the 20th century. At the end of The Terrace, you can make a short detour to get a feel of the village atmosphere of Barnes. Follow the High Street round to the right, and you will find the village green and the pond, not to mention:

The Sun, 7 Church Road, SW13 9HE. Tel: 020 8876 5256. Mitchell & Butler. Real ale and food. Traditional pub near the pond and The Green.

Otherwise, continue along Small Profits Dock. Past the roundabout, the road becomes Lonsdale Road.

The Bulls Head, 373 Lonsdale Road, SW13 9PY. Tel: 020 8876 5241. Youngs. Real ale and food, Sunday roast. Famous for live music, especially jazz.

The Thames Towpath splits from Lonsdale Road, and you can enjoy nearly two miles of woodland walking. Growth is quite dense on the riverside, and you rarely see much of the other bank.

Leg o' Mutton Nature Reserve. Lonsdale Road Reservoir was built in 1838 and was in use up to 1960. The nickname Leg o' Mutton comes from its shape. The site was earmarked for housing, but local groups successfully lobbied for a nature reserve. Apart from all the water birds, it is home to bats, tawny owls, woodpeckers, kestrels, and sparrowhawks. A walk, separate from the towpath, runs around the lake.

Looking across the river, you see Chiswick Pier with an orange RNLI lifeboat moored at the end; the Chiswick Ferry used to cross here. Then comes the long wooded Chiswick Eyot; at low tide, this hardly appears to be an island. You glimpse the tower of Chiswick Parish Church (St Nicholas) with its vestigial spire.

Old maps show the whole riverside from here to Hammersmith Bridge taken up by reservoirs and water treatment works. Two very different schools now occupy this space. The **Swedish School**, properly Svenska Skolan, was founded in 1907 in Marylebone. A co-educational independent school, it caters for 275 or so pupils and gets an outstanding rating from the OFSTED inspection organisation. Sweden, along with Finland, is often regarded as having the best public education system in Europe. Once, they said the same of Scotland.

St Paul's School was founded in 1509 by John Colet, Dean of St Paul's Cathedral on a site near the cathedral. The school moved to Hammersmith late in the 19th century and to this site in 1968. The school has just under 1000 pupils, all boys (a few boarders), and is notably high-achieving. During the Second World War, the former school buildings were taken over as headquarters of 21 Army Group comprising the British and Canadian armies preparing for the D-Day landings; in command was General B.L. Montgomery, himself an old boy of the school. Earlier old boys include Milton, Pepys, Judge Jeffreys, Halley (comet man), and G.K. Chesterton. It may be worth mentioning that British "public" schools are anything but public; entry is competitive, and the fees run up to £50,000 a year, more than four times a year's tuition fees at university.

Hammersmith Bridge

This was London's first suspension bridge, completed in 1827 to the design of William Tierney Clark. This was seven years after the Union Chain Bridge over the River Tweed linking England to Scotland. Clark later did the Chain Bridge over the Danube joining Buda to Pest.

The present bridge is a replacement designed by Sir Joseph Bazalgette and built in 1887. It stands on the same piers as its predecessor, and some may feel the classical Etruscan arches of the original preferable to the fussy Victorian ironwork. Greaves' marvellous painting of the old bridge on Boat Race Day is in Tate Britain (currently in the 1815 room). The clearance under the bridge is only 3.6m (12ft) at high tide.

Note the plaques at either end of the bridge, once painted in the proper heraldic colours. There is also a memorial plaque for an airman who dived from the bridge to rescue a drowning woman and consequently died of tetanus. The IRA have had three goes at blowing up the bridge, in 1939 and again in 1996 and 2000, some damage being done on the last occasion.

At the time of writing, the bridge is undergoing a heavy restoration occasioned by expecting a 19th century structure to carry 21st century traffic; this has disrupted both excursion boats and the University Boat Race. The bridge is now open to pedestrians and cyclists but will be closed to motor traffic until 2027.

Getting there. Hammersmith tube station (District and Circle Lines) is a ten-minute walk from the bridge via St Paul's Church and its Green.

Walking. Hammersmith Bridge to Putney Bridge is 2 miles (3.25km) on the north bank and 1¾ miles (3km) on the south bank.

11. HAMMERSMITH BRIDGE TO PUTNEY BRIDGE

North bank

On the approach to the bridge from Hammersmith tube station is:

Old City Arms, 107 Hammersmith Bridge Road, W6 9DA. Tel: 020 8748 2359. Real ale and (Thai) food. A real Victorian boozer.

On the riverside at low tide, you can see the remains of a slipway, possibly for the barge builders who operated at **Beckett's Wharf**; a small riverside garden marks the wharf. **Gun Wharf** was the site of a factory for boring gun barrels. Next is the old **Hammersmith Drawdock**, still used as a slipway for launching small boats.

Riverside Studios occupies the site of an iron foundry and was converted into film studios in 1933. Purchased by the BBC in 1954, early episodes of *Doctor Who* and *Hancock's Half Hour* were recorded here. The Beeb moved out in 1975, and the place is now run as an art centre by a charitable trust. Bar and restaurant. Events details: www.riversidestudios.co.uk

Continue to the **statue of Lancelot 'Capability' Brown**, who lived locally, and the pier of Fulham Reach Boat Club. Just downstream of the statue, **Stamford Brook** flows into the river. A stone above the arch is marked HP and FP 1865, showing the border between Hammersmith Parish and Fulham Parish, though you will only see this by mudlarking along the shore at low tide. Do not try this without expert guidance, the mud can be dangerous.

Thames Tideway Tunnel

By 2000, it was obvious that Bazalgette's Victorian sewer system had become inadequate. There were two causes: increased population density (by almost a factor of three) and the concreting over of natural drainage. This meant that even relatively modest rainfall – surface water has to drain through the sewage system

– could result in raw sewage running into the river, undoing the work of the last seventy years in cleaning it up.

The answer is a huge new "super-sewer" tunnel running under the river, the only place to put it. This is a colossal undertaking involving a tunnel 25km (16 miles) long and 7.2m (24ft) in diameter. The tunnel starts at stormwater tanks in Acton in West London; it joins the river near Hammersmith Bridge and runs to Beckton Treatment Works, where the effluent is pumped to the surface for treatment. The tunnel is 30m below the surface at Hammersmith and reaches a maximum depth of 70m (230ft). It leaves the river at Limehouse for Abbey Mills Pumping Station and then on to Beckton.

The work is being carried out by a consortium known as Bazalgette Tunnel Ltd and is scheduled for completion in 2025. The total cost is around £6bn. The many access points have caused disruption along the river banks, but this will improve as the work winds down.

Fulham, as a place name, was first recorded as Fulenham in AD707 when the manor was granted to the Bishops of London. The name means Fulla's settlement on a flood plain, but who Fulla may have been is unknown. As far as this walk is concerned, Fulham runs as far as Chelsea Creek.

Easily missed is a memorial to **William Tierney Clark**, who built the first suspension bridge here and also the Chain Bridge across the Danube in Budapest. He is buried in St Paul's Church between here and the tube station.

The Blue Boat, Distillery Wharf, W6 9GD. Tel: 020 3092 2090. Fuller's. Real ale and food. Modern building with outdoor seating. 'Distillery Wharf' tells you that this was the site of Hammersmith Distillery; that had displaced Brandenburgh House, a refuge of the slighted Queen Caroline (1768-1821).

The **Figurehead** sculpture by Rick Kirby resembles the figurehead of a ship riding its bow wave. Two other female forms play like dolphins. The sculpture is of small pieces of bronze welded together.

On this part of the walk, you look across to the former Harrod's Furniture Depository with its two cupolas, now apartments. The two blocks downstream are Holst Mansions and Handel Mansions.

The site of the **Thames Wharf Studios** was, until 1979, the home of a small oil refining company. Car enthusiasts of a certain age will remember Duckham's Q20/50, the first multigrade motor oil, and still made for older cars. The building took its present form as a showcase of Rogers Stirk Harbour + Partners. The late Richard Rogers, with his partners, was one of the outstanding British architects of the last 45 years, with the Pompidou Centre (Paris) and the Lloyds Building (London) to his name.

The River Cafe, Thames Wharf, Rainville Road, W6 9HA. Tel: 020 7386 4200. Famed Italian restaurant, but pricey. Details: info@rivercafe.co.uk

The Crabtree, 40 Rainville Road W6 9HA. Tel: 020 7385 3929. Metropolitan Pub Co. Real ale and food. Riverside patio and garden.

Past The Crabtree, a narrow path follows the river bank and then rejoins the more accessible path. Some nice little properties contrast with the often mediocre apartments. The undeveloped nature of the opposite bank is the London Wetlands Centre, once reservoirs.

Rowberry Mead is a small park decorated with scraps of old engineering. At Stevenage Park, you need to walk up to Stevenage Road and turn right to skirt around the ground of **Fulham Football Club**. The club was formed in 1879 and has been based here at Craven Cottage since 1896. The ground takes its name from a former royal hunting lodge. At the end of the long red brick facade is the statue of **Johnny Haynes** (1934-2005), Fulham's greatest player. Apart from his 20-year spell at Craven Cottage, he won 56 England caps, 22 of them as captain.

The Riverside Stand was being redeveloped at the time of writing; when completed, it will be possible to continue along the riverside. For the moment, take the pedestrian entrance to Fielder's Meadow, and return to the river.

The path enters **Bishop's Park** at steps down to the river. From here you can turn inland to the Tea House Café (good) and toilets. This leads to **Fulham Palace**. The palace dates in part from the early 16th century, though activity on the site goes back to pre-Roman times. It was built as a residence for the bishops of London and served as such until 1973. The palace, in the form of a quadrangle, is now a museum (free) set in attractive gardens with specimen trees. A late 19th century chapel stands nearby.

All Saints Church was heavily rebuilt in the late 19th century, and only the ragstone tower is original. The tower lost its wooden spire in 1845. After Chelsea Old Church (see below), All Saints is reckoned to have the finest collection of monuments of any outer London church. Ten bishops are buried in the churchyard.

Alternatively, continue along the river bank. **Bishop's Meadow** was embanked in the 1890s. By the second set of river steps is the pink marble **International Brigades Memorial** to local men who volunteered to fight on the nationalist side in the Spanish Civil War. There is more on this subject in the South Bank section 18. The **sculptures** on the green just before you reach the bridge are all by James Wedgwood (1886-1975).

South bank

Past a green open space, the huge building on your right is the former **Harrod's Furniture Depository**, a store for stock too large to be taken to the Knightsbridge shop. Now apartments, it is named William Hunt Mansions after the original architect. Behind are buildings named after Charles Harrod, the founder, and Richard Burbidge, who took over from him. Harrod's, incidentally, was known as Horrid's to generations of small boys dragged there by their mothers to buy school uniforms.

The following two blocks of mansion flats are named after those two German-sounding but very English composers, Handel (1685-1759) and Holst (1874-1934). Apart from all his other fine music, we should remember Handel for his *Water Music* written to be played on the Thames. Holst also has a local connection as he taught for many years at St Paul's School for Girls in Hammersmith.

London Wetland Centre is a nature reserve covering 105 acres (42ha). This used to be Barn Elms Waterworks, consisting of four large squarish reservoirs; now, there are two miles of footpaths and hides for watching the large numbers of aquatic birds. The visitor centre also has CCTV viewing. Access to the Visitor Centre (and the Red Lion pub) is via Queen Elizabeth Walk, though this is ½ mile (800m) from the river.

Roughly halfway down the Wetlands Centre, a monument to the Australian **Steve Fairbairn** (1862-1938) stands at the One Mile Post on the university boat race course. Like other members of his family, Fairbairn was a distinguished oarsman and rowing coach. After Cambridge University, he was a member of the London Rowing Club based a little downriver in Putney. Founded in 1856, it was the first club successfully to challenge Oxford and Cambridge.

Barn Elms House stood some way back from the river at the end of a tree-lined drive. The original manor house was lived in by Sir Francis Walsingham, spymaster of Elizabeth I. After the Restoration in 1660, it became popular for boating picnics; Pepys wrote enthusiastically about a visit. Later, the house, considerably enlarged, became home at various times to the Kit-Kat Club, the Ranelagh Club, and even Queen's Park Rangers football club. The house fell into disrepair and was demolished following a fire in 1954. The grounds became playing fields; the sinuous lake was the fish pond. In 1668, a duel was fought here between the Duke of Buckingham and the Earl of Shrewsbury, whom the duke had cuckolded. Shrewsbury was killed, and the evil duke took up full-time with the merry widow, an act which shocked even the libidinous Charles II.

Barn Elms Boathouse, the first of many between here and Putney Bridge, is a training centre where experienced scullers can hire boats.

Over the river is the new Riverside Stand of Fulham's **Craven Cottage** football ground with its flying roof.

Ashlone Wharf is where **Beverley Brook** joins the Thames. The brook rises in Worcester Park in south-west London and runs for 14 miles (23km) through Wimbledon Common and Richmond Park ponds. Recent work has improved the flood defences whilst allowing fish and eels to enter the brook from the Thames. Its name derives from *bever*, the European beaver which once frequented it and *ley*, a meadow. The pleasant market town of Beverley in the East Riding of Yorkshire comes from the same stem. There is a waymarked walk along the brook.

Leader's Gardens are named after John Temple Leader, a politician who formerly owned the land. The railings on the Embankment are the originals from 1903, a rare survivor of the drive for scrap iron and steel in the Second World War.

The statue *Exodus* marks the start of the **Putney Sculpture Trail**. All nine sculptures are by Alan Thornhill (1921-2020).

The first house after the gardens is **Bleak House**, though not the inspiration for Dickens' novel. The actual source of that is uncertain. A house in St Albans in Hertfordshire has been suggested, though it seems more likely to have been one of Dickens' favourite holiday haunts. Dickens is known to have roughed out the plot for *Bleak House* at Fort House in Broadstairs in Kent. Long after Dickens died in 1870, this became known as Bleak House and housed a Dickens museum.

A succession of famous **rowing clubs** has their boathouses along Putney Embankment. The river here is always busy with boats of all sizes accompanied by their coaches in dories.

Further along the Embankment, on either side of Putney Pier, are the sculptures *Horizontal Ambiguity* followed by *Load*, part of the **Putney Sculpture Trail**.

Duke's Head, 8 Lower Richmond Road, Putney, SW15 1JN. Tel: 020 8788 2552. Young's. Real ale and food (Sunday roast). Lavishly decorated Victorian pub.

J.R. Ackerley (1896-1967) was a true English eccentric who lived locally. With our interest in India we remember him best for his book *Hindoo Holiday* (1932), brought about through his friendship with E.M. Forster. A plaque on Star and Garter Mansions commemorates him.

The blue plaque on Kenilworth Court over the road is to **Fred Russell** (1862-1957), described as "the father of modern ventriloquism"; his dummy, Coster Joe, is denied a mention. Gockle o' geer, anyone?

Putney Bridge

When the first bridge opened in 1729, it was the only crossing, apart from ferries, between London Bridge and Kingston Bridge. The bridge was a 26-span wooden structure and a serious obstacle to navigation. This was not quite the first crossing here as the Parliamentarians had established a pontoon bridge in 1642. The bridge was altered to 23 spans in 1872 and replaced by Bazalgette's granite bridge in 1886. Water mains under the pavements replace an aqueduct. Putney Bridge has been the starting point of the **University Boat Race** since 1845. The crews race from here the 4½ miles (7.2km) upstream to Mortlake on a flood tide.

In 1795 Mary Wollstonecraft, the philosopher and early feminist, piqued at being abandoned by her lover, threw herself off the bridge. Had a waterman not rescued her, her daughter Mary would not have created *Frankenstein*.

Getting there. Putney Bridge tube station is on the north side of the road bridge. There is a footbridge on the downstream side of the rail bridge (Fulham Bridge). Thames Clipper RB6 makes its final stop at Putney Pier, but on weekday mornings and evenings only.

Walking. Putney Bridge to Wandsworth Bridge is 1½ miles (2.5km) on either bank, or 3½ miles (5.5km) to Battersea Bridge.

12. PUTNEY BRIDGE TO WANDSWORTH BRIDGE

North bank

After passing under Putney Bridge, turn sharp right back to the waterside. Alternatively, veer left for **Hurlingham Books**, 91 Fulham High Street, SW6 3JS. Tel: 0207 736 4363. Email: hurlinghambooks@gmail.com A traditional second-hand bookshop with a vast and eclectic stock. This path, beside the Premier Inn, also leads to the tube station.

Back on the river is a lovely weeping willow. Cross an old **drawdock**, now a nature reserve, and you are on Carrara Wharf, perhaps a clue as to what was landed here. A **mosaic** tells the story of the Oxford and Cambridge Boat Race which starts here.

The pretty **Fulham Railway Bridge** is pretty because the Act of Parliament authorising it said it had to be. It's certainly quite a contrast with some of the others, though its appearance is not improved by the water pipe attached to it. The odd thing about it is that it has never had an official name. The builders of this lattice girder bridge referred to it as Putney Railway Bridge, yet a recent plaque on the footbridge calls it Fulham Railway Bridge. This is of no concern to the locals who have always known it simply as "The Iron Bridge".

Now we need to make an inland detour to avoid private river frontage and the **Hurlingham Club**, *rus in urbe*, a country club in town. And jolly nice too. Membership is £1200 or so a year, but don't hold your breath. It costs money to go on the waiting list, and it's closed anyway.

From the river, walk beside the tracks until you reach Ranelagh Gardens, turn right under the bridge and continue to Napier Avenue, where you turn left. There is supposed to be a pillbox somewhere here, but it must be so well camouflaged that we missed it. At the end of Napier Avenue, turn right into Hurlingham Road. It is possible to take a short cut across the top end of **Hurlingham Park**, but there is no actual path. It is just as easy to walk to Broomhouse Lane, which leads down to the river, Broomhouse Pier, and the slipway. The only point of interest is a mock Jacobean building converted to yet more flats.

Follow the bank for a short distance before Tideway Tunnel works block the way, so join Carnwath Road. Rejoin the riverside path and walk along to Wandsworth Bridge. This last section was Trinidad Wharf, where tar from Trinidad's Pitch Lake was landed. The view across the river is of the mouth of the River Wandle and the adjacent waste transfer station.

Not the most exciting of walks. Of the 1½ miles (2.5km), you spend less than a third by the river. In fact, if you are going to walk just one bank, the other side is a better bet.

South bank

Church of St Mary the Virgin, Putney High Street, SW15 1SN. The tower, with its two clock faces and sundial, is 15th century. The rest was heavily rebuilt early in the 19th century, retaining some earlier elements. The rather odd interior layout stems from a severe fire in 1973. The fine Danish Marcussen organ was installed in 1982. Access to the church is through the café. Note the reference to Oliver Cromwell on the right as you enter, and the quotation on the gallery as you leave. Pepys heard 'a good sermon here' in 1667 but reckoned that the local girls were not very pretty. It was in this church (according to Dickens) that David Copperfield married Dora Spenlow.

The **Putney Debates** were held here in 1647 when the Parliamentarians (Roundheads) discussed England's constitutional future after the Civil War. Whilst actuality did not match the rhetoric, the debates had a considerable influence on future developments in England and, rather sooner, on formulating the American constitution. There is a permanent exhibition in the church.

The fine building with two caryatid figures over the road from the church was once the **White Lion Hotel**, built in 1887 and Grade II listed. Unused for several years, it is probably due a fire.

The **Memorial Cross** in Church Square is to the people of Putney, soldiers and civilians, who died in both World Wars. To the south of the square is *The Turning Point*, the fourth sculpture on the Putney Sculpture Trail.

The Rocket, Putney Wharf, Brewhouse Lane, SW15 2JQ. Tel: 020 8780 8970. Wetherspoon's. Real ale (cheaper than most) and food. Modern pub in a riverside setting. The building above The Rocket started as an uninspired 60s office block, the ICL Tower; amazing what a bit of imagination can achieve.

The *Punch and Judy* sculpture (2013) is followed by *Mother Figure* further along the river bank past the slipway.

Turn away from the river and follow the pleasant Deodar Road to the left. The **deodar**, *Cedrus deodara,* is a species of cedar common in the Himalayan foothills and the national tree of Pakistan. The deodar is mentioned in the Hindu epic *The Ramayana* and the oil used in ayurvedic medicine; no deodars here, but several other unusual trees. Over Deodar Road is Fulham Railway Bridge with its walkway to Putney Bridge tube station. Continue through the arch along Blade Mews to Wandsworth Park.

Wandsworth takes its name from the River Wandle, itself possibly named after a Saxon noble. The river once powered 68 water mills between here and its source in Croydon. On the left in **Wandsworth Park**, as the path regains the river, is Wandsworth Park River Terrace, maintained by the Friends of Wandsworth

Park, who have developed it as a sensory garden. The park is 20 acres (8ha) and was allotments until 1897. There are many fine trees, including the shady lime avenue along the river. A café and toilets are in the park inland from the far gate.

The barges moored at the low water mark provide roosting space for large birds like herons and cormorants, and have nesting boxes for sand martins and kingfishers. The *Pygmalion* sculpture at the end of the park is part of the Putney Sculpture Trail, as is *Nexus* by Putney Bridge Road in the south of the park.

Leave the park and follow Lighterman's Walk past the piers of Prospect Moorings. The *Fall* on Prospect Quay marks the end of Putney Sculpture Trail. Wandsworth Riverside Quarter Pier and boat moorings follow this.

Walk along the riverside from here to the River Wandle and cross the first footbridge. On the left is The Spit between Bell Lane Creek and the River Wandle. Walk down to see the **Sail sculpture** by Sophie Horton and the view across the river to a short length of riverside walk and the Thames Tunnel works.

From here onwards, the south bank became heavily industrialised during the 19th century. Cross the second footbridge, and to the right is the Wandsworth to Pimlico Cable Tunnel building. Walk along Smugglers Way to avoid the **Western Riverside Refuse and Recycling Centre**. Barges take the waste to be burned for electricity at Bexley 20 miles (32km) downstream. The Bexley plant deals with more than 500,000 tonnes of rubbish a year.

At the end of the recycling centre, Waterside Path to the left takes you to Nickols Walk along the river, and this brings you to:

The Ship, 41 Jews Row, SW18 1TB. Tel: 020 8870 9667. Youngs. Real ale and food. Started life in 1786 as the Thames Watermen's Inn. Burger bar behind the pub and ample seating overlooking the river.

The plant next to The Ship mixes the concrete for all the new flats few people can afford. Follow Pier Terrace to reach the bridge underpasS.

Wandsworth Bridge

Wandsworth and Albert Bridges were authorised on the same day in 1864, the last two private toll bridges to be permitted in London. Wandsworth Bridge was initially intended to be built on the same odd suspension principle as Albert Bridge, but the money would not run to that. The result was a narrow and weak lattice girder bridge that was a commercial failure. The present bridge, completed in 1940, is a decidedly utilitarian steel structure. The colour scheme is said to have originated in its camouflage against enemy bombers.

The traffic roundabout at the south end of the bridge, in 60s brutalist style, was used as a location in Kubrick's *A Clockwork Orange* (1971).

Getting there. Walkways under the roundabout lead to Wandsworth Town overground station, but this is not the easiest place to access public transport. Buses do run over the bridge, though there is still no easy access to a tube station.

Wandsworth Riverside Quarter Pier is on the Thames Clipper RB6 water bus route, though this operates only on weekday mornings and evenings.

Walking. Wandsworth Bridge to Battersea Bridge is 1¾ miles (3km) on either bank.

13. WANDSWORTH BRIDGE TO BATTERSEA BRIDGE

North bank

More road walking: from Wandsworth Bridge, walk up to the traffic lights and turn right into Townmead Road. The site on the right was once Swedish Wharf. John remembers it as a rather dodgy car auction where he once had the opportunity to buy the unmarked police Jaguar that had nicked him for speeding on the M4. He declined. Queen Mary I may have had Calais inscribed on her heart, but that registration SUU500F is etched on his brain more than fifty years later.

Follow Townmead Road past the office block of the former Kops Brewery, which occupied much of this area. A memorial plaque is on the wall. The business was started in 1890 by Polish-born Henry Lowenfeld to brew non-alcoholic ale and stout, mainly for export to the Empire. The same man built the Apollo Theatre in the West End and the Ocean Hotel on the Isle of Wight.

At the roundabout past Sainsbury, take Imperial Avenue down to the river. A lot of indifferent flats to start with, but at least it's unbroken riverside walking. **Imperial Park** is a much-needed slice of green; note the view along an avenue of trees to a fountain, and then the Sensory Garden. Out in the river is the Imperial Wharf Marina.

The Waterside, The Boulevard, Imperial Wharf, SW6 2SU. Tel: 020 7371 0802. Youngs. Real ale and food. Good location and nicely done. More a gastropub with prices to match.

Walking up the service road on the south side of Battersea Railway Bridge brings you to:

Roca London Gallery, Townmead Road SW6 2PY. Tel: 020 7610 9503. Zaha Hadid theme of flowing water inside. Billed as a funky designer venue. Modern architecture at its best – and London has plenty of the other kind. Details of events: http://www.rocalondongallery.com

Also here is Imperial Wharf overground station and a shortcut under the tracks to the Design Centre (see below).

Chelsea Harbour and Sands End. Looking around at the luxury flats and hotel, it is hard to believe that Chelsea Harbour was once a louche and cheap place to live. Until about thirty years ago, this was a scene of devastation of old gasworks and coal yards. The present marina and the creek were filled with houseboats, many based on old landing craft and patrol boats sold cheaply at the end of the Second World War.

Pass under Battersea Railway Bridge, another pretty one, and past Chelsea Harbour Pier (Thames Clipper RB6). The *Gateway of Hands* sculpture stands in front of the Belvedere Tower, which has a tide ball on its roof. Cross the lift bridge over the harbour entrance and stroll down to the harbour, where you find another sculpture, *The Fish*. The fine Harbour Yard building is now flexible office space. Behind the Chelsea Harbour Hotel is the:

Design Centre, Lots Road SW10 0XE. Tel: 020 7225 9166. A showcase and retail outlet for the best and brightest in British Design. Closed weekends (!). Details of events: www.dcch.co.uk

Follow the Thames Towpath up to the viewpoint at the mouth of Chelsea Creek, from where you can see the London Eye. The footbridge here is a shortcut to Lots Road. **Chelsea Creek**, more properly Counter's Creek (the name is a corruption of countess), rises near Kensal Green and flows into the river here. At one time, the river was converted into a canal as far as Olympia, but this was not financially successful. The route of the canal is still marked by the tracks of the railway company that bought it and filled it in, a process often repeated.

On the other side of the creek is **Lots Road Power Station**, built in 1902-04 specifically to power the underground railways; you can imagine what they were like with steam engines. Like all the other power stations along the Thames, it was located because of the ease of delivering coal; it burned 700 tons *a day*. At the time, it was said to be the largest power station ever built. It was converted to burn heavy oil in the 60s when it lost two of its chimneys, and to natural gas in the following decade. It was finally closed in 2002 and is being developed (very impressively) into apartments. Continue along Chelsea Creek, cross the footbridge, and turn right into Lots Road.

Lots Road, 114 Lots Road, SW10 0RJ. Tel: 020 7352 6645. Market Taverns. Real ale and food, Sunday roast. Imaginative menu. This pub was formerly known as the Balloon Tavern, taking its name from several balloon ascents nearby. As The Balloon, it featured in the 1966 flick *The Deadly Affair* starring James Mason.

Lots Road Pumping Station is a fine example of Edwardian municipal architecture. It deserves the same treatment as the power station.

Cremorne Gardens is a remnant of a large 19th century pleasure garden. It had a turbulent history (well worth reading about) and was eventually closed down as 'a nursery of every kind of vice'. Presumably, for that reason, Cremorne has lent its name to a series of spectacularly dirty books. The power station took over most of the gardens, leaving just this tiny part. An ornate set of gates from the original gardens has been restored and installed here. There are toilets. The views are good and appreciated by artists. The gardens lead onto first Cremorne Road and then Cheyne Walk. Welcome to the traffic! You'll be past St Katherine's Dock before you escape it again.

Blue plaques

The idea of linking famous people with the buildings where they lived or worked was instituted by the Royal Society in 1866. The oldest surviving plaque, to Napoleon III, dates from just a year later. This is also, incidentally, the only one ever awarded to a living recipient; the rule now is that a recipient must have been dead for twenty years, presumably to give journalists and biographers a chance to muck-rake. Around 1900, the scheme was taken over by the London County Council, which experimented with different designs, including some brown plaques, before settling on the standard blue ceramic pattern. British Heritage now runs the scheme, and their choice of subjects is pleasingly eclectic. There are some 950 official plaques at present and quite a few more unofficial ones.

Cheyne Walk was, for many years, one of the most prestigious addresses in London, and it probably has a higher concentration of **blue plaques** than any other street. The street is in several bits and pieces but has some very fine examples of domestic architecture dating back to the 18th century. The first section runs from №122 to №92.

№122 George Melly. Jazzer, Magritte collector, and fly fisherman.

№120 Sylvia Pankhurst (1882-1960), suffragette and socialist activist.

№119 (Turner's House) J.M.W. Turner (1775-1851), the painter, lived here as plain Mr Booth. Ian Fleming's mother, Eve lived here in the 1920s, and produced his half-sister courtesy of the artist Augustus John, who lived next door. And Ronnie Wood of the Rolling Stones.

№114 was, until 1990 or so the King's Arms pub, named after Charles II. An 18th century publican had the honour of being the King's Bunmaker. The tablet over the first-floor windows once bore the dread name Watneys.

№109 Philip Wilson Steer (1898-1942), painter.

№104 Hilaire Belloc (1900-05), satirist and poet (*Tarantella*). Before him, the painter Walter Greaves lived here 1855-97, best known for *Hammersmith Bridge on Boat Race Day* in Tate Britain.

№96-100 were built around 1670 as one property, Lindsey House, said to be the oldest house in Chelsea.

№98 Sir Marc Brunel and Isambard Kingdom Brunel, engineers.

№96 James McNeil Whistler (1834-1903), American artist. He painted *'Whistler's Mother'* here, now in The Louvre. The garden behind is by Gertrude Jekyll.

№93 Elizabeth (Mrs) Gaskell (1810-1865), writer, was born here.

№91 & 92 built in 1771 with Venetian-style windows

On the riverside is **Cheyne Pier** and its many houseboats. In **Battersea Bridge Gardens** is a statue of **James McNeill Whistler**. The Chelsea Arts Club intended to ask Rodin to do the statue when xenophobia struck, "Why" asked a member, "should the club pay a Frenchman for a statue of a Yankee in London?" And that was that for near enough a hundred years. This statue by Nicholas Dimbleby was eventually unveiled in 2005, 102 years after Whistler's death. The witty Whistler was a friend of Oscar Wilde, Monet, Rossetti, and many others.

South bank

This is a pleasant walk through well-kept gardens away from traffic. Look out for the lollipop trees.

The Waterfront, Baltimore House, Juniper Drive, SW18 1TS. Tel: 020 7228 4297. Young's. Real ale and food (Sunday roast). Modern building with outdoor seating.

The **Intertidal Terraces** were built as an ecological offset for the Riverside Development, and also as flood defence. An information board tells the story.

Plantation Wharf and Pier took its name from the sugar factory once here. The path continues as Clove Hitch Walk; the names of the streets leading to it are Coral Row, Calico Row, Cinnamon Row, Molasses Row, and Cotton Row, which gives an idea of the cargo landed here.

London Heliport. London's only heliport was opened in 1959 by the Westland aircraft company which, at that time, built the American Sikorski helicopters under licence. As a distant memory, in the early days, helicopters were limited to flying along the river because of their perceived unreliability and, accordingly, had to be fitted with flotation gear. Stringent noise regulations still restrict helicopter use over the city.

Cross **Falcon Brook,** now culverted but once used (as Battersea Creek) for transport by Price's candle factory. The brook usually drained into Bazalgette's Southern Low Level Sewer, but a pumping station would dump the wastewater into the river when that became overloaded.

Oyster Pier has another group of houseboats. These are far from cheap, but many look to have more living space than the average flat.

Battersea Railway Bridge is a double-track lattice girder bridge dating from 1863. The bridge needed extensive repairs after an errant refuse barge rammed it in 2003. The **Cremorne Footbridge**, to be attached to the rail bridge, was granted planning permission in 2013, and wrangling over money has gone on ever since. Completion was set for 2022, but in September 2022 work had yet to start. See the North Bank for the significance of Cremorne, a name once applied to the rail bridge as well.

Pass under the bridge and continue along Albion Quay past its pier, Vicarage Gardens, and a slipway to the: **Church of St Mary**, Battersea Church Road SW11 3LD. Much altered and rebuilt over the centuries, it is of interest mainly for the 17th century glass in the east window depicting Henry VIII and Elizabeth I. William Blake married here in 1782. Another window commemorates **Benedict**

Arnold (1741-1801), born in Norwich, Connecticut, who set the Continental Army on the road to victory by capturing Fort Ticonderoga during the American War of Independence. Considering himself slighted, he changed sides and was only just prevented from surrendering West Point. A plaque at 62 Gloucester Place, his former residence in Marylebone, describes him, rather controversially, as an "American Patriot". There is another memorial in the crypt of the church. In the vestry is said to be Turner's chair from which he sketched the river. Open for private prayer most mornings, www.stmarysbattersea.org.uk

In the river wall is a memorial to **Sir Roy Watts** (1925-1993), a former Chief Executive of British Airways and Chairman of Thames Water.

In Town is a pleasing sculpture by John Ravera (1941-2006) of a young couple holding up their child. The child had a small bird perched on its hand, but it has flown away. Ravera was a successful artist whose works can be seen elsewhere in London, and in Hong Kong, and Tokyo. This piece dates from 1983.

Battersea Bridge

The bridge dates from 1890; designed by Sir Joseph Bazalgette (what a work rate that man had!) in cast iron, it replaced a wooden bridge first built in 1772. The wooden bridge was the last of its kind over the river, and inspired artists, including both Turner and Whistler. Whistler's *Nocturne: Blue and Gold* is in Tate Britain, as is Turner's pencil and watercolour sketch with St Mary's Church in the foreground. This is the narrowest of London's bridges and carries little traffic these days; once trams, first horse-drawn, then electric, used to cross. Restoration in 1992 saw the bridge return to its original colour scheme with gilt spandrels; it had been blue and red for many years. Because of its location on a bend, it has often been rammed by boats.

Getting there. The 170 bus runs between the south side of the bridge and Victoria station for underground and overground connections. Plantation Wharf Pier, about 500m downstream of Wandsworth Bridge, is on the Thames Clipper RB6 route, though this operates only on weekday mornings and evenings.

Walking. Battersea Bridge to Albert Bridge is ¼ mile (0.5km) on either bank, or 1 mile (1.5km) to Chelsea Bridge.

14. BATTERSEA BRIDGE TO ALBERT BRIDGE

North bank

The first block over the road was part of the garden of Sir Thomas More when he lived at Beaufort House. More (1478-1536) was Lord Chancellor to Henry VIII and a staunch Catholic; he fell out with Henry over reformation of the church and was executed on Tower Hill for his pains. **More's Garden**, on the corner, is a block of flats built in 1904. A three-bedroom flat here went for £3½ million in 2022.

Sharing the block and, despite its Tudor appearance, 25 years younger is **Crosby Hall**. This was built in 1926 as the International Hostel of the British Federation of University Women; it takes its name from Crosby Place, a palatial 15th century house in the City and incorporates elements of that building. It has been owned since 1988 by Christopher Moran, who has spent a staggering amount of money making a facsimile of a Tudor palace. Pictures here:

https://www.christophermoran.org/crosby-hall/photos-of-crosby-hall/

Roper's Garden, part of More's orchard, was the dowry of his daughter Margaret when she married William Roper in 1521. It was later built over as Lombard Terrace and then destroyed by bombing in the Second World War. The sunken garden was the cellars and basements of the houses. Epstein's unfinished **relief of a nude girl** (1950) commemorates the time before the First World War when he had a studio here. The other statue is *Awakening* by Gilbert Ledward (1965); one has to say that Ledward's interpretation of the female form is prettier than Epstein's, unfinished or not.

Chelsea Old Church. The origin of All Saints is a Norman church dating from 1152. The chancel is 13th century and the nave and tower 17th century. Sir Thomas More, whose statue is outside, built his own chapel here and left a lovely tribute to a stepmother on the monument to his second wife. Sir Hans Sloane, an Anglo-Irish physician whose collections founded the British Museum, the British Library, and the Natural History Museum, donated six chained books, the only ones in London.

The church was destroyed in 1941, the damage thought to have been caused by a parachute mine; these exploded on the surface, rather than burying themselves first, and caused huge blast damage. The RAF later used much larger light-case blast bombs, and the press called them blockbusters because they could destroy a complete city block. Not a lot of people reading a blockbuster novel or watching a blockbuster movie know that.

The church was rebuilt, and most of the monuments pieced back together. This is a traditional church using the King James Bible and the Book of Common Prayer rather than the anaemic modern offerings. The church is open 1400-1600 Tuesday, Wednesday, and Thursday.

The **statue of More** stands in the semi-circular garden in front of the church. The elaborate lamp standard commemorates the building of the Chelsea Embankment, and the ornate drinking fountain is in memory of George Sparks, formerly a judge in Madras (now Chennai) in southern India.

The statue on the green is of **Thomas Carlyle** (1795-1881), the Scottish historian who rented 24 Cheyne Row for £35 a year. Here, he wrote his history of the French Revolution and biography of Frederick the Great. The house has been almost untouched since his death, no electricity even. Pre-booked tours through the National Trust on Wednesdays only.

Behind the statue is the excellent and pretty (but expensive) restaurant №
Fifty Cheyne. Mick Jagger and Marianne Faithfull lived at №48.

Carlyle Mansions is a block of flats built in the 1880s. It is named after
Thomas Carlyle but became known as Writers' Block as authors as diverse as Ian
Fleming, T.S. Eliot, Erskine Childers, and Somerset Maugham all lived here.
Another resident was Richard Addinsell, who wrote the *Warsaw Concerto*, of
which Spike Milligan was so unkind. Note the reliefs in white Portland stone, said
to be based on Aesop's fables.

The bronze of *Atlanta* just upstream of Albert Bridge is a memorial to the
prolific sculptor Derwent Wood (1871-1926). This is a cast of his own marble
original, now in Manchester Art Gallery. Wood helped the rehabilitation of men
who had suffered facial injuries in the First World War by making masks in a
semblance of their unwounded appearance.

The cabmen's shelter nearby was known as **The Kremlin** as it attracted a left-
leaning clientele. It has been restored recently but is not in use, mainly because of
the impossibility of parking nearby.

Over the road is ***Boy with a Dolphin***, a bronze by David Wynne (1975) on the
same theme as his *Girl with Dolphin* at Tower Bridge. The model in this case was
his son Roly, and the inscription tells a sad tale.

The approach road to Albert Bridge is Oakley Street. **Captain Robert Falcon
Scott** (of the Antarctic) lived at №56, the second house on the right (SW3 5HB),
and **Bob Marley** at №42 (SW3 5HA).

South bank

Battersea was a Saxon settlement first mentioned in AD693. The name derives
from 'Batrice's Ege', meaning Badric's Island; the land was low-lying and marshy.
The area was built up rapidly in the 19th century with a mixture of market
gardening and industry.

The path here is called **Albion Riverside**; it was formerly Anglo-American
Wharf. The sailing barge **Atrato** was built in 1898 by Forrest at Wivenhoe on the
Thames estuary. At one time converted to a motor barge, it is now re-rigged,
though the mast looks a little far back. There has been considerable argy-bargy
over the owner's right to moor Atrato here, which may interest maritime lawyers if
no one else.

Ransome's Dock took its name from Ransome of Ipswich, the famous
engineering company whose steamrollers and traction engines were exported
worldwide. Excavated in the late 19th century, it was later used to import ice from
Scandinavia, and then for actual ice-making. Having crossed the bridge at the
entrance, you can walk down the east side. Several large continental barges are
moored here as houseboats.

Albert Bridge

The bridge is pretty but a real oddball from an engineering point of view. As first built in 1873, the deck was made as a cantilever (i.e. it could support itself) with rigid staybars to take the loads imposed by traffic. The ornate towers and piers are cast iron made in Battersea, the piers the largest iron castings to that date. The bridge soon earned the name "The Trembling Lady", and Bazalgette had to add chains, thus making it more like a conventional suspension bridge. Finally, in 1972, the two central piers were added, making the centre section more like an ordinary beam bridge. The toll booths are still present (the only ones left in London), and an indication of the bridge's fragility is the signs telling troops to break step rather than march over in order. The bridge is attractively lit at night.

Getting there. The 170 bus runs from Victoria Station (tube and mainline) to the north side of Albert Bridge. Cadogan Pier is by the north side of the bridge, but Thames Clipper service only at peak times.

Walking. Albert Bridge to Chelsea Bridge is ¾ mile (1.2km) on either bank, or 2½ miles (4.5km) to Vauxhall Bridge.

15. ALBERT BRIDGE TO CHELSEA BRIDGE

North bank

More blue plaques along **Cheyne Walk**:

№27 **Bram Stoker** (1847-1912), the Irish author of *Dracula*.

№21 **James McNeil Whistler**, and at several other numbers, too.

№17 **Thomas Attwood**, who was a pupil of Mozart and organist at St Paul's.

№16 (Queen's House) In 1862**, Dante Gabriel Rossetti, Algernon Swinburne,** and **George Meredith** jointly took the lease. Their menagerie, especially the peacocks, distressed the neighbours. The house became an important meeting place for poets and artists.

№14 **Bertrand Russell**, philosopher and peace campaigner.

№13 **Ralph Vaughn Williams**, composer (*Lark Ascending* and much more).

№10 **Earl Lloyd-George,** aka The Welsh Goat. Successful prime minister during the First World War.

№4 **George Eliot**, the translator and author (*Middlemarch, The Mill on the Floss*), was actually Mary Ann Evans, obliged to adopt a man's name to be taken seriously in Victorian Britain. **Michael Bloomberg**, sometime mayor of the Big Apple, bought the house in 2015.

Chelsea Embankment Gardens, the green in front of the houses, has several sculptures.

59

The Boy David. The original statue here was a maquette by Derwent Wood of his Machine Gun Corps memorial at Hyde Park Corner; it was stolen in 1969, and this glass fibre replacement (not a copy) by Copnall installed in 1971.

The memorial fountain is to **Dante Gabriel Rossetti**. The bronze medallion is by Rossetti's friend Ford Madox Ford, better known as a writer (*The Good Soldier*). The empty plinth once bore *Boy with Cat*, a bronze by Philip Lindsay Clark. Missing, presumed stolen. You can see a photo and the story here: https://www.londonremembers.com/memorials/jacqueline-cockburn-missing-sculpture-image

Ralph Vaughan Williams (1872-1958). Composer remembered mainly for his shorter pieces like *Fantasia on a Theme by Thomas Tallis* and *The Lark Ascending*, but also for nine symphonies including *A London Symphony*. He was an avid collector of English folk songs which, along with a studentship with Ravel, influenced his style. He and Holst were great friends and fierce critics of one another's music. This is bound to upset a lot of people (including Colette), but Vaughan Williams was a truly British composer determined to shake off Teutonic influence. Elgar... well, lovely music, but let's just remember that the premieres of both *Enigma* and *Gerontius* were conducted by Hans Richter.

Chelsea Physic Garden, Swan Lane, SW3 4HS. Founded by the Apothecaries' Company in 1676 to grow medicinal plants. Seeds sent from here in 1732 began the cultivation of cotton in Georgia. It has the oldest heated glasshouse in Britain, and research continues. Sir Hans Sloane donated the land for the garden, and his statue stands in the centre. The original statue by Rysbrack (1732) was moved to the British Museum in 1985, and this is a fibreglass copy. Interesting but expensive. Note that while the address is given as Swan Lane, the only access is on Royal Hospital Road.

John Wolfe Barry, the civil engineer who built Tower Bridge, has a blue plaque on Delahaye House. There is a good view of the Peace Pagoda in Battersea Park over the river.

After the Great Indian Mutiny (or First War of Independence) in 1857-58, the British government took over the governance of India from the East India Company. Queen Victoria became Empress of India, and a viceroy was appointed to represent her in India. George Robinson, **Marquess of Ripon**, was one of the more enlightened holders of that post (1880-1884). His blue plaque is at 9 Chelsea Embankment, SW3 4LE.

From the Bull Ring Gate, you have a fine view of the **Royal Hospital Chelsea**. This was founded by Charles II to house army veterans, possibly inspired by Les Invalides in Paris, which had opened a few years earlier. Designed by Sir Christopher Wren, the first pensioners were admitted in 1688. The hospital still houses around 300 pensioners whose walking-out dress is a red coat and cocked hat..

The prominent obelisk is a memorial to the losses of the 24th Regiment of Foot (later the South Wales Borderers) at the **Battle of Chillianwalla** in 1849.

This was a sanguinary and indecisive clash during the Second Anglo-Sikh War. The battlefield is now in Pakistan, and the memorial there remembers the dead of both sides. Behind that is a gilded **statue of Charles II** in the garb of a Roman general. The lawns in front of the hospital host the Chelsea Flower Show every year. Visitor centre and shop, enter by Chelsea Gate on Royal Hospital Road. Guided tours: https://www.chelsea-pensioners.co.uk/visit

Behind the Hospital is the **National Army Museum**, Royal Hospital Road, SW3 4HT. Tel: 0207 730 0717. Free entry. Frequent lectures, etc. https://www.nam.ac.uk/

The **Westbourne River** rises in West Hampstead and flows almost entirely underground down to Hyde Park. In the 18th century, it was dammed to form The Serpentine lake. Leaving there, it becomes the Ranelagh Sewer and, having passed through Sloane Square tube station in a huge iron duct, joins the river directly in front of the hospital.

Ranelagh is a corruption of the Irish Raghnallach, a seat of the Earl of Ranelagh, who also had a house here. An upmarket pleasure garden with a huge rotunda operated here from 1742 to around 1800. The gardens then became part of the grounds of the Royal Hospital. In the corner of Ranelagh Gardens is the **Carabiniers Memorial** to their losses in the Boer War. The Carabiniers were the 6th (Inniskilling) Dragoons; dragoons were heavy cavalry (call them mounted infantry at your peril), and the name refers to the carbines or short rifles they carried.

Some way north of here (it's too good a story to leave out), **Thomas Crapper** established his sanitary engineering business. Contrary to popular belief, the rather vulgar noun is not a play on his name; it came into use in the 15th century from the Middle Dutch *krappe* meaning chaff. Funny thing, language.

South bank

The 200 acres (81ha) of **Battersea Park** neatly fill the whole space between Albert and Chelsea Bridges. A low-lying marshy area, the land was stabilised with 750,000 tons of material excavated to form Surrey Docks. The public park was opened in 1853 by Queen Victoria.

Following the riverside path, Terrace Walk, you come to the **Japanese Peace Pagoda** (1985), one of 80 odd put up around the world between 1947 and 2000 by the Nipponzam Myohoji Buddhist Order. Whimsical, though not a patch aesthetically on their sublime stupa at Rajgir. The park, however, has a lot more to offer and would be easier to enjoy if there were any signposting.

Near where you entered the park are a **Herb Garde**n and an **Old English Garden**. By the Old English Garden stands a statue of a rather woebegone terrier. This refers to the **Brown Dog Affair**, a celebrated libel case in 1903. By that time, great strides were being made in medical science, but at the cost of animal experimentation and vivisection. Two Swedish women observed one of these lecture demonstrations and alleged that the dog was inadequately anaesthetised, implying that this was deliberate.

Stephen Coleridge, a barrister and great-grandson of the poet, repeated their allegations in a speech. One of the surgeons sued for libel and won his case to the tune of £5000 for damages and costs, the thick end of £800,000 today. Then, as now, Britain's libel laws are a rich man's game. A *Daily Mail* appeal raised £5700 to refund Coleridge.

That was just the start of the trouble. A monument topped by a much perkier-looking bronze dog was raised in Latchmere Recreation Ground, about 300m south of here. London's medical students (traditionally an unruly bunch) considered the descriptive plaque provocative, and full-scale riots ensued. Eventually, the statue was surreptitiously disposed of in 1910. The unveiling of this rather pathetic replacement in 1985 had the medical profession in a tizz all over again, with words like 'libellous' bandied about.

Past the two gardens is an ornamental lake with fountains. Elsewhere are an adventure playground, children's zoo, and extensive sports facilities. Past the pagoda and a little away from the river are toilets and a snack stall. The left fork of the lane past the snack stall leads to a decent café beside the boating lake.

Around the lake (added in 1860) are the sculptures *Three Standing Figures* by Henry Moore (1948) and *Single Form* by Barbara Hepworth (1962). The sub-tropical garden (1864) at the western end of the lake was set up by John Gibson (1815-1875) after a plant-hunting trip to India. The **Pump House Gallery** is located in the building (1861) that supplied water to the cascades; it is more an event venue than the art gallery its name may suggest.

In Elizabethan times, before clay pigeons were invented, this was a popular place for shooting real sparrows and pigeons. Anti-aircraft guns installed here in both world wars aimed at larger game.

John's rather hazy memories are of the funfair that was here from the time of the Festival of Britain (1951) until 1974. At that time, the pubs closed on Sunday between 2.00PM and 7.00PM – but not here. So it was a ride on the Big Dipper, a quick go at a shooting gallery, and into the bar for pints of Dortmund Union. The only possible excuse is that lager was a novelty at the time.

Chelsea Bridge

The present bridge was built in 1934. Human remains and many Roman and British weapons were found when the foundations of its predecessor (also a suspension bridge) were dug in the 1850s, suggesting a battle had taken place here. A new footbridge under the north end of Chelsea Bridge leads into the space between that and the Grosvenor Rail Bridge.

Getting there. Buses 11 and 211 run up Chelsea Bridge Road to Sloane Square for the tube network. Battersea Power Station Pier, in front of the power station, is served by the Thames Clipper RB6 service.

Walking. Chelsea Bridge to Vauxhall Bridge is 1 mile (1.7km) on the north bank and 2 miles (3km) on the south bank.

16. CHELSEA BRIDGE TO VAUXHALL BRIDGE

North bank

Chelsea Embankment has now become Grosvenor Road. The Grosvenor family stems from Normans who accompanied William the Conqueror to Britain in 1066. An auspicious marriage in 1677 brought them ownership of much of what is now the West End, Belgravia and Pimlico, mostly open fields at the time. As London expanded they developed their land for housing and commercial use. Despite punitive death duties, they have hung on to most of it and are regarded as benign landlords. The last non-royal dukedom (of Westminster) was created for them in 1874. Winston Churchill, incidentally, was offered a dukedom in 1945 but declined, preferring to stay in the House of Commons and not prejudice his son's and grandson's political careers.

The **Western Pumping Station** on the north side of **Grosvenor Road** was part of Bazalgette's scheme for sewage and safe drinking water. Built in 1872-75, it is of a simple Italianate design; the chimney was for the boilers that fed the steam pumps, redundant since 1936 when they were replaced by diesel pumps. The lock gates mark the entry to the **Grosvenor Canal**; started in 1725, it supplied water to reservoirs in Hyde Park and Green Park. Once extending past Ebury Bridge, it was progressively shortened as land was taken for housing and for Victoria railway station. Its last use, up to 1995, was for loading refuse barges. Steps lead down to the canal basin and locks.

Just downstream is the railway **Grosvenor Bridge** which takes the tracks from Victoria station over the river. First built in 1860, it was much altered over the years and finally completely rebuilt and widened to take ten tracks a hundred years later.

Lupus Street, over the road, is named after Hugh Lupus Grosvenor, the first duke. Lupus is Latin for a wolf. Before we knew the true origin, we went off on a flight of fancy trying to connect the hospital for women and children that once stood in this street with an unpleasant disease. The condition was named lupus by Rogerius of Salerno in the 12th century and affects far more women than men. Thus are conspiracy theories founded.

We now enter **Pimlico**, a low-lying area of market gardens and osiers up to the 1830s. The name is thought to have come from one Ben Pimlico, a publican who served a fine nut-brown ale. **Churchill Gardens** is a large post-war housing development providing 1600 homes and relevant amenities. It was built on the site of bomb-damaged Victorian terraces and, unlike so many post-war schemes, on a human scale. The flats and maisonettes were heated by surplus hot water from

Battersea power station over the river; plumes of water vapour always hovered over them. Heating still comes from a central source, quite unusual in Britain.

King William IV, 111 Grosvenor Road, SW1V 3LG. Tel: **020 7834 9689.** Fine Victorian pub rebuilt in 1880. Green tile exterior. Seating outside. Appears to be closed.

By way of contrast, **Dolphin Square** is decidedly swep'up. The 1310 flats and studios were built in 1935-37 and are much favoured by MPs, civil servants, spies, and other ne'er-do-wells. The square encloses a communal 3½ acre (1.4ha) landscaped garden.

Westminster Boating Base offers training in most forms of waterborne activity. Experienced canoeists and kayakers can join expeditions on the river: details at https://www.westminsterboatingbase.co.uk/

Pimlico Gardens is on the riverside opposite St George's Square. *The Helmsman* bronze sculpture (1996) is by Andre Wallace who also did the roller skating girl on Vauxhall Bridge Road. At the end of the gardens is a statue of **William Huskisson MP** in the garb of a Roman senator, a popular theme at the time. In 1830, he was the first person in the world to be killed in a railway accident. The accident was witnessed by his sworn political enemy, the Duke of Wellington. A quixotic lot, the English. The little Latin tag on the base tells you that the statue is the work of John Gibson in 1836, which must have been a lot easier to inscribe than MDCCCXXXVI.

The long narrow green strip past Dolphin Square is the wooded St George's Square. At its head is the **Church of St Saviour**, Pimlico. Built in 1860 and much enhanced since, this is a richly decorated Anglo-Catholic church. Laurence Olivier was a choirboy, Compton Mackenzie (*Whisky Galore*) was married here, and Lady Diana Spenser worked in the kindergarten before marrying the then Prince of Wales.

Behind St Saviour is Pimlico tube station. A modern sculpture (fun!) on Bessborough Street by Paolozzi disguises an air vent, and there is also a statue of **Walter Clopton Wingfield**, who formulated the modern game of lawn tennis on Lupus Street. More walking away from the river. Over the road is:

The Grosvenor, 79 Grosvenor Road, SW1V 3LA. Tel: 020 7821 8786. Free house. Real ale and food. Highly rated. Attractive 1920s building that appears to have had a block of flats built over it.

Past Tyburn House is access to **Crown Reach Riverside Walk** which takes you all the way to Vauxhall Bridge. You get a good view of the figures on Vauxhall Bridge and of the SIS building.

South bank

Between the two bridges is Chelsea Bridge Wharf. The railway **Grosvenor Bridge** takes the tracks from Victoria station over the river. First built in 1860, it was much altered over the years and finally completely rebuilt and widened to take ten tracks a hundred years later. There are toilets under the bridge.

Battersea Power Station was, in effect, two power stations built side-by-side. Construction of the first started in 1929, though the second was not completed until 1955, having been delayed by the Second World War. Sir Giles Gilbert Scott (1880-1960), who designed the traditional red phone box and Liverpool Cathedral, is usually credited as architect, though he was brought in quite late to prettify the exterior. The station burned 1,000,000 tons of coal annually, mostly brought from the South Wales coalfields in specially designed ships. Two cranes, which stood on the Coaling Wharf (open 1000-1300), could handle 480 tons an hour.

London fogs

Shakespeare wrote "drooping fogge as blacke as Acheron" in *Midsummer Night's Dream*, and Dickens (in *Bleak House*) coined the phrase 'London particular'. By the 16th century London depended on coal for fuel, brought mainly by coaster from the north-east of England. Things got worse with the growth of industry, and the final straw was the building of coal-fired power stations all along the river. The result, London being in a natural depression, was smog.

This was no ordinary fog; it was dense to the point that you literally could not see your hand in front of your face. I remember my father telling me that in the 1920s he once became so disorientated within a few hundred yards of his parents' home that he had to knock on the first front door he could find. He was taken in for the night. Fogs could last for weeks at a time, and the effect on people's health was appalling. Eventually, in 1956, the Clean Air Act passed through Parliament, and things began to improve.

At its peak, the station produced 1500GW of electricity. Scrubbers were installed to reduce sulphur dioxide emissions, but the resulting sulphuric acid was dumped back into the river, which was probably even more harmful. The flats over the river used surplus hot water for heating, and one always saw plumes of water vapour above them.

The station finally closed in 1983, and several false starts at redevelopment left it badly damaged and derelict. Finally, after nearly 40 years, work is nearing completion to provide residential, office, and retail space, and a park.

The station's distinctive (oops, nearly said iconic) design has seen it appear in many films, from Hitchcock's *Sabotage* (1936) through The Beatles' *Help* (1965) and *The Battle of Britain* (1969) to Monty Python's *The Meaning of Life* in 1983. It was featured on Pink Floyd's *Animals* LP sleeve in 1977.

The best news is one of the chimneys now houses a glass lift (elevator) for the view from 100m (330ft) up. Booking at https://lift109.co.uk/

Battersea Power Station may be in fine fettle again, but construction of the Tideway Tunnel and other projects have disrupted the riverside walk. From the block on the riverside path, follow the hoardings to Cringle Street.

Behind the hoardings on the other side is (or was) **Battersea Pumping Station** which was built in 1840 for the Southwark Water Company and extended in 1856. It housed a series of Cornish engines (a form of steam-powered beam engine) used for pumping water from the Thames. At one time, the pumping station housed the largest Cornish engine ever built, with a cylinder of 112″ (2.84m) diameter. After 1855, extracting domestic water from the tidal Thames was illegal. Water had to be brought from reservoirs out to the west and pumped to consumers. The company's reservoirs occupied the site of the power station. You can see similar engines working at the London Museum of Water and Steam in Brentford (see North Bank walk). The building is listed, but the developers at the power station want to demolish it, so it may well be gone by the time you read this.

A waste transfer station will likely be a block on the riverside path even when all the construction work is complete. Continue along Cringle Street to Battersea Park Road and bear left. Some way away to the right is:

Battersea Dogs and Cats Home, 4 Battersea Park Rd, SW8 4AA. Tel: 0800 001 4444. It was founded in 1860 and has been located here since 1871. This is London's main home for abandoned and unwanted dogs and cats. All the animals are available for adoption – if you meet their criteria. Visits by appointment only. www.battersea.org.uk

Where you see an Indian elephant with a howdah, you can turn left to:

Battersea Barge, Nine Elms Lane, SW11 8PZ. Tel: 020 7582 1066. Closed Monday and Tuesday. Floating pub on a Dutch barge with an interesting history. Real ale but no food at present. Live music and cabaret.

The path is again blocked, this time by the **Heathwall Pumping Station,** one of the stations for the new Tideway sewage tunnel under the Thames. At this point the tunnel is 46m (151ft) under the river.

You eventually regain the river on **William Henry Walk**, named after a borough engineer in the 1980s who died of cancer at an early age. The mural relief of **Father Thames is** by Stephen Duncan.

Between 1960 and 2018, the **United States Embassy** was housed in an elegant Eero Saarinen building on Grosvenor Square. The Duke of Westminster leased the site at a peppercorn rent. When the U.S. offered to buy the freehold, the Duke suggested exchanging it for an ancestral property lost during the American Revolution – the city of Miami. The Grosvenor Square site was deemed to be insecure after the 9/11 attacks in New York, and a long search for a new site began. Eventually, in 2018, the new embassy on the other side of Nine Elms Road was opened.

The cylindrical **St George Wharf Tower** has 49 storeys and is 181m high. From its foot is a panorama of some of the dreadful buildings put up in London in the 1960s and 70s.

The path under Vauxhall Bridge and in front of the MI6 building is at present blocked, so walk down towards:

Vauxhall Transport Interchange, designed by Arup. has an inclined solar panel roof. This is a bus station close to Vauxhall tube and mainline stations. Demolition was approved in 2019 with the intention of building two tall blocks of social housing, but it's still there. Cross over and follow Albert Embankment (road).

Vauxhall Bridge

Construction started here in 1811 on a stone bridge, but the company switched to a cheaper cast iron one completed in 1816. This, known initially as Regent's Bridge, was the first iron bridge over the Thames. It was replaced by the present one, a five-arched steel job on granite piers, in 1895-1906. The eight bronze figures on the piers are not visible from the bridge. The four on the upstream side are by Frederick Pomeroy and represent, from left to right, *Agriculture*, *Architecture*, *Engineering*, and *Pottery*. The four on the downstream side are by Alfred Drury and represent *Science*, *Fine Arts*, *Local Government*, and *Education.* And yes, it's a long story, but Vauxhall, or more appropriately вокзал, is the Russian word for a railway station.

Getting there. Pimlico tube station on the north side. Vauxhall tube and mainline stations on south side. St George Wharf Pier (London Clipper service) is a short distance upstream of the bridge.

Walking. Vauxhall Bridge to Lambeth Bridge is ½ mile (1km) on either bank.

17. VAUXHALL BRIDGE TO LAMBETH BRIDGE

North bank

Millbank, as the road becomes after Vauxhall Bridge, is named after a mill owned by Westminster Abbey that stood here. The mill was long gone by 1796 when a young artist sat and painted *Moonlight, a Study at Millbank*. The young man was J.M.W. Turner who could not have guessed (or could he?) that exactly 100 years later a gallery in which his work would be prominent would stand here.

The chunk of veined rock by the steps down to the path is **Shapes in the Cloud II** by Peter Randall-Page. A children's play sculpture stands in front of a pleasant coffee shop, and another a little further on are by Pablo Reinoso.

In **Riverside Walk Gardens** is the sculpture *Love Locking Piece* by Henry Moore (1898-1986), cast in 50 or so pieces and then brazed together. **Millbank Penitentiary** (an unsuccessful attempt at prison reform) has a memorial at the end of the gardens; this is a stone bollard bearing a plaque that tells the tale. With the exception of these two, sculptures here seem to be transient. Over the road on the corner of Ponsonby Terrace is:

Morpeth Arms, 58 Millbank, SW1P 4RW. Tel: 020 7834 6442. Youngs. Real ale and food. Outside seating. The pub was supposedly built for the warders at Millbank Penitentiary. Under it are the remains of cells and tunnels used to transfer prisoners from the penitentiary to boats for deportation to Australia; CCTV cameras watch for ghosts.

At the end of the next block is the sculpture **Jeté** by Enzo Plazzotta (1975), modelled on the dancer David Wall.

When we first heard about **Millbank Bridge** being knocked up from wooden stakes and a bit of old angle-iron, we suspected a spoof. In fact the British Government was so concerned about Thames bridges being destroyed by bombing that they built two (some say four) such emergency bridges from 1940 onwards. The Millbank one used hefty wooden piles and steel truss units; it would support a tank. The bridges were all dismantled by 1947, and no visible trace remains. The bridge went from somewhere near the gardens to near the slipway over the river. The steel sections of the Millbank bridge ended up in North Rhodesia (now Zambia) where they bridged a tributary of the Zambesi. The prominent white and green building over the river is the headquarters of the Secret Intelligence Service, commonly referred to as MI6.

The **Tate Gallery** was built on the site of the Millbank Penitentiary (1821-1890), an unsuccessful attempt at prison reform. The gallery was founded and endowed by Sir Henry Tate (1819-1899), a sugar millionaire of humble beginnings; the successor company, Tate and Lyle, still refines sugar and makes its famous golden syrup downstream at Silvertown. Tate's own art collection formed the basis for the gallery, and other endowments have seen it greatly expanded. Well worth a browse to see the work of artists mentioned in here, and much more.

For nearly 100 years, the gallery was simply 'The Tate'; now that it has offshoots (Bankside, Liverpool, and St Ives), it has become the rather ugly 'Tate Britain'. Once showing the art of all nations, The Tate now concentrates on British art from 1500 to the present day. Foreign modern art has been moved to Tate Modern on Bankside. Visiting the Tate today is still enjoyable, but it is easy to feel that, like so many museums, it has been captured by the wokerati.

Brock's fine statue of **Sir John Everett Millais** (1829-1896), which once stood in front of the gallery, was disliked by more than one Director and has been dumped around the back. Millais was instrumental in setting up the Tate and was one of the founders of the British Pre-Raphaelite Brotherhood. You will find examples of this style and of his later move to realism in the gallery. Aesthetes criticised him for letting his painting *Bubbles* be used for advertising Pears Coal

Tar Soap. Millais was of Jersey stock; asked by the author Thackeray when England had conquered Jersey, he replied, 'Never! Jersey conquered England'. Jerseymen had indeed accompanied William of Normandy in 1066.

Look across the river from here for a nice view of the Shard framed by other buildings. The brightly coloured barge is a pub.

Past Millbank Pier is the ugly **Millbank Tower**, built in 1963 for Vickers, the engineering and armaments company. At the time, it was the tallest building (119m/390ft) in London, though soon surpassed by the Post Office Tower.

Approaching Lambeth Bridge you can walk through Victoria Tower Gardens South. The large building over the road, **Thames House**, is the office of the Security Service, Britain's internal security organisation, commonly referred to as MI5. This and the next block date from 1929 and were designed by the same architect.

South bank

The **River Effra** joins the Thames just below Vauxhall Bridge. Another of London's lost and buried rivers, it rises in Upper Norwood near Crystal Palace. Various fanciful interpretations of the name include the Celtic *yfrid*, meaning a torrent. It is more likely a corruption of Heathrow, a small manor in nearby Brixton (and nowhere near the airport).

The riverside path is closed, mainly due to Tideway Tunnel works, and you must walk down from the bridge to Albert Embankment (Road). The **Albert Embankment** itself was part of Bazalgette's scheme of land reclamation, though the project was carried out (1865-68) by his subordinate John Grant. Unlike its equivalent Victoria Embankment it does not accommodate major sewers or underground railways.

The **Secret Intelligence Service**, colloquially known as MI6, is Britain's overseas intelligence organisation. After many years in cramped and insecure offices (it was illegal even to publish the address) it was decided to build a proper headquarters. This site was formerly part of the Vauxhall Pleasure Gardens, but by 1980 a post-industrial mess. The architect was Terry Farrell, and the front overlooking the river (best seen from the bridge or the opposite bank) is a fun combination of 1930s industrial modernism and a Mayan temple. The landward side is plainer but equally impressive. Apparently, some locals unkindly christened it Ceausescu Towers, and another critic referred to the whole area as Dubai-on-Thames.

The **Millbank Bridge** (see the north bank walk for a description) joined this bank at **Lack's Dock**. This is a slipway once used by tourist vehicles based on Second World War DUKW amphibious lorries. The dock is currently inaccessible.

Albert Embankment Gardens marks the actual start of the Albert Embankment, opposite Tinworth Street to be precise, rather than at Vauxhall Bridge. And it runs for the whole mile from here to Westminster Bridge. The embankment south to Vauxhall Bridge is decidedly utilitarian by comparison. The naming of Albert Embankment Road causes the confusion. In the gardens is a bust of **Basaveshwara**, a 12th century South Indian statesman, poet, and social reformer.

The Rose, 35 Albert Embankment, London SE1 7TL. Tel: 020 7735 3723. Free house. Real ale, cocktails, and food. Sunday roast and live jazz. Attractive Victorian street corner pub. Spectacular view of the Houses of Parliament from the upstairs room. Good music (I can hardly believe I'm writing this) played at just the right level.

Tamesis Dock is a floating pub on a brightly coloured Dutch barge.

Boat skeletons on the other side of the road from the path is a series of sculptures. Behind them is **White Hart Dock**, used by Doulton china works to bring in raw materials and export finished goods. The dock is ancient, and the Albert Embankment had to be arched to provide access. A short detour down Black Prince Road will take you to the ornate Victorian **Doulton Office Building**. Their pottery works dominated this area until 1956 when clean air regulations forced them to move to Staffordshire.

The former **London Fire Brigade Headquarters**, opened in 1937 by King George VI, is a large, rather plain 1930s office block with some fine friezes of firefighters at work. This may become a museum for the fire service. In the river is **Lambeth River Fire Station** and Pier.

The **Copper Boat Prow** projects from the building of the International Maritime Organisation on the other side of road, worth a closer look.

Lambeth Bridge

The approach road on the north bank is called Horseferry Road because that is what was here before the bridge. Not a horse-hauled ferry, but one that could take a coach and horses. The crossing was not without its perils; the ferry sank as Oliver Cromwell's coach and horses crossed in 1656. The first bridge was a suspension one built in 1862. The present steel bridge replaced it in 1932.

Getting there. Thames Clipper service at Millbank Millennium Pier on the north bank, this runs to the Tate Modern at Bankside. No convenient public transport. Walk the half mile to Westminster Bridge or take a taxi if it's raining.

Walking. Lambeth Bridge to Westminster Bridge is ½ mile (1km).

18. LAMBETH BRIDGE TO WESTMINSTER BRIDGE

North bank

We are now in Westminster, the heart of the United Kingdom's government and administration. Strictly speaking we entered the City of Westminster at Chelsea Bridge, but this is the area best known as Westminster.

Until the time of Edward the Confessor (1042-1066) the royal presence was in either the Tower of London or in Winchester on the south coast. Edward, however, decided to build his Collegiate Church of St Peter here. As this took shape Edward also built a palace which stood on the site now occupied by the Houses of Parliament. Westmunster, as recorded in AD785, means 'western monastery'.

From the end of Lambeth Bridge, the building on the other side of the roundabout is the former head office of ICI (Imperial Chemical Industries), once Britain's largest employer in the days when we actually made stuff. The building dates from 1929 and has some interesting sculptural details on the facade.

Victoria Tower Gardens is a long triangular open space stretching from Lambeth Bridge to the Houses of Parliament. It takes its name from the Victoria Tower at the south-western corner of the Houses of Parliament. The gardens must have been extended since 1897 as a map of that date shows the southern part occupied by buildings. The gardens contain, from the south, a children's playground and sand pit. The **Buxton Memorial Fountain** commemorates Sir Thomas Buxton (1786-1845), who founded the Anti-Slavery Party in 1823. The following year he was the founding chairman of what was to become the Royal Society for the Prevention of Cruelty to Animals. The fountain was set up by his son in 1865 in Parliament Square and reinstalled here in 1957. The statuettes of British monarchs are glass-fibre replicas of the bronzes stolen in 1960. Buxton also has a memorial in Westminster Abbey nearby. From the memorial, you see down Dean Stanley Street to St John's, Smith Square. And across the river are the ornate buildings of the older part of St Thomas' Hospital.

The **Burghers of Calais** is a cast of Rodin's group in Calais. During the Hundred Years War Edward III of England besieged Calais in 1347. To save the town further punishment six burghers offered themselves with nooses around their necks. Edward was so impressed he spared their lives, but Calais remained an English possession until 1558.

Statue of **Emmeline Pankhurst** (1858-1928) who, from an early age, was an activist for women's right to vote. Finding moderate action ineffective, she turned, to all intents and purposes, to terrorism, leading her followers to imprisonment and forced feeding when they went on hunger strike. During the First World War her encouragement of women's service, notably in armaments factories, probably had more effect than terrorism. Women over 30 were granted the vote in 1918, and ten years later, the age was reduced to 21, the same as for men. The plaque to her daughter, Dame Christabel Pankhurst (1880-1958), was added in 1959. On the other side is the Women's Social and Political Union prisoners' badge, a broad

71

arrow (as used to be printed on prison uniforms) superimposed on a portcullis representing the government.

A proposal to build a **Holocaust Memorial** and education centre in the gardens is proving controversial because of the loss of open space. Exit the gardens onto Abingdon Street, as Millbank has become. Over the next few hundred yards, it will become Old Palace Yard and then St Margaret Street. On the other side of the road on College Green is the Henry Moore sculpture *Knife Edge Two Piece*. Dating from 1965, it was cast in Berlin and has a twin in Vancouver.

Had you walked up Millbank rather than through the gardens, Dean Stanley Street on the left leads to **St John's, Smith Square**. This former church, built in the English Baroque style with four corner towers is well worth a quick look. Dickens (in *Our Mutual Friend*) was pretty uncomplimentary – "some petrified monster, frightful and gigantic, on its back with its legs in the air" – but we think it's fun. Burned out by incendiary bombs in 1941, it was restored as a concert hall with fine acoustics. A restaurant occupies the crypt. Walk down the continuation of Dean Bradley Street on the south side of Smith Square, and you come to:

The Marquis of Granby, 41 Romney Street, SW1P 3RF. Tel: 020 7227 0941. Nicholson's. Real ale and food. Like many restaurants and shops around here, this pub has a Division Bell; when it rings to announce a division (i.e. a vote), members have precisely eight minutes to make it back to The House. There are many pubs of this name in London and around the country. Granby was a successful and popular general during the Seven Years' War (1756-1763). He set up many disabled soldiers as publicans out of his own pocket.

Black Rod's Garden, to the north of Victoria Tower Gardens, is part of the Houses of Parliament and not open the public. The office, the official title is Gentleman (or Lady) Usher of the Black Rod, dates back to 1350 and involves responsibility for security and order in the House of Lords. The name comes from the staff of office with which Black Rod knocks on the door of the Commons to summon them to the Lords' Chamber for the state opening of parliament. Steps, with a little pavilion at the top, lead up from the river to the garden.

The present Houses of Parliament, properly the **Palace of Westminster**, were built between 1837 and 1858 following a disastrous fire in 1834. They replaced an agglomeration of unsuitable buildings, some dating back to before the Norman Conquest of 1066. Turner made a watercolour sketch of *The Burning of the Houses of Parliament* in 1834; it is in the Tate but not on display; see: https://www.tate.org.uk/art/artworks/turner-the-burning-of-the-houses-of-parliament-d36235. The two oils that Turner worked up from this sketch are in the USA.

The architects were Barry and Pugin, and the style was Victorian Gothic. The stone used was yellow limestone from a quarry in Yorkshire, chosen on grounds of cost. London's appalling air quality, right up to the 1960s, meant that deterioration was apparent even before the building was complete. Recent work has used a more durable stone from Rutland. The buildings are showing their age; annual maintenance is over £130 million, and estimates for a full restoration run up to £1 billion.

Victoria Tower was built between 1843 and 1860 to house parliamentary records. Its load-bearing structure is of cast iron clad in stone. Updated over the years, it is now an air-conditioned store over twelve storeys. The tower is 98.5m (323ft) high, excluding the 22.3m (73ft) flagstaff, which makes it slightly taller than the Elizabeth or Clock Tower ('Big Ben') at the other end of the palace. The tower covers the Sovereign's Entrance used by the king or queen every year for the state opening of Parliament.

At the beginning of the 20th century the **House of Lords** was composed of some 600 hereditary peers, plus 26 bishops of the Church of England. Also there were the most senior judges, known informally as the Law Lords, who formed the ultimate court of appeal. The powers of the Lords had been gradually reduced during the 19th century, and a major stand-off over the Budget in 1909 reduced it to pretty much a reviewing role in 1911. Life peers were introduced in 1958, and this marked the introduction of women to the House. A half-baked reform in 1999 reduced the number of hereditary peers to 92 and the bishops to 25, the rest being appointed. The result has been a core of competent and hard-working members and a rump of mainly political hacks and cronies. It is said that some sign on to collect their £313 daily attendance allowance (members are otherwise unpaid) and then retire to one of the 30 or so subsidised bars in the Palace. The House, at around 800 members, is the second largest legislative body in the world; some way behind the 3000-strong National People's Congress of that bastion of democracy China.

The statue of **Richard the Lionheart** (Richard I, 1189-1199), by Baron Marochetti, was placed in Old Palace Yard in 1851. A bit of Victorian romanticism, it symbolises bravery, zeal, and a quest for justice. Really? This was a man who rebelled against his father and spent only six months of his reign in England. He regarded England as a source of money whilst he campaigned on the Third Crusade and tried to subdue his lands in France, of which he had more than the King of France. A great man of his time but hardly a *beau idéal*. Richard took as his arms the three lions couchant-guardant, still a symbol of England (and Jersey) and its sports teams. A bomb in 1940 damaged the window of St Stephen's Porch behind the statue and bent Richard's sword.

Westminster Hall survived the fire of 1834 and was incorporated in the new palace. It was built by William Rufus, the son of William the Conqueror, in 1097 as a banqueting hall. It was heavily rebuilt in the time of Richard II (1377-1399) when it acquired its magnificent hammer-beam roof, a feat of engineering that did away with the need for support pillars and left an unencumbered floor space 73.2m (240ft) by 20.7m (68ft) and 12m (39ft) high. The outward load this puts on the walls accounts for the hefty buttresses you see outside. The oak timber came from various sources and was worked at Farnham in Surrey. Replacement timber needed in the 20th century was from 600-year-old trees planted to replace the originals. Some steel reinforcement had to be sneaked in at the same time. In the

13th century the hall housed law courts and shops, a use that continued up to 1882. Sir Thomas More, Anne Boleyn, and Charles I were all sentenced to death here, and after the Restoration the heads of Cromwell, Ireton, and Bradshaw were displayed on pikes. Coronation festivals were held here when the king's champion would ride into the hall on horseback and throw down his gauntlet as a challenge to any dissenter. St Stephen's Porch, added to the south end of the hall during the rebuilding, connects to the House of Commons. Latterly, the hall has seen the lying in state of sovereigns and prominent citizens.

Behind Westminster Hall is the **House of Commons**. The Commons has evolved from the 13th century and probably takes its name from the Anglo-Norman (and modern French) *commune*. It currently has around 650 members; their constituencies are adjusted to have 70,000 to 77,000 voters, and are independent of local government boundaries. Members are paid £84,000 plus office expenses, and the Prime Minister £164,000. Voting is by simple paper ballots, mostly by personal attendance on election day, and counted manually. Postal voting on demand, allowed for the first time in 2000, introduced an unwelcome opportunity for fraud. The Commons chamber was bombed and gutted in May 1941 during the Blitz; reconstruction took until 1950.

Glimpsed through the railings outside Westminster Hall is a statue of **Oliver Cromwell** with a sword in one hand and a bible in the other. Members of Parliament refused to pay for the sculpture as Cromwell's men had decimated the captives taken at Drogheda and Wexford in Ireland. Lord Roseberry, a former prime minister, himself paid the sculptor Sir Hamo Thornycroft for his work.

At the northern end of the palace is the Clock Tower known the world over as **Big Ben**. This was the last part of the palace to be completed, not least because the clock proved too big to be hauled up inside the tower. The tower itself is 96m (318ft) high on a base 12m (40ft) square. The tower leans 24cm (10") to the north-west but is stable. The tower was renamed in 2012 as the Elizabeth Tower to mark the late Queen's Diamond Jubilee, the 60th anniversary of her accession.

The clock faces are 7m (23ft) in diameter, and the minute markers are 30cm (12") square. The minute hands are 4m long; they had to be cast hollow in copper to get the weight down to the 100kg that the mechanism could cope with. The weights that drive the clock weigh 2½ tons; electric gear replaced the efforts of two manual winders in 1913. The pendulum is 4m long, weighs 310kg, and is adjusted by adding or removing old pennies that weigh only 9.5g (⅓ of an ounce).

Strictly speaking, Big Ben is the largest of the five bells in the tower and the one that strikes the hour. The first bell cracked as soon as it was tested, not least because the clock designer Denison insisted on a massive 660kg clapper. A new bell was cast in Whitechapel and hauled to Westminster by a team of 16 horses; it weighed 13½ tons, and the founder specified a 200kg (440lb) clapper. After a few months it too cracked. It turned out that Denison had used a 335kg (740lb) clapper, and that is why the bell sounds flat to this day. So why Big Ben? You can choose between the civil servant Sir Benjamin Hill and the bare-knuckle prizefighter Benjamin Caunt. We know whom our money's on.

Visiting. The whole interior of the palace is a work of art and well worth seeing. Guided tours are available when the Houses are not sitting. The Commons and the Lords both have public galleries where you can watch debates for free. The entrance is by Cromwell's statue. Full information on guided tours and so on: https://www.parliament.uk/visiting/

Opposite Victoria Tower is the **Jewel Tower**, built around 1365 for the king's wardrobe and valuables. It was later used for parliamentary records and by the Weights and Measures Office. It is now a small museum, free for English Heritage members.

The first **Westminster Abbey** was built by Edward the Confessor starting around 1050 on or near the site of a Benedictine monastery. This church seems to have been similar to the Abbey of Jumièges in Normandy, the ruins of which still stand. Edward's church was demolished in 1245 to be replaced by the present building begun by Henry III. Since the time of Elizabeth I, the Abbey has been a Royal Peculiar, responsible to the sovereign rather than the church hierarchy. For near enough a thousand years it has been the traditional location of coronations and royal funerals. What we see from here, of course, is the east end of the Abbey, actually the Chapel of Henry VII, built during his reign (1485-1509). The grand front and entrance are around the corner on Broad Sanctuary. If you do walk around there, the two towers which dominate the front were finished off by Hawksmoor in the first half of the 18th century.

Parliament Square was laid out in 1868 by Sir Charles Barry. Despite the awful traffic it has become the place for statues and demonstrations. The statues are listed in anti-clockwise order starting with Churchill.

Winston Churchill (1874-1965). Britain's inspirational leader during the Second World War, and an author and artist of note. Bronze (1976) by Ivor Roberts-Jones.

David Lloyd George (1863-1945). Welsh Liberal politician and social reformer. He was Prime Minister 1916-1922 and influential in the First World War, the Paris Peace Conference, and the founding of the Irish Free State. Bronze by Glynn Williams (2007).

Field Marshal Jan Christian Smuts (1870-1950). South African soldier and statesman. A rebel in the Boer Wars and staunch ally in both World Wars. His political and humanitarian views defy short description. He and Gandhi held one another in high regard. Bronze by Jacob Epstein (1956).

Viscount Palmerston (1784-1865) was a statesman who was almost continuously in office between 1807 and his death, first as a Tory and later as a Liberal. He was a popular and effective politician, being prime minister 1855-1858 and 1859-1865. The apparent anomaly of a peer sitting in the House of Commons is explained by his inherited title being in the Irish peerage which did not entitle him to a seat in the House of Lords. Statue of 1876 by Thomas Woolner.

Derby was Edward Smith-Stanley, 14th Earl of Derby (1799-1869), a Conservative politician three times Prime Minister between 1852 and 1868.

Benjamin Disraeli (1804-1881), later Earl of Beaconsfield, was Prime Minister 1874-1880. Disraeli was the first, and so far only, person of Jewish birth to be Prime Minister. Disraeli was also, in his time, a well-regarded novelist. The statue by Mario Raggi was unveiled in 1883.

Sir Robert Peel (1788-1850). Conservative politician and prime minister. A notable reformer (emancipation of Roman Catholics), free trader, and founder of the modern police force. This 1876 statue by Matthew Noble replaces (and uses the same metal) as an earlier and larger one by Baron Marochetti.

Nelson Mandela (1918-2013). Lawyer and anti-apartheid campaigner, he was convicted of sabotage in 1962 and spent 27 years in gaol, mostly in inhumane conditions. Eventually freed, he negotiated the move to a fully democratic South Africa and became its first president. Bronze by Ian Walters (2007), the same man who did the bust of Mandela on the South Bank.

M.K. Gandhi (1869-1948). Gandhi's given names were Mohandas Karamchand; Mahatma was an honorific meaning Great Soul. Gandhi turned the independence movement in India from a middle-class waffle group into an effective mass movement. After the achievement of independence he was assassinated by Hindu fundamentalists. Amitabh Bachchan, the Bollywood heartthrob, spoke at the unveiling. We watched him once compering the Indian version of *Who Wants to be a Millionaire?*; slipping effortlessly between Hindi and English, he made the best impression of Chris Tarrant you could imagine. Bronze by Philip Jackson (2015).

Millicent Fawcett (1847-1929). Leader of the National Union for Women's Suffrage Societies, the largest movement for women's voting rights. She was also a social activist involved in outlawing incest, raising the age of consent to prevent child abuse, and improving women's opportunities for higher education. The first statue of a woman in Parliament Square and the first by a woman, Gillian Wearing (2018).

Over the road to the west are two more statues:

George Canning (1770-1827). Tory politician who was prime minister for 119 days until his death, an unenviable record for brevity only recently eclipsed. Father of 'Clemency' Canning, first Viceroy of India.

Abraham Lincoln (1809-1865) was the 16th president of the United States and leader of the North during the Civil War. This statue is a copy of the one in Chicago by Saint-Gaudens.

Behind the statue of Lincoln is the new-fangled (and politicised) **Supreme Court**, set up in 2009 as another ill-thought-out attempt at reform. The job had previously been done perfectly well by the Law Lords. More notable is the building itself; Middlesex Guildhall was built in the early 20th century as the base of Middlesex County Council. The style has been referred to, seriously, we think, as art nouveau gothic.

Church of St Margaret, on the south side of Parliament Square, has been the parish church of the House of Commons since 1614. It was first built around 1150 and demolished and rebuilt in the time of Edward III (1327-1377). We are lucky the church is still here. In 1549, the over-mighty Protector Somerset, regent to the young Edward VI (1547-1553), decided to appropriate the stones to build a house for himself. His men were quickly disabused by parishioners and the London mob. It was damaged several times in the Second World War. Pepys, Milton, and Churchill were all married here.

On the corner of Parliament Street (which leads into Whitehall) is the **Houses of Parliament Shop** selling souvenir knick-knacks. Further down is:

The Red Lion, 48 Parliament Street, SW1A 2NH. Fullers. Spectacular Victorian pub with a long political history, being only a three-minute walk from Downing Street or the Houses of Parliament. Another political pub with a Division Bell. The terracotta head of Charles Dickens at second-floor level attests to his having been a regular here.

The attractive **Portcullis House** with its many chimneys (actually vents for an eco-friendly ventilation system), provides office space for Members of Parliament and their staff. It stands over Westminster tube station and was completed in 2001 in a modern Gothic Revival style.

Between Big Ben and the river is **Speaker's Garden**, more a builder's yard during the renovation work on the Elizabeth Tower.

South bank

In the fork between Lambeth Palace Road (along the river) and Lambeth Road lies the former **Church of St Mary-at-Lambeth**, now the **Garden Museum**. The two John Tradescants, father and son, were gardeners and naturalists to King Charles I (1625-1649) and Queen Henrietta Maria. They travelled widely, including to Russia, the New World, and North Africa, searching for new plants. Common spiderwort, a popular garden plant which they brought from North America, is named *Tradescantia* after them. After the death of the younger John in 1667 their collection was acquired by Elias Ashmole; he bequeathed it to Oxford University in 1683, forming the base of the Ashmolean Museum, where some items can still be seen.

A monument to the two men stands in the churchyard, and Ashmole is buried in the church. Another famous seafarer buried here is **Vice-Admiral William Bligh** (1754-1817), formerly captain of HMS Bounty. A mutiny aboard ship caused Bligh to be cast adrift in a small open boat with eighteen members of his crew. Bligh crossed 4000 miles (6,500km) of ocean to safety. The remaining twenty-five crew settled on Tahiti and Pitcairn Island where a few descendants still live. Bligh's tombstone is of Coade stone, like the lion on the south side of Westminster Bridge. Bligh lived nearby at 100 Lambeth Road, SE1 7PT, as evidenced by a blue plaque. Beside the museum is the **Knot Garden**, a formal garden of aromatic plants and culinary herbs.

Continuing a little further along Lambeth Road, you find the **Imperial War Museum**, SE1 6HZ, which commemorates the involvement of British and Commonwealth forces in the wars of the 20th century. The two 15" naval guns in front of the museum were fitted first in battleships during the First World War, and later saw service in the Second World War. Each gun weighs 100 tons (102t) and could fire a 1900lb (862kg) shell 16¾ miles (27km).

The displays inside are impressive but, as with most museums these days, it is hard to avoid the feeling that things have been dumbed down. The museum has an extensive reserve collection of war art, which is fascinating, but you need to make advance arrangements. The building is the central block of the old Bethlehem Royal Hospital, a polite euphemism for a lunatic asylum. This place, or Bethlem as it was usually pronounced, is the origin of the word bedlam.

And, if you have walked this far, it is well worth visiting the **Tibetan Peace Garden**. The Samten Kyil, to give it its proper name, is Tibetan for Garden of Contemplation. Completed in 1999, it was opened and consecrated by the Dalai Lama. Charming place, but does feel a little fort-like for the real religion of peace.

Sticking to the river, you pass the pier of **Thames River Cruises**, who run dinner, Sunday lunch, and afternoon tea cruises. There is also a bar on the pier. www.bateauxlondon.com/

Lambeth's **Millennium Tree** is just past here, a *quercus ilex* or evergreen holm oak.

The **Special Operations Executive** was set up in 1940 to organise the resistance to Nazi Germany and, later, Imperial Japan in the countries they had occupied. This memorial commemorates all those who undertook this deadly work. The bust is of Violette Szabo, an Anglo-French woman married to a Hungarian who fought with the Free French forces. He was killed during the Battle of El Alamein; she was captured by the Germans on her second mission to France and eventually executed at Ravensbruck concentration camp in 1945. Virginia McKenna played Violette Szabo in the 1958 film *Carve Her Name with Pride*.

Lambeth Palace has been the London residence of the Archbishop of Canterbury since 1197. The buildings date from that time up to the present day. This is, in effect, the head office of the Church of England. Over to the right is Morton's Tower, one of the gates to the palace. Cardinal Morton built it in red brick in the Tudor style in around 1490. As you follow the path, you can see the Great Hall (rebuilt in 1663 after Civil War destruction) with the lantern on top, and the ragstone Lollards' Tower (1435). Lollard comes from an old Middle Dutch word meaning a mutterer; it came into English as a derogatory term for a follower of John Wycliffe (ca1328-1384), a Christian fundamentalist and nationalist who taught that the only authority was the Bible. This made him, as a kind of proto-Protestant, a heretic in the eyes of Rome. Wycliffe, rather surprisingly, avoided the stake and spent the last part of his life directing a translation into Middle English of the Latin bible. The tower, more properly known as the Water Tower from the Water Gate below it, only assumed its modern name in 1647.

Within the palace precincts is the **Library**, reckoned to be the largest collection of ecclesiastical documents outside the Vatican. There are research facilities. The design of the new red brick building appears to have been cribbed from a 1920s power station. See below for details of guided tours. The palace is closed at present for refurbishment, though open days of the fine gardens still take place. Details for visiting all three venues: https://www.archbishopof-canterbury.org/about/lambeth-palace/visit-lambeth-palace

A memorial plaque to **Lieutenant-Colonel John By** (1779-1836) is on the wall to the right. A Royal Engineer educated at the old Royal Military Academy in Woolwich, he rebuilt and modernised the Royal Gunpowder Mills (in Waltham Abbey in Hertfordshire) after a huge explosion. He is best known for constructing the 126-mile (202km) Rideau Canal from Kingston on Lake Ontario to Ottawa. He founded Bytown to house his workers which, in due course, became Ottawa, Canada's federal capital.

Behind the wall here is **St Thomas' Hospital**, founded in about 1106 on a site in Southwark. After various ups and downs, it was established here in new buildings in 1871, and the medical school was established at the same time. Expansion and bomb damage account for the mixture of building styles. Note the elaborate water tower. Within the grounds is (for the moment anyway) a marble statue of Sir Robert Clayton by Grinling Gibbons. He was Lord Mayor of London in 1679 and a benefactor. An earlier Lord Mayor, Richard (Dick) Whittington, had founded "a new chamber for young women who had done amiss, in trust of a good amendment".

Florence Nightingale (1820-1910), the Lady with the Lamp, made her reputation tending to wounded soldiers during the Crimean War (1853-1856). She professionalised nursing and set up the first secular school of nursing here at St Thomas's. It's worth reading more about her – a fascinating character. The original bronze statue was stolen in 1979 and was replaced by this composite copy.

Florence Nightingale Museum, St Thomas' Hospital, 2 Lambeth Palace Road, SE1 7EW.

The riverside wall of the hospital forms memorials to Covid and Human BSE victims. The French artist **Monet** (1840-1926) painted his famous series of the Houses of Parliament from the terrace in front of the hospital. Nineteen paintings are known to survive, none, as far as we can tell, in London.

Westminster Bridge

The idea of a bridge at Westminster was first mooted soon after the Restoration in 1660 but was shot down by vested interests, notably the watermen and the Archbishop of Canterbury, who owned the horse ferry a little upstream. The first bridge (of multi-arched stone) was completed in 1750, and earned those people hefty compensation. This was the first bridge between Old London Bridge and Putney Bridge eight miles away. It was the view from this bridge that inspired Wordsworth to write:

> *Earth has not anything to show more fair:*
>
> *Dull would he be of soul who could pass by*
>
> *A sight so touching in its majesty:...*

And Canaletto painted it, though the attributed date of 1747 is at odds with the completion date of 1750. The painting is in the Yale Center for British Art in New Haven. Two paintings by Richard Wilson (1713-1782) of the bridge under construction are in Tate Britain, in the 1720 room.

The first bridge suffered settlement problems throughout its life, and a cast-iron bridge of seven arches eventually replaced it in 1862. This bridge was unusually wide (84ft/26m) for its time and remains as built. The green colour is said to reflect the leather benches in the House of Commons, whilst the red of Lambeth Bridge upstream is the colour of the seating in the House of Lords.

In the Bond film *Spectre*, Blofeld's helicopter crashes into the bridge.

Getting there. Westminster tube station. Waterloo mainline and tube stations are a short walk from the far end of the bridge. Pier for Thames Clipper services is just downstream of the bridge on the north side of the river.

Walking. Westminster Bridge to Waterloo Bridge is ½ mile (1km).

19. WESTMINSTER BRIDGE TO WATERLOO BRIDGE

North bank

The bronze statue by the bridge is of *Queen Boudicca*; in AD61 she led a rebellion of her Iceni clan against the Roman occupiers and burned down the town of Londinium. The group is by Thomas Thornycroft, a member of the family better known later as shipbuilders and engineers. Boadicea, as the Romans called her, is accompanied by her two daughters; it was their abuse by Roman soldiers that sparked the rebellion. Thornycroft started the statue in the 1850s, intending it for Decimus Burton's grand entrance to Hyde Park. After fifty years of money trouble, it was eventually installed here in 1902.

On the base of the statue, and usually hidden by a tourist tat stall, is a London County Council Bridges By-laws notice dated 1914 imposing a 15-ton weight limit. Behind and below the statue is the odd little **Tide Kiosk**, a copper-clad housing for tide recording instruments. Originally fitted with a pen and drum recorder, it now sends a message to the Thames Barrier Control Room every quarter hour.

The riverside walk here is the **Victoria Embankment**; before Sir Joseph Bazalgette constructed this in 1865-70, the river was much wider; just how much wider becomes clear when we reach the Embankment Gardens. This was a multi-purpose land reclamation to accommodate Bazalgette's new sewers and a roadway to relieve congestion on The Strand and other city streets. Under the road is the cut-and-cover tunnel for the District Line underground railway.

Over to the left are the buildings of **New Scotland Yard**, headquarters of the Metropolitan Police, responsible for the whole Greater London area. The original New Scotland Yard in red brick and white Portland stone (1890) is now called the Norman Shaw Buildings after its architect. They were built over the foundations of the Grand National Opera House, never completed due to lack of finance. Next door is the new New Scotland Yard in the modern Curtis Green Building.

It is little known that London also suffered air attack to a lesser extent in the First World War. Zeppelins (huge, lighter than air airships) and Gotha biplane bombers wandered over the city, dropping relatively small bombs more or less at random. Damage caused by one of these attacks can be seen at Cleopatra's Needle. Civilian casualties amounted to around 1400.

The Blitz

The Blitz is the name by which the air assault on London and other British cities, beginning in the summer of 1940, became known. The name derives from the German *blitzkrieg* (*blitz* = lightning + *krieg* = war). Germany overran Poland in 1939 by a combination of fast-moving armoured columns and crushing air superiority – not to mention Soviet connivance. In May 1940, it was the turn of Denmark, Norway, The Netherlands, Belgium, and France. This put German bombers within easy reach of London.

To mount an improvised seaborne invasion, the Germans needed air superiority, and that was what the Battle of Britain was all about. The Luftwaffe (the German air force) started attacking the Royal Air Force's airfields by day and moved on to strategic targets such as aircraft factories and London Docks. When that did not work, they switched to indiscriminate night bombing.

The main blitz ended in Spring 1941 as the Luftwaffe turned its attention to Operation Barbarossa, the invasion of Soviet Russia. Intermittent raiding, supplemented in 1944 by the V1 cruise missiles and V2 ballistic rockets, continued into early 1945. By that time, London was a very battered and war-weary city. Civilian casualties over the whole war were about 40,000, half of those in London. http://bombsight.org/ maps where the bombs fell, including the one on John's mother's home in Hanwell.

It is little known that London also suffered air attack to a lesser extent in the First World War. Zeppelins (huge, lighter than air airships) and Gotha biplane bombers wandered over the city, dropping relatively small bombs more or less at random. Damage caused by one of these attacks can be seen at Cleopatra's Needle. Civilian casualties amounted to around 1400.

The **Battle of Britain Memorial** (2005) commemorates every one of the nearly 3000 airmen from fifteen different nations who took part on the British side. Five hundred and forty-four were killed during the battle, and another 795 did not survive the war. Contrary to popular belief, not all the pilots were public school toffs; as far as we can tell, between a third and half of them were non-commissioned officers, sergeants and flight sergeants. The website https://bbm.org.uk lists all the aircrew involved. The badges of all the RAF squadrons involved are on the memorial, as are those of 302 and 303 squadrons of the Polish Air Force.

The monument has two bronze plaques in deep relief that repay scrutiny. RAF fighter pilots at rest and scrambling dominate, but you also see the armourers with belts of ammunition reloading the aircraft and all those on the ground who backed them up. Control was an essential factor in the battle, and you see the radar stations, the Observer Corps, and the control rooms. There are social aspects too; St Paul's Cathedral surrounded by flames symbolises a nation's defiance, and there is the part played by women. And, of course, that essential part of British life, especially in adversity, the brew-up of tea. As the Duke of Wellington said of the victory over another tyrant, it was *"the nearest-run thing you ever saw in your life."* Around the base is Churchill's famous tribute: *"Never in the field of human conflict was so much owed by so many to so few".*

From here, there are two routes to Waterloo Bridge, the official route along the river and an alternative through the gardens with many reminders of British history. The far edge of the gardens marks the old river bank.

Along the river

The **Royal Air Force Memorial**. The Royal Air Force was formed on 1 April 1918 by merging the Royal Flying Corps (of the Army) and the Royal Naval Air Service, making it the first independent air force in the world. This memorial was unveiled in 1923 to commemorate the casualties of the First World War and later altered to include more recent conflicts. The RAF motto *Per Ardua Ad Astra* (initially that of the Royal Flying Corps) translates as "through struggle to the stars".

Tattershall Castle, Victoria Embankment, SW1A 2HR. Tel: 020 7839 6548. Real ale and food. The *Tattershall Castle* is a paddle steamer built in 1934 by William Gray & Co of Hartlepool for the London & North-Eastern Railway. She was a passenger and vehicle ferry across the River Humber in the days before the bridge was built. Tattershall Castle itself is a fine 15th century red brick tower in South Lincolnshire.

Over the road is a memorial to **Samuel Plimsoll** (1824-1898). He was a Bristol-born politician and social reformer. He noticed that merchant ships were frequently overloaded, affecting their seaworthiness; even worse were the 'coffin ships' sent to sea to gain insurance money regardless of the deadly results for their crews. His parliamentary bill for a safe loading mark to prevent this was voted down by vested interests in 1867, but eventually forced the government to act in 1876. A 'Plimsoll mark' is on the base of the memorial, which was funded by the National Union of Seamen in 1929. Note the seahorses on the railings to either side; we were amazed to learn that there are seahorses in the Thames.

At the time of writing, access to the riverside past the *Tattershall Castle* is limited by works on the Thames Tunnel sewer. A relief bust of **Sir Joseph Bazalgette** is on the river wall just before Hungerford Bridge. The Latin motto *flumini vincula posuit* translates literally as 'he put chains to the river'.

R.S. Hispaniola, Victoria Embankment, WC2N 5DJ. Tel: 020 7839 3011. Bar and restaurant, located here since 1973. Originally called the *M.V. Maid of Ashton*, she was built in 1953 by Yarrow in Glasgow for the River Clyde ferry services run by the Caledonian Steam Packet Company. Interesting-looking menu and reasonably priced for the location.

The garden walk

As an alternative to the riverside, you can walk through the **Victoria Embankment Gardens**. The first part of the gardens is below the former Air Ministry, now the Ministry of Defence, built on the site of the old palace of Westminster. Accordingly, these memorials are all of a military nature.

Chindit Memorial. The Chindits (chindit comes from the Burmese *chinthe*, a lion or temple guardian) were elements of the British and Indian armies that fought the Japanese in Burma. Landed behind enemy lines, their task was to attack the enemy's lines of communication. Opinions differ as to their effectiveness, mainly because of the high casualty rate. They certainly proved, however, that Allied soldiers could fight in the jungle. On the reverse is a memorial to their leader, Major-General Orde Wingate, a charismatic soldier and Zionist.

Iraq and Afghanistan Memorial to the British personnel who lost their lives in two unnecessary and unwinnable wars, wars that left the inhabitants of those benighted countries in an even worse state than before, and increased the risk of terrorism in the West.

Lord Trenchard (1873-1956) was a professional soldier sometimes described as Father of the Royal Air Force for his part in forming and nurturing that force. Four plaques on the base represent his varied career: the Royal Scots Fusiliers, the WAFF (West African Frontier Force) in Nigeria, the Royal Air Force, and the Metropolitan Police.

Korean War. At the end of the Second World War Korea, which had been annexed by Japan in 1910, was divided on the 38th parallel between the Soviet-dominated North and the Western-inclined South. In 1950 the North invaded the South; communist China intervened later that year, and after bitter fighting, United Nations forces (predominantly South Korean and American) pushed them back to the border. An armistice was agreed in 1953, though the war has never been formally ended. This was a dirty war with total casualties of around 3,000,000, mostly civilians. British casualties amounted to around 1100.

The Fleet Air Arm is the Royal Navy's aviation component. The Royal Naval Air Service became part of the Royal Air Force when it was formed in 1918, so the development of aircraft carriers in the 1920s necessitated the forming of the Fleet Air Arm. The FAA played a distinguished role in the Second World War (and afterwards) despite struggling for much of the time with obsolete and unsuitable aircraft. The **Fleet Air Arm memorial** depicts a naval aviator as Daedalus, a name also used for the FAA's main shore establishment at Lee-on-Solent in southern England. According to the Roman poet Ovid, Daedalus was an architect and inventor. He built the Minotaur's labyrinth for King Minos of Crete but was imprisoned there with his son Icarus. Fashioning wings from feathers and wax, the pair escaped. Icarus, overcome by excitement, flew too close to the sun which melted the wax and pitched him into the sea.

Portal is Marshal of the Royal Air Force Lord Portal. After a distinguished career as a bomber pilot in the First World War, he served as Chief of the Air Staff from 1940-45; the CAS is the professional head of the RAF and the man who had to mediate between the politicians and his sometimes unruly subordinates.

General Charles George Gordon (1833-1885) was otherwise known as 'Chinese' Gordon from his time as an officer of the Emperor of China. In later service in Egypt and the Sudan, he made great efforts to suppress the slave trade, at that time the basis of the local economy. A difficult subordinate, he finally came unstuck in Khartoum where he was murdered by the soldiers of Ahmed bin Abd Allah, an Islamic leader popularly known as the 'Mad Mahdi'. It was this event, *inter alia*, that brought Winston Churchill to prominence. Older readers may recall Charlton Heston playing Gordon in the 1966 flick *Khartoum*. Behind the statue of Gordon is what appears to be the steps of a watergate, either from the Palace of Whitehall or the townhouses that were later built here. Cross Horse Guards Avenue and enter the next part of the gardens, known as Whitehall Garden.

William Tyndale (ca1494-ca1536) produced in 1526 the first English translation of the New Testament of The Bible based on the Hebrew and Greek texts. Another work encouraged Henry VIII to break with Rome and become head of the Church of England, as is the current sovereign and why you find *FID:DEF* or *F:D* (*Fidei Defensor* or Defender of the Faith) on every British coin. Falling out with Henry over his divorce from Catherine of Aragon, he moved to the Continent. A follower of Luther, he was martyred in Belgium, then under the control of the Holy Roman Empire.

Sir Henry Bartle Frere (1814-1881) was a colonial administrator who laid the foundations of the postal service in India and encouraged literature and education in Sindh (now a province of Pakistan). His subsequent career in South Africa was less successful.

Sir James Outram Bt (1803-1863) was a successful and popular soldier in the Bombay Army of the East India Company, campaigning in Sindh, Afghanistan, and the Relief of Lucknow. Like Havelock, Outram appears in a *Flashman* novel; he was played by Richard Attenborough in Satyajit Ray's *The Chess Players* (1977).

Near here at Hungerford Stairs, possibly now under the site of Charing Cross station, was the dark, satanic mill (actually a rat-infested slum) of Warren's Blacking Warehouse, where boot polish was made. **Charles Dickens**, at the age of twelve, worked ten-hour days here to help out his indigent father. Walk under Hungerford Bridge for the next part of the garden or rejoin the riverside walk.

Northumberland Avenue, on the left before Hungerford Bridge is the start of the Trafalgar Square detour; see section 20 below. **Hungerford Bridge** takes Southern Region trains over the river into Charing Cross station, the railways actually call it Charing Cross Bridge. The ramshackle walkway on the downstream side was replaced by the twin Golden Jubilee Bridges in 2002, acknowledging The Queen's 50 years on the throne. The earlier bridge here was a suspension road bridge by Brunel. When it was demolished in 1845, the chains were used for the spectacular Clifton Suspension Bridge over the Avon Gorge near Bristol. Monet produced 37 paintings of the bridge 1899-1905, none, as far as we can tell, in London. The viewpoint may have been his room at The Savoy; no freezing garret for Monet!

Along the river

A bust of **W.S. Gilbert** (1836-1911), the librettist of the Gilbert and Sullivan light opera partnership, is opposite Embankment tube station. Nearby is **Embankment Pier** for Thames Clipper services.

Cleopatra's Needle. Ancient Egyptian rulers set up obelisks outside their temples, the inscriptions puffing their reigns. Fourteen over 15m high (and a lot more smaller ones) still exist, many in Italy. This one, 21m high, dates from around 1450BC and was set up in Heliopolis, now part of Cairo. Its tenuous connection with Cleopatra (69BC-30BC) is that the Romans moved it to a temple she had built to Julius Caesar or perhaps Mark Anthony (her affairs with both inspired plays by Shaw and Shakespeare) at Alexandria. After toppling, it lay for nearly 2000 years before the ruler of Egypt gifted it to Britain in 1819 to commemorate the victories of Nelson and Abercrombie over Napoleon at the Nile. And there it lay for another 50 years due to government parsimony.

Eventually, it was towed to Britain in an iron tube made by the Thames Iron Works at the mouth of the River Lea. It was set up in 1878, thirty years after the French had installed their Luxor Obelisk in the Place de la Concorde. Items included in a time capsule in the base include a box of cigars, photographs of the best-looking women of the day, and a Bradshaw Railway Guide.

The bronze sphinxes are Victorian and said to be the wrong way round; they should be facing away from the obelisk to guard it. That on the upriver side bears the shrapnel scars of a bomb dropped from a German aircraft in 1917. On the river side of the obelisk base is a memorial to the six seamen who lost their lives in the Bay of Biscay trying to reattach the broken tow. This pillar's twin is in Central Park in New York. From the river side you can also see the magnificent mooring rings along the river, like mammoth door knockers. The setting of the column, along with the sphinx and camel seats and dolphin (actually sturgeon) lamp standards, was done by G.J. Vulliamy (1817-1886). The Vulliamys were a talented family who had started out as Swiss clockmakers.

Opposite is the **Anglo-Belgian Memorial**, a token of thanks from the estimated 250,000 Belgian refugees who fled the German occupation of their country during the First World War. The bronzes are by Victor Rousseau in a setting designed by Sir Reginald Blomfield. The shields are the arms of the provinces of Belgium.

Queen Mary II (a steam passenger ship built in 1933) was moored as a restaurant here 1981-2009; she is currently being refitted in Glasgow, where she will remain.

In the river wall just before Waterloo Bridge is a plaque to **Sir Walter Besant** (1836-1901), the historian and novelist. In case you were wondering, Annie Besant, the theosophist, activist for Irish and Indian independence, and social reformer, was his sister-in-law.

The garden walk

As before, it is possible to walk through gardens, now **Victoria Embankment Gardens**, rather than along the river. **Gordon's Wine Bar**, 47 Villiers Street, WC2N. (Right in the north-west corner of the gardens). Claims to be London's oldest wine bar. Great atmosphere in the original building, and you can interpret that as you will. Now greatly expanded outside. Almost next door, at 43 Villiers Street, is a blue plaque to **Rudyard Kipling** (1865-1936), the poet and storyteller.

The back gardens of houses on the Strand used to have watergates giving access to the river. The **York House Watergate** can still be seen at Watergate Walk. Looking south towards the river gives you an idea of how wide the river was before the building of the embankments. Just behind the watergate, in Buckingham Street, is a plaque to **Samuel Pepys**, who lived in a house on that site. There are many more memorials in the gardens.

The **Imperial Camel Corps Brigade** was formed in Egypt in 1918 to campaign against the Ottoman Empire (Turkey). It had four battalions: two Australian, one British, and one Indian. Assistance and mounts came from the Bikaner Camel Corps already in the area. The Indian princely state of Bikaner, an area now bordering Pakistan, had used camel-mounted troops since the 15th century. Their successors still take part in state occasions in New Delhi, though now part of the Border Security Force rather than the Indian Army.

Robert Burns (1759-1796) is widely regarded as the national poet of Scotland. A serious literary influence, the author of *Auld Lang Syne* and *Tam o'Shanter* is celebrated worldwide on 25 January (his birthday).

The fountain is part of the memorial to **Major-General Lord Cheylesmore** (1848-1925), soldier, sportsman, and local administrator. Cheylesmore is buried in Highgate Cemetery, and this memorial was designed by Sir Edwin Lutyens. Behind it is the Anglo-Belgian Memorial and Cleopatra's Needle.

Sir Wilfrid Lawson (1829-1906) was an anti-imperialist member of parliament. He was also an advocate of temperance; as other dedicated men and women around the world have discovered, a lost cause if ever there was one. On the plus side, he had a GSOH, as a good sense of humour is described in singles' ads.

Henry Fawcett (1833-1884) was blinded in a shooting accident in 1858, an event which seemed to have little effect on his career as a social reformer, economist, and Member of Parliament, altogether a remarkable character. The memorial fountain (1886) is by Mary Grant.

Robert Raikes (1736-1811) was a philanthropist and educationist. He greatly expanded the Sunday school movement, using it to teach reading and writing to deprived children. Churchmen pilloried him for teaching on the Sabbath but he was, in effect, a founder of universal education in England.

Behind the Raikes statue is Carting Lane, referred to by the vulgar as Farting Lane, with some good reason as it has London's last surviving **lamp powered by sewer gas**, mainly methane.

The **Coal Hole**, Carting Lane (top end by the Strand) WC2R 0DW. An Edwardian recreation (1903) of a traditional London pub. Reputedly named after an earlier incarnation frequented by coal-heavers from the river. The Wolf Room is named after a club for repressed husbands, specifically those forbidden to sing in the bath.

Back in the gardens is the suitably melodramatic memorial to **Arthur Sullivan** (1842-1900). He was a major composer in his time but destined to be remembered for the twelve "Savoy" comic operas produced in partnership with W.S. Gilbert.

The **Savoy Hotel**, Strand, opened in 1889 and extended in 1903, is London's premier hotel. It was established by Richard D'Oyly Carte, who also staged the Gilbert and Sullivan operettas at the adjacent Savoy Theatre. The site was previously occupied by the Savoy Palace, destroyed during the Peasants' Revolt in 1381. Henry VII had the palace rebuilt as a hospital for the poor. In front of the riverside entrance to The Savoy is a memorial planter to **Richard D'Oyly Carte**, topped by an armillary sphere; John thought it was an astrolabe.

The Savoy interests us mainly for two reasons. Its main entrance on the Strand is the only place in Britain where traffic is obliged to drive on the right, and in 1953 Mr E. Drury won a bet by casting a line into the river from the roof. This is a good 90m (100yds) and quite a feat in the days before composite rods.

As you exit the gardens, over to the left is a statue of **Michael Faraday** (1791-1867), the pioneer in electromagnetism and much more. The lighthouse and a replica of his laboratory at Trinity Buoy Wharf are a further memorial.

Walk up Savoy Street for the **Savoy Chapel**. When the Savoy Palace was rebuilt as a hospital, it included a Chapel of St John the Baptist. Much altered over the years, it eventually became the Chapel of the Royal Victorian Order, an order of knighthood in the gift of the Sovereign. The chapel was the first place of worship to have electric lighting and first to provide church marriage to divorcees. It is still a Royal Peculiar outside the authority of the local bishop. The chapel, a quiet refuge from the traffic on the Embankment, is open from 0900-1600 Monday to Thursday (but closed August and September) and for choral service at 1100 on Sunday.

South bank

The Queen's Walk, which runs from here to Tower Bridge, was laid out for the Queen's Silver Jubilee in 1977. This was quite an achievement, considering it would have been impossible to walk almost any part of it up to then. The walk is just short of 2½ miles or 4km and marked by plaques in the pavement.

Coade stone

Coade stone is usually referred to as an artificial stone; it is, in fact, more like a ceramic as it needs long firing at an intense heat. A man called Richard Holt first patented the process in the 1720s. The material is weatherproof and harder wearing than many forms of natural stone; this was assumed to derive from the inclusion of ground glass and quartz. Coade stone was used both for statues and building components such as keystones and decorative panels.

The material takes its name from the two Mrs Eleanor Coades. The mother, a widow, bought an existing business in 1769 (where the Festival Hall now stands). She is thought to have perfected the formula before handing on the business to her daughter. The young Eleanor, who was unmarried but assumed the *Mrs* title as was proper in Georgian England, ran the business until her death in 1821. The successor business went bust in 1840 as fashions changed, and the formula was assumed lost. The name and the product have been revived recently.

The **South Bank Lion** was made from Coade Stone in 1837 and for many years adorned the Lion Brewery; it was admired by Zola, amongst others. The brewery was demolished in 1949, and the site is now occupied by the Festival Hall. Stripped of its red paint, the lion was installed here in 1966. Inscribed on one of the paws is "W.F.W. Coade 24 May 1837." This relates to the sculptor W.F. Woodington; the same man made two other smaller lions, which also decorated the brewery. One (now gilded) stands at the Rugby Football Union's stadium in Twickenham; the other has disappeared, possibly due to a fire at the brewery in 1931.

County Hall accommodated the London County Council from 1922 to 1965, though the council dated back to 1889. Its successor, the Greater London Council covered a much larger area including outer London. Oddly enough, the GLC was always held by the party in opposition to the central government in Westminster; the resulting friction led to its abolition in 1986. The separate London boroughs assumed its functions. A successor body (of sorts) is mentioned a few miles further on.

The building stands on the site of a flour mill and a Crosse & Blackwell food factory. Excavation of the foundations revealed a Roman boat, now preserved in the Museum of London. The riverside part of the building with the colonnade opened in 1922, and the north and south blocks behind it were added in 1936-39. Current occupants of the building include two hotels, an aquarium, the London Dungeon, and Shrek's Adventure.

Behind County Hall and buried under the 20 or more railway tracks and platforms of Waterloo Station is **Leake Street Graffiti Tunnel**. And if you have found this, Lower Marsh Street, with its shops and restaurants, is worth a look.

The Millennium Wheel, later the **London Eye**, was opened in 2000. Using components from Britain and all over Europe, it was assembled flat over the river and then hauled upright. At the time, its 135m (443ft) made it the world's tallest Ferris wheel. The 32 capsules take 30 minutes for a full rotation, and the views are spectacular. You can see the BT Tower, where the rotating restaurant of fond memory, was somewhat higher (158m/520ft), and The Shard, where the open viewing platform is at 244m/800ft; prices for the Eye and the Shard are much the same. Blackrock is the current owner of the London Eye.

Jubilee Gardens was first laid out for the Queen's Silver Jubilee in 1977 and revamped in 2012. Within the gardens is the **International Brigades Memorial**. A memorial service is held here on the first Sunday in July.

The Spanish Civil War

This war (1936-1939) was fought between the Republicans, an elected leftist regime in Madrid, and the Nationalists, an alliance of militarists and conservatives. The Soviet Union backed the Republicans, and Italy and Germany the Nationalists. Many volunteers (perhaps 40,000) joined in, those on the Republican side forming the International Brigades. Four thousand British volunteers, including George Orwell, took part, mainly on the Republican side. Around 600 Irishmen also went to Spain; their sympathies were with the Nationalists because of the Republicans' perceived anti-clericalism.

An American diplomat described the war as a dress rehearsal for the Second World War. It was certainly a very messy war. Apart from the 100,000 or more combatants killed, the Republicans killed perhaps 40,000 non-combatants, mostly clerics, landowners, and petits bourgeois. The Nationalists killed perhaps twice as many (plus another 50,000 after the war had ended), just about anyone suspected of leftist sympathies and Protestant clerics. Prisoners of war were routinely murdered. Investigations continue to this day, and it is thought that over 100,000 bodies still lie in unmarked graves.

The tall building behind the gardens is the **Shell Centre**, constructed in 1957-62 after the Festival of Britain had been cleared from the site. Groundworks revealed a never-finished pneumatic railway between King's Cross and Waterloo Stations. The traditional Portland stone cladding has weathered much better than the raw concrete round and about.

The Jubilee Gardens and the rest of the space to Waterloo Bridge were the site in 1951 of the **Festival of Britain**. On the anniversary of the Great Exhibition of 1851, the government planned a festival to lighten the gloomy economic mood. Six years after the Second World War ended, Britain was war-ravaged, short of dollars and everything else, and still subject to food rationing. Much of the design, some of it startlingly modern, was done by refugees from either Nazi Germany or Soviet Russia. The gardens occupy the site of the Dome of Discovery, the main building. The dome was 365ft (111m) in diameter and 93ft (28m) high. The dome, of aluminium was at the time the largest in the world. This is about one-third the size of the Millennium Dome further downstream; the displays were, by all accounts, more intellectually challenging.

Nearby was the **Skylon**, a rocket-shaped sculpture to symbolize progress and the way forward; it was supported 15m (50ft) above the ground on wires and rose to 90m (nearly 300 ft) at its tip. I remember, as a highly impressed eight-year-old, looking up at it from directly underneath. I wonder if the little disc marker is still in the pavement? There is a model of the Skylon in the Museum of London.

Despite the morale boost, recovery took a long time; even fifteen years later, there was no shortage of bomb-site parking space in central London. Britain finally paid off its war debt to the USA in 2006.

Hungerford Bridge takes Southern Region trains over the river into Charing Cross station; in fact, the railways call it Charing Cross Bridge. The ramshackle walkway on the downstream side was replaced by the twin Golden Jubilee Bridges in 2002, acknowledging the Queen's 50 years on the throne. Monet produced 37 paintings of the bridge from 1899-1905, none, as far as we can tell, in London. Street food stalls operate under the bridge.

The space between Hungerford Bridge and Waterloo Bridge was also part of the Festival of Britain. The **Southbank Centre** now occupies the site; this is the largest performing arts centre in Europe, putting on more than 2000 events and attracting an audience of over four million annually. The collective name covers several venues, of which the **Royal Festival Hall** is the only surviving building of the Festival. Matthew and Martin designed it and it has a seating capacity of 3000. The hall is run imaginatively, and there is always something going on; well worth a shufti when you are passing. The **Poetry Library** is on Level 5 of the Royal Festival Hall.

A bust of **Nelson Mandela** is down the walkway to the right of the hall. Many restaurants and cafes here, and more choice in the food market below.

The **statue of Chopin**, installed on the other side of the hall in 1975, is by his fellow Pole Kubica and was paid for by Poles in this country and Poland.

The **Queen Elizabeth Hall & Purcell Room** were built in 1967 to provide space for smaller ensembles and audiences, 900 in the QEH and 350 in the Purcell Room. Architecture was by GLC staff, though Lasdun usually gets the blame for this, as well as the National Theatre the other side of Waterloo Bridge. The building stands on the site of a shot tower, circular on plan and 50m/165ft high, demolished after the Festival. During the Festival, it carried a dished radio beacon antenna. Skateboarders and graffiti artists are very active below the building. The **Zemran** sculpture by William Pye (b.1938) is in front of the Queen Elizabeth Hall.

Behind the QEH, the **Hayward Gallery** of the same vintage and provenance hosts shows of modern art. An icon of brutalist architecture, they say. The neon tower was added in 1970. **BFI Southbank** (formerly the National Film Theatre) has its entrance under Waterloo Bridge. It incorporates the Museum of the Moving Image.

Waterloo Bridge

The first crossing here was a granite nine-arched bridge completed in 1810. When Old London Bridge was removed in 1830, the increased flow caused scour damage to the supporting piers, and to other bridges too. Makeshift repairs were made in the 1920s, but replacement was inevitable. The new bridge, an advanced concrete box-girder affair, was opened in 1942 and finished properly in 1945 once the war was over. The whole was clad in Portland stone, and jacks in the piers deal with any settlement. This was the only bridge to suffer other than superficial damage by bombing.

Constable's painting of the opening of the first bridge is in Tate Modern. **Monet** painted 41 images of the same Waterloo Bridge as seen from his room at

The Savoy. A **second-hand book fair** takes place under the south end of the bridge every day.

On 7 September 1978, **Georgi Markov**, a dissident Bulgarian who worked for the BBC, sustained a tiny injury in his leg on Waterloo Bridge. Four days later he died, and a post mortem found an airgun pellet less than 2mm in diameter that had probably been impregnated with ricin. Blame was aimed at the Bulgarian secret police, probably aided by the KGB.

The entrance to the Proud Cabaret under the north end of the bridge once led into a tram underpass to Southampton Row.

Getting there. Westminster tube station, cross the bridge for the south bank walk. Embankment tube station is adjacent to Hungerford Bridge. Waterloo Bridge is equidistant between Embankment and Temple tube stations.

Walking. Waterloo Bridge to Blackfriars Bridge is ½ mile (0.8km).

20. TRAFALGAR SQUARE DETOUR

Just before Hungerford Bridge on the left is Northumberland Avenue, which was opened up in 1875. This involved the demolition of Northumberland House which stood at the far end. The lion you may have seen at Syon House in Brentford stood over the portico of this house. Charles Dickens mentions the lion in his essay *Gone Astray* (1853). The main reason for this detour, of course, is Trafalgar Square and Nelson's Column, but from Northumberland Avenue bear right into Craven Street to find:

Benjamin Franklin House. 36 Craven Street, WC2N 5NF. Former home of Benjamin Franklin (1705-1790), who was one of the Founding Fathers of the United States. He lived in London from 1757-1775, representing the colony of Pennsylvania. Apart from this, he was a true polymath and a pioneer in physics and electricity.

At 25 Craven Street is a blue plaque to **Herman Melville** (1819-1891), the author of *Moby Dick*. At №32 is a bronze plaque to **Heinrich Heine** (1797-1856), the poet and essayist who lived here in 1827 whilst in exile from German censorship. He disliked the English, concurring with Napoleon's view of them as a nation of shopkeepers, and spent the rest of his life in Paris. Cut through Craven Passage to:

Sherlock Holmes, 10 Northumberland Avenue WC2N 5DB. Tel: 020 7930 2644. Greene King. Real ale and food. A shrine to the great detective; upstairs is a replica of the front room at 221b Baker Street. Also see: www.sherlock-holmes.org.uk/

From the top of Northumberland Avenue, cross onto the traffic island for a panoramic view. You share the island with a **statue of Charles I** (1625-1649), and this has quite a tale to tell. Made by Hubert Le Sueur, who also did the statue of

Diana in Bushy Park, it first stood at the country house of one of Charles' ministers. The statue was pulled down after the English Civil War and sold for scrap to a brass founder. This enterprising soul, John Rivet, made a good living selling artefacts supposedly made from the statue's metal. In fact, he had hidden the statue and sold it back after the Restoration of the monarchy in 1660. This was the first equestrian statue in London, and Charles looks down Whitehall towards his place of execution. Remember the nursery rhyme about seeing a fine lady on a white horse at Banbury Cross?

As I was going by Charing Cross,

I saw a black man upon a black horse;

They told me it was King Charles the First -

Oh dear, my heart was ready to burst!

This island was the site of the last of twelve Eleanor Crosses; each marked the overnight resting place of the body of Queen Eleanor of Castile (1241-1290), wife of Edward I. She was buried in Westminster Abbey, where her fine gilt bronze effigy may still be seen. The original cross was removed in 1647, but a more ornate replacement (1855) stands nearby in front of Charing Cross station. A **plaque** in the ground tells you that this is the point from which distances from London are measured.

Behind you to the left is **Admiralty Arch** (1912), leading to The Mall and Buckingham Palace. A short distance through Admiralty Arch, on either side of The Mall, are a statue of **Captain James Cook** and a memorial to the **Royal Marines**. At 21-24 Cockspur Street is a statue of **St Olaf** dating from when the building was the Norwegian Chamber of Commerce.

When John was a youngster everything here, including the National Gallery, was black with the soot of the power stations, industry, and home fires. It looks a lot nicer now.

Trafalgar Square

Trafalgar Square was laid out around 1840 following demolition of the stables and offices of the Royal Mews. It took its present form when it was pedestrianised in 2003. From its inception it has been dominated by Nelson's Column, the monument to Britain's greatest naval hero.

Napoleon Bonaparte, already a seasoned general for the French revolutionaries, seized power from the Directory in 1799 and became, in effect, dictator of France. The Napoleonic Wars that he then unleashed were to cost the lives of something between three and six million civilians as he fought, like a later dictator, to dominate Europe, including Great Britain. Napoleon had two British nemeses, at sea Horatio Nelson, later Admiral Lord Nelson, and on land Arthur Wellesley, later the Duke of Wellington. Nelson's tomb is in the crypt of St Paul's Cathedral, along with that of the Duke of Wellington and many other naval and military commanders.

Nelson won a series of great naval victories, often achieved by his loose interpretation of the orders of his superiors. His last battle was at Trafalgar in 1805, when he was killed by a bullet from a French sniper. His renown led to a rash of memorials. Glasgow had a 44m (144ft) tall obelisk as early as 1806, and there were others in places as diverse as Montreal and Great Yarmouth. Dublin had one, too, but the IRA blew it up in 1966.

London's monument was late on the scene. It was only started in 1838 when a public subscription was opened. Construction was protracted, partly due to lack of funds, and the lions were not installed until 1867. The competition for the design was won by William Railton (1800-1877), an architect better known for his churches and country houses. He had recently placed fourth in the contest to design the new Houses of Parliament.

The fluted column itself is of Devonshire granite. The Corinthian capital is bronze cast from guns salvaged from *HMS Royal George* which, incidentally, led to the discovery of the wreck of the *Mary Rose*. The statue of Nelson, 5.5m (18ft) tall, is of hard sandstone quarried near Edinburgh. It was sculpted by E.H. Baily and installed in 1843. The overall height is said to be the above-deck height of *HMS Victory's* mainmast – something to think of as you look up.

The reliefs on the base, 5.5m (18ft) square, were cast from cannons captured during Nelson's victories. That on the side facing Whitehall depicts his death at Trafalgar; note George Ryan, a Caribbean crew member, standing at the left edge of the plaque. Going clockwise from there are the battles of Cape St Vincent (1797), the Nile (1798), and Copenhagen (1801). The St Vincent relief saw the partners of the founding company locked up for adulterating the bronze material.

The lions were another epic. Railton rejected the granite originals sculpted by Thomas Milnes as being too small. Sir Edwin Landseer (1802-1873), the most prominent animal painter of his time, was commissioned to produce bronze lions instead. As he was inexperienced as a sculptor, the commission was shared with Baron Marochetti with whom he did not get on. Delay was piled on delay, and the whole thing became a London joke. The lions were eventually modelled on Barbary lions, a sub-species of the Asiatic lion, and once kept at the Tower of London. Landseer's lions, all identical (or near enough) and rather tame, are not a patch artistically on Milnes', which can still be seen at Saltaire in Yorkshire. The lions were set in place in 1867, nearly 25 years after the statue of Nelson. Ballantine's painting of Landseer at work on one of the lions is in the National Portrait Gallery (see below). Lutyens, architect of New Delhi and much more, was christened Edwin Landseer after his godfather.

From its beginning, Trafalgar Square has been a venue for all sorts of revels and protests that the police needed to keep an eye on. Accordingly, in the southeastern corner of the square is what is often said to be the smallest police station in London. Survey and restoration around 2006 showed that the monument was 51.5m (169ft) high rather than the usually quoted figure of 56.4m (185ft).

Hitler, in the event of a successful invasion of Britain, planned to move the whole monument to Berlin.

Other monuments in the Square

General Sir Charles Napier (1782-1853) was a soldier who served in the Peninsular War against Napoleon's forces and in the 1812 campaign in America. He went to India in 1841 and conquered Sindh the following year. It is said (probably apocryphally) that he sent a one-word despatch *Peccavi* – I have sinned, in Latin. Surprisingly perhaps, he proved an enlightened administrator.

Sir Henry Havelock (1795-1857) was a soldier of analytical bent who campaigned successfully in India, Afghanistan, and Persia (as Iran was then called). As a result of one of those imperial cock-ups known, according to persuasion, as the 1857 Indian Mutiny or First War of Independence, the British residency in the city of Lucknow was besieged. Havelock led the first relieving force but died there of dysentery. His name is remembered by pubs and streets around the country and sympathetic appearances in a couple of George Macdonald Fraser's *Flashman* novels.

King George IV (1820-1830), one of our less successful monarchs, commissioned this statue of himself to go on top of Marble Arch, which, at that time, stood in front of Buckingham Palace. After his death, it was put up here for no better reason than to fill the space on the plinth.

The **fourth plinth** was intended for a statue of George's successor, William IV (1830-1837), but he failed to supply either a statue or the funds. Since 2001, it has had several occupants, apparently chosen on a woker than thou basis. Busts on the north wall of the square follow a naval theme:

Admiral Viscount Cunningham, commander in the Mediterranean in the Second World War; **Admiral Earl Jellicoe,** Commander of the British Grand Fleet at the Battle of Jutland in 1916; and **Admiral Earl Beatty**, commander of the Battlecruiser Squadron at Jutland. Beatty famously remarked, "There seems to be something wrong with our bloody ships today", as two of his battlecruisers exploded catastrophically due to inadequate protection of their magazines. *HMS Indefatigable* had only two survivors from a crew of 1019, and *HMS Queen Mary* nine survivors out of 1275. Below the bust of Beatty are Imperial standards for the foot and the yard. The present fountains were completed in 1948 as memorials to Jellicoe and Beatty; the originals are in Canada. Note the plaque in the terrace between the fountains.

North of the square

The square is bounded to the north by the National Gallery, flanked by two fine statues. That of **James II** is by Grinling Gibbons (1648-1721), better known as a wood carver. James was a lot less aware of public opinion than his brother Charles II, whom he succeeded, and lost his throne after only three years (1685-1688) due to his absolutism and overt Catholicism. The companion statue of Charles II, also in Roman garb, stands outside the Royal Hospital in Chelsea.

George Washington (1732-1799) was a Founding Father of the United States of America and the first president between 1789 and 1797. This statue is a 20th century bronze cast of the marble original in Richmond, Virginia made from life by Houdon. It was a gift of the Commonwealth of Virginia and installed here in 1921. One guesses that the statue of James II, which had stood in various places beforehand, was placed here at the same time.

The present **National Gallery** was opened in 1838 to show the United Kingdom's collection of old masters from the 13th century and now up to 1900 or so. The collection may be smaller than other great galleries, but it is representative; "from Giotto to Cézanne", they say.

The modern left wing stands on the site of a department store destroyed in the Blitz. The Sainsbury supermarket family put up the cash, but the first design was described by the then Prince of Wales (now King Charles III) as a "monstrous carbuncle on the face of a much-loved and elegant friend"; a comment that attracted opprobrium from architects and anti-royalists and a sigh of relief from just about everyone else. This comment led to the annual Carbuncle Cup, a spoof award run from 2006 to 2018 for the worst building constructed in the United Kingdom. Other London winners and nominations are mentioned elsewhere.

The main entrance and vestibules are decorated with mosaics by the Russian-born Boris Anrep (1885-1969). Anrep used real people and events as models, note Greta Garbo, Bertrand Russell, sporting events, and a Christmas pudding. Churchill, representing the virtue of defiance, is seen defying a swastika-shaped beast. The gallery is easily worth a rainy day. Many people, given the scope of this book, will be happy to see just Turner's *Fighting Temeraire*.

The **National Portrait Gallery**, behind the National Gallery, has reopened recently after essential works. Apparently, this included 'Establishing a learning centre', 'Connecting with young people', and 'Working with communities'. And, who knows? We are even allowed to look at portraits again, or at least those that have escaped cancel culture.

The statue of **Minerva** on the east side of the square was started as Britannia by one sculptor to be placed on top of Marble Arch. He died, and the job was finished by another who had to convert Britannia's trident into a spear. Finally, look across to South Africa House, at the south-eastern corner of the square, for a statue of **Bartolomeu Dias**, the 15th century Portuguese explorer who was the first European to round the Cape of Good Hope.

Getting there. Turn right out of Embankment tube station and under Hungerford Bridge to Northumberland Avenue for the start of the detour. From 1906 to 1979 Trafalgar Square had its own tube station on the Bakerloo line. The opening of the Jubilee line in 1979 saw the Trafalgar Square platforms integrated into Charing Cross station. There is still an entrance/exit on the square.

21. WATERLOO BRIDGE TO BLACKFRIARS BRIDGE

North bank

Just downstream of the bridge is the **Tower Lifeboat Station**, once a River Police station. The best view is from the bridge. Apparently, they rescue more people cut off by the tide than have fallen into the water. Take heed if thinking of mudlarking!

Somerset House, the first purpose-built government offices (1780s and later extended), was built on the site of a royal palace. Today, it houses the Courtauld Institute Galleries, a fine collection of modern art and, in winter, an open-air ice-skating rink.

A statue of **Isambard Kingdom Brunel** stands, half-hidden by trees, on the end of an island between Victoria Embankment and Temple Place. Walking up Temple Place by the statue, you find a cabbies' shelter, a place for a good, inexpensive meal and a non-alcoholic drink (if you are a cabbie). This shelter, here since 1880, is one of only thirteen left in London. Once, there were 61. On the terrace over the tube station entrance is a colourful artists' garden. The small garden below contains statues of Forster the educationist, Lady Somerset a temperance advocate, and J.S. Mill the economist.

Bar & Co. Temple Pier, Victoria Embankment WC2R 2PN.Tel: 020 7836 7594. info@barandcompany.com is a Thames spritsail barge (built in 1926 in Greenwich), now a party venue, and dog friendly. **The Yacht** (actually named St Katherine), also moored here, was a restaurant and wedding venue which seems to have been finished by the Covid epidemic. A shame as this is a historic vessel built in 1927 by Philip & Co. of Dartmouth for the Port of London Authority.

W.T. Stead (1849-1912) was a campaigning journalist who turned the stuffy *Pall Mall Gazette* into a proto-tabloid. Between 1883 and 1885, the House of Commons failed three times to pass the Criminal Law Amendment Bill to raise the age of consent from thirteen to sixteen. The purpose of the bill, already passed by the House of Lords, was to reduce child abuse and child prostitution. There was also a belief that British girls were being shipped as 'white slaves' to the Continent for prostitution. Stead ran a series of lurid articles on the subject detailing how he had bought a twelve-year-old girl, Eliza Armstrong, from her mother for £5 (about £600 today). The girl was handed to the care of the Salvation Army, and the incident became known as the Armstrong Scandal.

The Commons was forced to pass the bill into law, but the Establishment soon had its revenge. Stead and others involved were arraigned on charges of abduction. Stead spent a comfortable three months in Holloway Prison; some of the others were less lucky. Stead's later career included publishing affordable condensed classics and children's books. As you may have guessed from the date of Stead's death, he was a passenger on the *Titanic's* maiden and only voyage. He was last seen giving his life jacket to another person. The Criminal Law Amendment Act, incidentally, was the means Labouchère used to criminalise *any* sexual contact between men (see Twickenham).

HQS Wellington (Sloop 1934) was built by Devonport Dockyard in Plymouth, Devon as an escort vessel for the Royal Navy. After four years on the New Zealand station, the Second World War saw her escorting North Atlantic convoys both in the Western Approaches and around West Africa when based at Freetown in Sierra Leone. She escorted 103 convoys and steamed nearly 250,000 miles. She was acquired by the Honourable Company of Master Mariners in 1947 to act as their livery hall. The engines and boilers were removed during her conversion to a floating clubhouse. Now open to the public, booking at: https://hqs-wellington.arttickets.org.uk/ The flying of a white-bordered union flag on the jackstaff is a red rag to nautical pedants.

Two other historic warships were for many years moored along this stretch of the river, both used as Royal Naval Reserve drill ships. They became redundant with the building of the HMS President facility (traditionally referred to as a stone frigate) at St Katharine's Dock.

HMS Chrysanthemum (Sloop 1917). Built by Armstrong Whitworth in Newcastle. One of a large class of Flower (or Herbaceous Border) class sloops built during the First World War as convoy escorts. She was used in the film *Indiana Jones and the Last Crusade*, but scrapped in 1995. This class of ship was the first built specifically for anti-submarine warfare.

HMS President *(ex-HMS Saxifrage)* (Sloop 1918) Built by Lobnitz & Company in Renfrew, Scotland. Of the same basic class as Chrysanthemum, she was finished as an *Anchusa* class Q ship; these were submarine decoy ships, and *Saxifrage* engaged nine U-boats during her short military career. She is currently in Chatham on the River Medway, hopefully for restoration. The prolific Flower class corvettes of the Second World War re-used both these names.

The **RRS Discovery** was built to take Scott and Shackleton to Antarctica in 1901. After a hard life, she was moored here for around forty years before being returned to Dundee, her port of building, in 1986. This is not, incidentally, the ship that took Scott to Antarctica for his doomed expedition (1910-12) to the South Pole; that was the *Terra Nova*.

Temple Stairs Arch was built in 1868 as part of Bazalgette's design for the Embankment. The face in the keystone is of Neptune, not Father Thames as you might expect. Within the arch is a memorial of King George V's Silver Jubilee in 1935.

The **dragons** bearing shields tell you that you are leaving the City of Westminster and entering the City of London, the Square Mile. These cast iron dragons, dating from the 1840s, once decorated the Coal Exchange on Lower Thames Street and were moved here when that was demolished in 1960. They are the models for the smaller boundary markers elsewhere.

The **National Submariners War Memorial**. The Royal Navy, despite an admiral who called them "underhand, unfair and damned un-English", commissioned its first submarine in 1901. The submarine service was effective in both World Wars; most notably, it kept the German High Seas Fleet bottled up in the First World War, and cut off supplies to the Axis armies in North Africa during the Second. The Navy lost 54 boats during the First World War, 82 in the Second, and several more in peacetime accidents. This memorial, erected first in 1922, commemorates those personnel who lost their lives serving in submarines. The central part of the plaque depicts a submarine crew at work; it is flanked to the left by nereids or sea nymphs. It is harder to account for the male figures to the right as the 50 nereids had only one brother.

The **Inner Temple Gardens** over the road used to run down to the river. The gardens mark the western limit of the Great Fire of London in 1666. You can reflect as you walk along that four-fifths of the buildings between here and the Tower of London were destroyed by the fire.

The view across the river is dominated by the Oxo Building. Just before Blackfriars Bridge, the riverside path becomes known as **Paul's Walk** and runs as far as Broken Wharf House. Before the Great Fire and the advent of newspapers, Paul's Walk was a kind of paseo up and down the nave of Old St Paul's Cathedral, said by some to be the longest in Europe. The object was to exchange news and gossip and to conduct business. Crown and Church inveighed against the practice, to little effect. The riverside path from here to the bridge is blocked by Tideway Tunnel works, so cross the road.

At the bottom of John Carpenter Street is one of London's odder statues. *Taxi!* by Seward Johnson Jr (1930-2020) is said to have fooled more than one black cab driver. Its position near the Unilever Building is enigmatic; Johnson was a scion of the rival Johnson and Johnson company.

The facade of the **J.P. Morgan Building** (1991) is the restored City of London School built in 1880, though the school itself was founded in 1442. Statues of four British worthies on the face of the building look towards Blackfriars Bridge. From left to right they are: **Francis Bacon** (1561-1626), philosopher, statesman, and oddball, said by some to have written Shakespeare's plays. **William Shakespeare** (1564-1616) who probably did write Shakespeare's plays. **John Milton** (1608-1674) is best known as the poet of *Paradise Lost* and *Paradise Regained* but was a major political thinker and freedom of speech activist of his time. **Sir Isaac Newton** (1642-1727) was the mathematician and physicist who promulgated the laws of motion and gravity. He is often regarded as one of the greatest scientific thinkers of all time.

On the west wall, all on his own, is **Sir Thomas More** (1478-1535), lawyer, philosopher, and statesman, at one time Lord Chancellor to Henry VIII. He fell out with the King over the Reformation and paid for it with his life, being executed on Tower Hill. The Catholic Church regards him as a martyr and a saint.

The **Unilever Building** next door also has some interesting statuary typical of its period (1933). It stands on the site of the **Bridewell Palace**, a rambling brick structure put up in 1515-20 for Henry VIII. Charles V, the Holy Roman Emperor, was entertained here in great style. Later leased to the French ambassador, Holbein set his painting *The Ambassadors* here; the painting is in The National

Gallery (Room 12). In the reign of Edward VI (1547-1553), the palace was given to the City of London and degenerated into a workhouse and **prison**. Public floggings were a popular entertainment; a ducking stool was installed on the river bank in 1628, followed by stocks ten years later. The buildings were destroyed in the Great Fire of 1666 but replaced. By 1788, prisoners were provided not only with beds but with straw for them, a luxury unknown in other prisons at the time. The Bridewell was eventually closed in 1855.

Blackfriars takes its name from the Dominican Blackfriars Monastery. Founded in 1221, it was dissolved in 1538, and its buildings granted to Sir Thomas Cawarden, Keeper of the Royal Tents and Master of the Revels.

The Thames has several tributaries in the London area, mostly now running underground. The **Fleet River** runs from Kenwood and Hampstead Ponds down to the Thames. It takes its name from the Anglo-Saxon word for a tidal inlet, but originally this was only the lowest part of the river. Further upstream it was the Hole Bourn, from which Holborn is derived, and Turnmill Brook from the many water mills along its banks. In the 12th century, stones for the old St Paul's Cathedral were brought upstream, but not long after this it had become, and remained, an appalling open sewer. By the time of the Great Fire in 1666, it was impassable to boats, mainly because of the many 'houses of office' or latrines built over it. When London was rebuilt after the fire, the lower 640m (700yds) of the river were remodelled as a dock with wide wharves on either side. It was little used, however, and soon reverted to a noxious sewer. The Fleet's course in the Holborn area was covered over in 1733 and the lower part in 1766. The **medieval wall** of London, though not the Roman one, followed the Fleet down to the river. There is no trace here, the best extant fragment being by Tower Hill tube station.

South bank

Royal National Theatre. The idea of a national theatre was first proposed in 1848 and began to be taken seriously a century later. Princess Elizabeth (the future queen) laid a foundation stone in 1951, and it took another twenty-five years to build. The architect was Denys Lasdun (1914-2001), arch exponent of concrete brutalism. The building contains three theatres with capacities from 400 up to 1150. Whatever you think about it, Betjeman liked it.

To the right is Connor's statue of **Sir Laurence Olivier** as Hamlet. Apart from his acting career, Olivier was the first artistic director of the National Theatre Company. Directly in front of the theatre is the sculpture *London Pride.*

The **IBM Building**, completed in 1985, was also designed by Lasdun as a complement to the National. It is now owned by Middle Eastern interests; recent plans to alter and modernise the building were scuppered by its being granted listed status. The double-sided **seat** carved from the trunk of one tree has a touching inscription.

The former **London Television Centre** is a 70s building with the architectural distinction of at least making the IBM Building and the National Theatre look

100

interesting. Scheduled for demolition, it was bought by Mitsubishi and refurbished as office space. There is a good riverside viewpoint here of St Paul's Cathedral and The City.

Old Bargehouse Stairs take their name from the sheds where the royal barges were built and stored. The Royal Barge Master had a house here in the 16th century, and there was also a tavern called the King's Barge House.

Ernie's Beach is named after John Hearn, hence Ernie, who campaigned to preserve the old river wall and thus the beach. A plaque tells the story.

Gabriel's Wharf takes its name from Christopher Gabriel, an 18th century maker of woodworking tools. His family extended the business into a timber yard based here. The singer and songwriter Peter Gabriel, once of Genesis, is a distant descendant. Craft shops and restaurants now occupy the area.

Bernie Spain Garden. Like Ernie, Bernadette Spain was a local resident who campaigned against developers to provide affordable housing and open space. The landscaped gardens are owned and run by Coin Street Community Builders.

We now come to one of the most interesting buildings on the south bank, though you can only see it properly from the other bank. **The OXO Tower** has a history as odd as its design, a history that will probably upset both vegetarians and animal lovers. Ranchers in Argentina would slaughter cattle for the hides and throw away the carcasses. Refrigerated ships made it possible for the Liebig Meat Extract Company to import the carcasses and process them to produce meat extract, a forerunner of the modern stock cube. As a one-time chef, incidentally, I would advise anyone using these things (whatever the brand) to look carefully at the ingredients beforehand.

Liebig bought an old power station with a red brick and Portland stone facade and added a tower. The company wanted to spell out the OXO brand name in lights, an idea rejected by the planners. The architect got around this by clever design of the windows to achieve the same effect. You can see the remains of the cranes for hauling in the carcasses.

Disused by the 70s, the building passed to Coin Street Community Builders. It is now a lively community space with many eateries, art galleries, and five floors of social housing. A free viewing platform is on the seventh floor, though the tower itself is closed. The top floor is occupied by a restaurant, brasserie, and cocktail bar operated by Harvey Nicholls, the Knightsbridge department store.

The uninspired modernist **Sea Containers House** was designed as a hotel but completed in 1978 as offices, taking its name from the original tenant. Part has now become a hotel; cocktails in the rooftop bar cost £12.50, not bad for the location. By comparison, the **River Court** apartment block next door seems a throwback to concrete brutalism.

Doggett's Coat and Badge, 1 Blackfriars Bridge, SE1 9UD. Tel: 020 7633 9081. Nicholson's. Real ale and food. Interesting menu, prices typical for the area, and Sunday roasts. Multi-storey operation with fine views. Very popular, booking advisable. The name is that of the prize for a race instituted in 1715 for young watermen and the oldest annual event in the British sporting calendar.

Blackfriars Bridge

The first bridge was built in 1760-69 of Portland stone, its British architects heavily influenced by the work of Piranesi. Officially titled the William Pitt Bridge, the public never called it other than Blackfriars Bridge. The present structure of one hundred years later is of wrought iron faced with cast iron; the piers are granite. Plans to adorn the bridge with four equestrian statues of English kings came to nothing. Note the birds carved on the piers, freshwater birds on the upstream side, and marine birds downstream. The bridge was widened on the west side in 1907-10.

Roberto Calvi (1920-1982) was dubbed 'God's banker' for his ties to the Vatican Bank. Unfortunately for him, his ties also extended to the Mafia and a dodgy Masonic lodge. When Banco Ambrosiano, of which he was chairman, collapsed with huge debts, he fled to London. Shortly afterwards, he was found hanging under the bridge, his pockets full of bricks. It was 2002 before it was finally determined that he had been murdered rather than committing suicide. A murder trial in Italy in 2005 predictably resulted in no convictions. *The Vatican at War* by Philip Willan makes interesting reading on the subject.

Getting there. Embankment tube station is the best starting point.

Walking. Blackfriars Bridge to Southwark Bridge is ½ mile (1km).

22. BLACKFRIARS BRIDGE TO SOUTHWARK BRIDGE

North bank

The Blackfriar, 174 Queen Victoria Street EC4V 4EG. Tel: 020 7236 5474. Nicholson's. Real ale and food. Fairly recent construction (1875) on the site of Blackfriars Monastery, and the only Art Nouveau pub in London. The pub is built on a wedge-shaped site and richly decorated inside and out. Seating outside. Located just over the road from Blackfriars tube station, the pub is tiny inside, so phone ahead if you plan to eat.

Returning to the bridge from the pub you pass a **Temperance drinking fountain** that has run dry. This was originally set up in the City in 1861 by the Metropolitan Free Drinking Fountain and Cattle Trough Association, and moved here later. Sockets in the base once held three bronze dolphins.

Blackfriars Railway Bridge was built in 1884-86 to carry trains from St Paul's station; the name was changed to Blackfriars in 1937. The platforms are actually on the bridge and extend the full width of the river. The materials are wrought iron faced with cast iron. The piers of an earlier bridge are just upstream.

One might assume that **Puddle Dock** was a derisory name for something small and shallow; in fact, according to one 17th century record, it may have been named after a man called Puddle. It was, by all accounts, a filthy place where barges were loaded with dung and abattoir waste. The dock, filled in during redevelopment in the 1970s, was just east of the rail bridge. Its name is perpetuated by a street called Puddle Dock. This is pretty much where the south-western part of the old city wall met the riverside.

The **Mermaid Theatre** at Puddle Dock was the creation of a much-loved English character actor called Bernard Miles. Opened in 1959, it was converted from the shell of a bombed-out warehouse. This made it the first new theatre in the City of London (as opposed to the City of Westminster) for 300 years. Unfortunately, property development shenanigans (shark-infested waters in 1970s London) engulfed the project, and the theatre has latterly been used mainly as a conference centre. Its architecture, and most of that around it, is all too typical of the period. Its future is uncertain.

The **City of London School** traces its origins to 1442. It is a public (i.e. private and fee-paying) school for 900 boys; it employs around 100 academic staff and is reckoned to be in the top ten high-achieving schools in all Britain. Previously on a site the other side of Blackfriars Bridge (see above) it moved here in 1986. The rather pleasing red brick buildings incorporate some stained glass and sculpture from the old building. Daniel Radcliffe is a former pupil, as was Kingsley Amis.

There is a good view across the river to the former Bankside power station (now the Tate Modern art gallery) and the thatched Globe Theatre.

St Benet Paul's Wharf Church, Upper Thames Street, is reckoned to be one of Christopher Wren's prettiest. Built in 1683, its predecessor (which dated from 1111) was destroyed in the Great Fire of 1666. It is one of only four City of London churches to escape bomb damage in the Second World War. St Benet's is the Metropolitan Welsh Church in London and also associated with the nearby College of Arms. Sunday service at 1100 is held in Welsh. Otherwise, the church is open only on Thursdays 1100-1500. To get to the church, leave the riverside path by the end of Blackfriars Pier and follow White Lion Hill.

The **Millennium Bridge** links Bankside and the Tate Modern on the south bank to St Paul's Cathedral and offers marvellous views. The bridge opened on 10 June 2000 (late and over budget) and closed again two days later. In that short time, it had been rechristened the 'Wobbly Bridge'. The attractive underslung suspension design allowed too much lateral sway. To be fair to the designers, this was a newly discovered phenomenon where pedestrians instinctively adjust their pace to the movement of the bridge, thereby making it worse. The solution, which took two years, was to install eighty-odd dampers of five different designs; the most visible are the round section ones attached to the piers fastening the deck to the cables. The bridge appears in *Harry Potter and the Half-Blood Prince* and in *Guardians of the Galaxy*. Between 1851 and 1941 many plans were floated for a grandiose **St Paul's Bridge** close to where the Millennium Bridge now stands. They all foundered on the rocks of war or lack of funding.

Broken Wharf takes its name from the time in the 13th century when it collapsed into the river. Two clerics (the church owned much of London before the Reformation) argued for forty years over who should pay for the repairs.

Here you have to leave the river; walk up to High Timber Street and turn right. Glance back to see the tower of **St Mary Somerset** (the nave was demolished in 1871 when the church became redundant), and continue past the end of Stew Lane which leads to:

The Samuel Pepys, Stew Lane EC4V 3PT. Tel: 020 7489 1871. Shepherd Neame. Real ale and food. This is a modern pub with a balcony overlooking the river. The church's property holdings included many brothels, "stew" being an old word for a knocking shop. Stew Lane is not worth walking down unless you want to visit the pub.

Continue to **Queenhithe** (street) and turn right. *Hithe* is Old English for a landing place or small harbour, usually on a river, though there is Hythe in Kent on the sea. The 'Queen' part of the name comes from the right of the queen to collect customs dues on goods landed here. A wharf here was in use at least from the time of King Alfred, this was once one of the busiest docks in London. Queenhithe preceded Billingsgate as a wharf for fishing vessels. As ships grew larger in the 15th century the docks began their progressive move downstream.

Along the side of the dock is the **Queenhithe mosaic** telling the story of the area from 50BC to the present day. Just after the mosaic, the **Alfred plaque** records the resettlement of London in AD886 after Viking invasions.

The riverside path from here to Southwark Bridge is **Three Barrels Walk**. That Vintner's Hall is behind here is perhaps a clue to the name. Since 1947, 'Three Barrels' has been a popular brand of brandy, though not a cognac. The producer was founded in 1814 and, more recently, has been owned by the Grant's whisky firm.

South bank

Southwark's rather dubious reputation as a place of entertainment and naughtiness goes back to Roman times, a gladiator's trident having been found there. Here were the inns that fed the pilgrim routes to Canterbury and beyond, the theatres of Shakespeare, Marlowe, and Jonson, the strong alehouses, and the notorious stews or brothels.

Between the road and rail bridges is the **Rennie Garden**, named after the engineer who had built a corn mill on this site. The hoardings for the Bankside Yards development currently hide this; the stated aim is to replace outdated buildings and provide more open space.

Blackfriars Railway Bridge was built in 1884-86 to carry trains from St Paul's station across the river. The materials are wrought iron faced with cast iron.

The name was changed from St Paul's to Blackfriars in 1937. The piers of the earlier bridge, built in 1862-64, can be seen just upstream. Note the badge of the London, Chatham and Dover Railway.

Bankside is the name of the path and ancient street along the river and has become the name of this area.

Founders Arms, 52 Hopton Street, SE1 9JH. Tel: 020 7928 1899. Youngs. Real ale and food. Modern pub overlooking the river. Outdoor seating.

Bankside Gallery, 48 Hopton Street, SE1 9JH. Tel: 020 7928 7521. Modern gallery home to the Royal Watercolour Society and the Royal Society of Painter-Printmakers. Changing exhibitions. Good for affordable art, well worth a look. Online sales at: https://www.banksidegallery.com/

Tate Modern, Bankside, SE1 9TG. Tel: 020 7887 8888. Britain's premier gallery for modern and contemporary art. The building started life as a power station built between 1947 and 1963.

In 1891 **Bankside Power Station** was sited on what was once the Great Pike Gardens, which had supplied fish to the local religious institutions. Having eaten pike on several occasions – sooner them than me. The station started producing DC current for the arc street lights in Queen Victoria Street over the river. Two years later, the completed Bankside A also produced AC power for homes and offices. Blackfriars and Southwark Bridges carried the cables. By 1946, the thermal efficiency of Bankside A was down to 16% and, worse, it was dumping 235 tonnes of grit and soot per square mile on the surrounding area *every month*.

Bankside B, which replaced the A station in two phases, was designed to burn oil from the start. The oil, it burned 67 tons per hour, was delivered by barge from the Shell Haven refinery on the Thames estuary in Essex. Exterior design was by Sir Giles Gilbert Scott, who had done Battersea Power Station; the chimney, at 99m (325ft) was deliberately kept lower than St Paul's Cathedral over the river. As at Battersea, scrubbers were installed, but this traded air pollution for river pollution. Generation ceased in 1981, mainly due to the increase in oil prices. Unfortunately, all the machinery was removed before the Tate Gallery took over the building. Conversion to the art gallery cost £134 million and took 4½ years. The multi-angular Switch House was added in 2016 by Herzog and de Meuron, the Swiss architects who did the initial conversion.

Tate Modern is one of the world's leading modern art galleries. Their remit is from around 1900 to the present day and includes all modern art forms. You can even visit the vast tanks that held the oil for the power station. Entry is free, though there is a charge for special exhibitions. Full details: https://www.tate.org.uk/visit/tate-modern. Thames Clipper water buses run between Tate Britain at Millbank and here.

Keep your eyes open; peregrine falcons frequent the roof and do their best to keep pigeon numbers under control. More than twenty pairs of these wonderful birds nest in Central London.

The **Millennium Bridge** links Bankside and the Tate Modern on the south bank to St Paul's Cathedral and offers marvellous views. The bridge opened on 10 June 2000 (late and over budget) and closed again two days later. In that short time, users had rechristened it the 'Wobbly Bridge'. The attractive underslung suspension design allowed far too much lateral sway. To be fair to the designers, this was a newly discovered phenomenon where pedestrians instinctively adjust their pace to the bridge's movement, thereby increasing the movement. The solution, which took two years, was to install eighty-odd dampers of five different designs; the most visible are the round section ones fitted to the piers attaching the deck to the cables. The bridge appears in *Harry Potter and the Half-Blood Prince* and in *Guardians of the Galaxy*.

Between 1851 and 1941, many plans were floated for a grandiose **St Paul's Bridge** close to where the Millennium Bridge now stands. They all foundered on the rocks of war or lack of funding.

Past the Millennium Bridge on the right are two old houses. First is **The Deanery**, home of the Dean of Southwark Cathedral. Cardinal Cap Alley, which separates this from Cardinal House, leads to a secret garden; opening details: https://londongardenstrust.org. A plaque on **Cardinal House** relates how Sir Christopher Wren lived here and watched the cathedral slowly being built. Not to be taken as historical fact, it seems.

Samuel Wanamaker (1919-1993) was an American actor and director of Ukrainian Jewish extraction. During the McCarthyite witch hunts against alleged communist sympathisers he established himself in Britain. Here, he was surprised to find no replica of a Shakespearian theatre, whilst there were several in the USA and even one in Buenos Aires. Starting in 1970, Wanamaker experienced resistance from just about everybody who might have been expected to enthuse over such a project. The use of authentic (and combustible) materials such as timber and thatch did not help; **Shakespeare's Globe** is the only thatched building to have been allowed in London since the Great Fire of 1666. Wanamaker persevered, and Shakespeare's Globe opened in 1997, sadly after his death.

The **Sam Wanamaker Playhouse** opened in 2014 and is an enclosed theatre, effectively a generation on from the Globe. The design is based on plans for a Jacobean theatre drawn in 1660, the oldest known. The theatre is richly decorated especially the ceiling.

Note the fine wrought iron gates and the explanatory plaque to the left. Short of attending performances, the only way to see the two theatres is a guided tour: https://www.shakespearesglobe.com/seasons/guided-tours/

Past Pizza Express, you can walk down **Bear Gardens**, an indication that bear (and bull) baiting was a popular entertainment. Cromwell tried to ban it, and Pepys thought it 'a very rude and nasty pleasure'. It was not finally banned until 1835. Also here (at SE1 9HA) is the **Ferryman's Seat**, the last of many. This was a kind of misericord (fancy word for arse-prop) for ferrymen waiting for fares to be taken across the river. Turn left at the far end of Bear Gardens into Park Street.

The **Rose Theatre** was built in 1587, the first on Bankside. It operated until 1605, when the lease ran out. The site has been excavated since 1989. At the time of writing, it was not possible to visit, but there is an excellent digital recreation here: https://losttheatres.net/rose

The original **Globe Theatre** stood on the other side of Southwark Bridge Road. William Shakespeare (1564-1616) was an actor and entrepreneur as well as a playwright. His troupe, The Lord Chancellor's Men, built The Globe in 1599 and again in 1614 after a fire. It lasted until 1642 when all theatres were closed by the Puritan-dominated Long Parliament. Part of the foundations was discovered in 1989, though most are under later listed buildings, so can not be excavated. A fine relief bronze plaque depicting Shakespeare, The Globe, and Old London Bridge stands in a fragment of wall.

Southwark Bridge

The first bridge, of cast iron, was built by a private company in 1819. It bankrupted the iron founders who made it, and in 1864 it bankrupted the owners, probably because they charged a toll, whereas the bridges to either side were free. Ownership passed to Bridge House Estates (see Tower Bridge), who built the present bridge in 1912-21. A plaque in the centre of the bridge (upstream side) tells the tale. Except when other bridges are closed, Southwark Bridge carries less traffic than any other London Bridge.

Getting there. Blackfriars tube and overground stations are adjacent to the north end of the bridge. Blackfriars Pier is just downstream of the bridge on the north bank. Bankside Pier for Thames Clippers is outside Shakespeare's Globe, otherwise it is easiest to walk to London Bridge tube and mainline stations.

Walking. Blackfriars Bridge to Southwark Bridge is ½ mile (1km).

23. SOUTHWARK BRIDGE TO LONDON BRIDGE

North bank

The first part of the path is **Three Cranes Walk**, named after three wooden cranes that stood here in the 17th century.

The **Little Ship Club**, Three Cranes Walk, Upper Thames Street, EC4R 3TB. Tel: 020 7236 7729. A weekday watering hole right on the river. Membership reasonable.

Walbrook Wharf leads you under a large travelling crane for loading rubbish containers onto barges for transfer downstream. This was the site of **Coldharbour**, a building used by the Watermen's Company as their livery hall. Later, the site was occupied by the City of London Brewery, sadly destroyed by German bombing in 1941.

The Banker, Cousin Lane EC4R 3TE. Fuller's. Built into the abutment of Cannon Street railway bridge. Outdoor terrace, great views. Closed Saturday and Sunday. Glance up Cousin Lane to see a couple of cannons.

Cannon Street Station is built on the site of the Hanseatic Merchants' warehouses and yard, which operated from the 10th century up to 1598, when their monopoly was broken. The property, known as The Steelyard from the huge scales for weighing imported goods, actually remained in German hands up to 1852 when sold to the South-Eastern Railway. As at Blackfriars the platforms extend over the river. The path under the bridge is called Steelyard Passage.

London Stone, 111 Cannon Street EC4N 5AR in front of the station. Said to have been hereabouts since at least AD1198 and thought by some to be the Roman milestone from which all distances in Britannia were measured. The Roman governor's residence was under where the station now stands. This is quite a detour, and the stone is hardly imposing.

Emerging onto **Hanseatic Walk** you have a panorama of mostly old buildings across the river. Winchester Wharf, Pickford's Wharf, a yellow modern lump (that looks better close up), and, hard up against London Bridge, Glaziers' Hall. Rising above are the tower and pinnacles of Southwark Cathedral. Hanseatic Walk leads into Oystergate Walk, where you can, in fact, buy oysters at the **Oyster Shed**. *Regalia* was a floating pub moored at Swan Pier. Closed in 2011 or so, it is now rusting away downstream at West Silvertown.

After Swan Lane the path runs along Fishmongers' Hall Wharf. **Fishmongers' Hall** itself was built in 1671 to replace its predecessor burned down in the Great Fire. The Fishmongers' Company is one of many City Liveries, guilds to protect the interests of a particular trade. These days it functions as a charity aiding the industry and fishermen. The hall houses a large art collection and other interesting items. Guided tours are available: https://fishmongers.org.uk/contact/

South bank

You emerge from Southwark Bridge with a good view of the two towers of Cannon Street station. Follow Bankside along the river to:

Anchor Inn, 34 Park Street, SE1 9EF. Greene King. There has been a pub on this site for over 800 Years. This one dates from 1676, and Shakespeare probably knew its predecessor. Minstrels' gallery and viewing platform. This may have been the point from which Pepys watched the fire of 1666 consume Old St Paul's Cathedral. David Garrick the actor, Oliver Goldsmith the poet; and Dr Johnson, the essayist and lexicographer, were all regulars.

Pass under **Cannon Street railway bridge** (sometimes called Clink Street Bridge), and you are now in Clink Street.

Clink Prison Museum, 1 Clink Street, SE1 9DG. Tel: 020 7403 0900. This part of Southwark was owned by the Bishops of Winchester and known as the 'Liberty of the Clink'. The bishops derived considerable rental income from their property, not least from the many brothels, which is why the sex workers were called Winchester geese. The brothels were regulated, and miscreants could find themselves in the bishops' private prison, The Clink. Hence the expression 'in clink' for in prison. First mention of the prison is in 1509, but it was probably older, perhaps 12th century. It was burned down in the Gordon Riots of 1780 and not rebuilt. A separate entrance for debtors on Stoney Street gave rise to the expression 'stony broke'. The museum stands on the original site.

A feel of the stews, as the brothels were called, may be derived from Thomas Nashe's bawdy poem *The Choise of Valentines*; penned in 1592, it introduced the word dildo to the language. Nashe (1567-ca1601) was quite a lad; he is thought to have worked with Shakespeare on *Henry VI Part 1*, and got his co-author Ben Jonson jailed when the authorities took a dim view of their play *The Isle of Dogs* (since lost). He even spent some time in Newgate Prison himself for, as usual, offending authority.

Winchester Palace. In addition to their business interests, the bishops often held high office in the royal court. This required a comfortable place to stay and to entertain. Construction started in the 1130s, and the palace was enlarged over time. It fell out of use around 1700 and was mostly destroyed by fire in 1816. All you can see today is part of the Great Hall, dating from 1136, though the rose window is a 14th century addition. The three doors led to the buttery, the pantry, and the kitchen; they were level with a floor over a vaulted cellar.

Old Thameside Inn, Pickfords Wharf, SE1 9DG. Tel: 020 7403 4243. Nicholson's. Real ale and food. An old spice warehouse. Outside seating by the river.

St Mary Overie Dock takes its name from Southwark Cathedral, which is dedicated to St Saviour and St Mary Overie; Overie or Overy meaning over the river from the main part of London. More fanciful accounts of the name exist. Who built the dock and when is unknown, but it is old enough to be in the Domesday Book of 1086.

In the dock is a replica of Sir Francis Drake's privateer, the *Golden Hinde*, built in Devon in the 1970s using traditional methods and materials. Like its namesake, it is seaworthy and has circumnavigated the globe. Drake's ship started life as the *Pelican*, but he renamed it in favour of his patron, Sir Christopher Hatton, whose crest is on the stern. The motto translates as "Virtue is the safest (tutissima) helmet". The original *Golden Hinde* rotted away in 1668 in Deptford Creek, and some of its timber went into a chair for the Bodleian Library in Oxford and a table in the Middle Temple. The previous occupant of the dock, the *Kathleen & May*, a topsail cargo schooner built in 1900, is now in Albert Dock in Liverpool.

Minerva House is one of those modern buildings that look better close up rather than from a distance. It was built in 1979-83 as the headquarters of Grindlays, one of those famous old colonial banks. Grindlays has since merged with Standard Chartered Bank, another of its kind.

Statue of Minerva, Montague Close. Alan Collins (1928-2016) was a prolific sculptor and teacher in both Britain and the USA. Much of his work is religious in nature, notably at Guildford Cathedral in Surrey. This Minerva seems very aggressive for the Goddess of Wisdom but, apart from many other attributes, she was also the goddess of strategic or defensive warfare. The statue is thought to have been commissioned by Grindlays.

A **terrace** off Montague Close looks across the river to Fishmongers' Hall and has a fragment of the London Bridge now in Arizona.

The first church on the site of **Southwark Cathedral** was recorded in the 7th century. This, the fourth church, was started in 1220. It has been much altered over the centuries, not least because the stone vaulted roof collapsed in 1459 and was replaced by a wooden one. Traces of this Parish Church of St Mary Overie survive in the south aisle, as does the carving of a cardinal's hat and coat of arms on a pillar in the south transept. The retro-choir behind the high altar is the oldest surviving part of the church; note the 2012 window for the Queen's diamond jubilee.

During the counter-reformation in the reign of Mary Tudor (1553-1558), seven martyrs (out of a total of 280) were condemned here to be burned at the stake. Excavation of one of the walls revealed a 17th century kiln for firing English Delft ware.

The present church is mainly a late 19th century job. The Prince of Wales (later Edward VII) laid the foundation stone in 1890. Many ancient monuments remain, including one to John Bingham who was saddler to Queen Elizabeth I and King James I. Across the transept, you can see the old arms of England with the three leopards and the fleur-de-lys of France. There is even a 20th century memorial to Shakespeare.

Harvard Chapel in the north transept opened in 1907, endowed by Harvard University alumni. Among the many plaques is one to Oscar Hammerstein, the writer and librettist who partnered with Richard Rodgers to produce such notable musical plays as *The King and I* and *The Sound of Music*. In the fine stained glass window, the shield with three books reading Veritas is the arms of Harvard University.

The Mudlark, Montague Close, SE1 9DA. Tel: 020 7403 7364. Nicholson's. Real ale and food. Mudlark was the nickname for scavengers who scoured the river at low tide for anything of value. Still popular as a pastime, but get a PLA licence before picking up anything!

Glazier's Hall, Montague Close, SE1 9DD. The home of the Worshipful Company of Glaziers & Painters of Glass, and the only livery hall south of the river. Like most city livery companies, it has charitable funds to spend on training in its field; it also rescues and recycles stained glass. The building dates from 1808, originating as a warehouse, and is now a popular events venue. The rear is right on the river and best seen from London Bridge. The Scientific Instrument Makers' Company shares the hall.

London Bridge

Julius Caesar made two expeditions to Britain in 55BC and 54BC during his Gallic War campaigns. On the second occasion, he forded the Thames with the help of a war elephant, though the exact location is unknown. It was another hundred years before the Romans returned, and this time they stayed for nearly 400 years.

The Romans' next incursion in AD43 saw them building a bridge in what was to become Londinium. Their first effort was probably a bridge of boats or pontoons, a method still used by military engineers. It was followed, not long after, by a permanent wooden bridge. Others followed it, some destroyed by accident, others by war between the English kingdoms or against the various Nordic invaders. A Norse epic written after one of these incidents later evolved into the nursery rhyme *London Bridge is falling down*.

The first stone bridge was started in 1176, and it is known that houses had been built on it by 1206. At one point, there were over 100 houses, some of four or five storeys with a shop on the ground floor. A gatehouse and drawbridge at the southern end defended the bridge. It was on this gatehouse that the heads of traitors (and not a few unfortunate innocents) were displayed impaled on pikes. The heads were parboiled and dipped in pitch to ensure they were a lasting deterrent. A chapel to St Thomas à Becket was in the centre of the bridge, attended by four priests. This bridge was composed of nineteen arches; the piers for these constricted the flow of water, and it was dangerous, except at slack water, to take a boat under the bridge.

The houses were removed by 1762, and the bridge widened. By this time, however, it was in a pretty poor state, and thoughts turned to a new bridge. Ambitious plans for a single-span cast-iron bridge were rejected, and a more conventional five-arched granite bridge was completed by Sir John Rennie in 1831. The new bridge stood about 30m upstream from the old, which remained in use during construction. Rennie's bridge now stands at Lake Havasu City in Arizona. The joke that the buyer thought he was getting Tower Bridge was just that, a joke. The new approach was named King William Street after the monarch who opened the bridge; the old bridge lined up with Fish Hill.

By the 1950s, it was clear that Rennie's bridge was sinking by about an inch (2.5cm) every eight years; worse, one side was sinking more than the other. The answer was to replace it with the modern stressed concrete box-girder bridge that you see today, a task completed in 1972. The pavement on the upstream side from the south has a plaque telling the history, and a dragon shows that you that you are entering the City of London. A model of the old bridge is in the Church of St Magnus.

The southern approach to London Bridge is **Borough High Street**, and this is worth a detour.

Frost fairs

On occasions in the past, the River Thames froze so hard that impromptu festivities could take place on the ice. Two factors were at play here: the first was the Little Ice Age, a period of cooling in the Atlantic region between roughly AD1400 and AD1850, and the other was the restricted flow of water through Old London Bridge. One might note that the Little Ice Age had been preceded by the Medieval Warm Period, a corresponding period of warming.

The festivities were quite something. On at least two occasions a whole ox was roasted, archery and dancing, and carriage races took place. Access to the ice was controlled by the watermen (or ferrymen) deprived of their regular source of income. The most extreme fair was in the winter of 1788-89 when the river was frozen all the way from Putney Bridge to Rotherhithe, about eight miles (13km) and a scene of unbroken jollification.

The last great frost fair was in the winter of 1813-14. The removal of Old London Bridge in 1831, and later embanking, meant that the flow was too rapid for ice to form.

Getting there. Cannon Street tube and mainline station is between Southwark and London Bridges. Bankside Pier (Thames Clippers) is upstream of Southwark Bridge.

Walking. London Bridge to Tower Bridge is ¾ mile/1km.

24. THE BOROUGH DETOUR

This district is called The Borough simply because, at the time, it was the only borough south of the river. The High Street was the main road to the south, and because Old London Bridge was so narrow and congested, it became the terminus for stagecoaches on routes to the Channel ports and Portsmouth. This meant that there were many coaching inns here.

Set off down the left side of the street, a bit grotty, but worth persevering. Several buildings here are worthy of restoration.

George Inn, 77 Borough High Street, SE1 1NH. National Trust. The last remaining galleried coaching inn in London. The present building dates from 1676, but an inn existed here long before that. The inn was more extensive, but the northern and central wings were demolished in 1899 to make space for the tracks to London Bridge station. Dickens mentions The George in *Little Dorrit*, and summer sees performances of The Bard's plays in the courtyard.

South of the George is Talbot Yard. The **Tabard Inn**, well known to Chaucer and other Canterbury pilgrims, once stood here. The inn was demolished in the

19th century, mainly due to the railways taking over from the stagecoaches. A blue plaque marks the spot, but we've seen cleaner places in third-world cities.

The **John Harvard Library** is named after the local man who was one of the early benefactors of Harvard University in Cambridge, Massachusetts. More information under Southwark Cathedral, where the Harvard Chapel seems a more fitting memorial. The **Local History Library** is within the library, but both were closed for refurbishment when we visited.

Angel Yard, beside the library, has half a dozen plaques associated with Charles Dickens and his father, who was locked up for debt in the Marshalsea Prison here. These plaques are all in the pavement and could do with cleaning.

A little further on is:

Church of St George the Martyr, Borough High Street, SE1 1JA. Much rebuilt and altered since its foundation in 1122. Oliver Cromwell's body is said to have been brought here before lying in state at Somerset House, which seems odd as he died in Whitehall. The cherubs on the ceiling were added in 1897, and the frieze is composed of the arms of the city livery companies that contributed to the work. The church was last restored in 1951-52; the east window represents the Ascension and includes the figure of Little Dorrit who (according to Dickens) was baptised and married here. The clock in the tower has four faces, three of them illuminated. The fourth, facing Bermondsey, is black, reputedly because the people there were too mean to pay for the lighting.

You can continue down Borough High Street as far as Trinity Street. Turn left, and you soon reach Trinity Square. The former church is now the **Henry Wood Hall**; Henry Wood (1869-1944) was the conductor of the inaugural Promenade Concert ("The Proms") season in 1895, and this hall is his memorial. In the garden is a statue of **King Alfred the Great** (886-899), said to be the oldest outdoor statue in London and until 1826 installed at Westminster Hall. Recent restoration has shown that the lower half of the statue is of Roman origin, probably Minerva and dating from around AD150. The Alfred part may date from the time of Richard II (1377-1399), but how and when the two parts came together is still a mystery.

Walk back towards London Bridge on the other (west) side of the street. Opposite the church is an Italian grocery shop **Prezzemolo & Vitale**, possibly the best deli you will see. Seating outside for coffee and a snack.

You pass **Little Dorrit Court**, and then at 166, the site of the **Duke of Suffolk's Palace** (16th century). At 88 is the **Whisky Exchange**, an incredible selection of every kind of spirit you can think of; you could even splash out £15,000 for a bottle of old Macallan.

A short walk down Union Street brings you to **Crossbones Garden**, a former paupers' burial ground, where many of the unfortunate Winchester Geese ended up.

Several alleyways on the left have old buildings, though right of way is a moot point. Maidstone Buildings Mews has some interesting old warehouses. The building behind **50 Borough High Street**, once the Goat Inn dated 1542, is probably the only one surviving in London with an overhanging upper floor. Access is through Harding's property, though there is no right of way; the building is timber framed but rendered and of minimal interest.

Where Borough High Street forks, bear left. The **War Memorial** is a fine bronze statue of a soldier of the First World War erected in 1924. On the plinth are bronze reliefs, one of biplanes and the other of warships. Behind the gun turrets of the warship in the foreground is a three-funnelled battlecruiser. All the sculpture is by Philip Lindsey Clark (1889-1977), who won the DSO as an infantry officer in the First World War.

The **Hop Exchange**, 24 Southwark Street, SE1 1TY. The brewing of beer requires hops for flavouring. Most in Britain are grown in the county of Kent and used to be brought to London either by barge or rail. The Hop Exchange was built in 1867 as a central market for hops. Since fire damage in 1920, it has been offices. The covered central courtyard is a spectacular space; the ornate cast iron balconies display the white horse of Kent. The building was saved from demolition by the late Martin Birrane, a businessman and successful amateur racing driver. He went on to rescue the Lola racing car company, which is why you see a working replica of the Lola T90 Red Ball Special in which Graham Hill won the 1966 Indianapolis 500. If the gates are closed, you can still glimpse the courtyard.

Southwark Tavern, 22 Southwark Street SE1 1TU. Tel: 0207 403 0257. A fine Victorian boozer (food too). The exterior offers Meux's Famous Stout and Perfect Ales, but you'll be lucky; there's been no real Meux ales for 60 years. The building was once a debtors' prison (yes, until 1869 you could be locked up in very unpleasant conditions just for owing money).

Borough Market, 8 Southwark Street, SE1 1TL London's major food market has been here or hereabouts for a good 1000 years. London's foodie revolution has seen the market develop in the last twenty years, and good restaurants have moved in, too. Basically a wholesale market, retail customers are now welcome, and there are usually plenty of free tastes.

Getting there. Monument tube station to the north, and London Bridge tube and overground to the south of the bridge.

114

25. LONDON BRIDGE TO TOWER BRIDGE

North bank

Past London Bridge the path becomes Grant's Wharf Quay. From here you can see and walk through to:

St Magnus the Martyr, Lower Thames Street EC3R 6DN. A church stood on this site by the 11th century; that, or a successor, was destroyed in the Great Fire of 1666, being close to where the fire started. T.S. Eliot reckoned that the interior was one of the finest of all Wren's churches and mentioned it (and other places along the river) in *The Wasteland:* www.poetryfoundation.- org/poems/47311/the-waste-land

The archway through the base of the tower is a relic of the footpath over Old London Bridge with which it aligned. The stump of wood in the porch is part of the piling of a Roman river wall. Note too what appear to be fire marks in the porch. Stones from the old bridge can be seen in the churchyard.

The fabulous interior is more like a Russian palace than an English church. The statue in the south aisle is of Magnus, Earl of Orkney, killed in ca1116 in a feud with his cousin. Also here is Our Lady of Walsingham, a clue to the strong Anglo-Catholic tradition followed here. You would not be surprised to hear a Latin mass. St Magnus is the guild church of the Worshipful Company of Fishmongers and the Worshipful Company of Plumbers; their arms, along with those of the Coopers' Company, appear in the stained glass. The church itself was pretty much complete by 1676 but the spire, similar to that of St Carolus Borromeus in Antwerp, was added between 1703 and 1706. And finally the clock was installed in 1709.

After the Great Fire, 47cwt (2.40t) of melted bell metal was recovered and used to cast new bells, and others were replaced over the years. In 1976 ten old cracked bells were recycled to cast many of the Bells of Congress that were then hung in the Old Post Office Tower in Washington, D.C.

From St Magnus cross Lower Thames Street and walk up Fish Street Hill, the approach road to Old London Bridge. This brings you to **The Monument.** London has suffered many fires, but the most devastating was the Great Fire of 1666. The fire started in Farryner's bakery in Pudding Lane. A plaque on Farynors House, a fine example of modern architecture just to the east, marks the spot. The fire destroyed 13,000 houses, 87 churches, and 44 livery halls. Things might have been even worse but for the King and his brother the Duke of York (later James II) using gunpowder to blast fire breaks.

An Act of Parliament decreed a monument to the fire and the rebuilding of the city. Wren proposed first a pillar with flames (of bronze) coming from the slit windows and with a symbolic phoenix on top, all in gilt bronze. The next idea was a statue of Charles II in Roman dress; Charles demurred because "I did not start the fire". Eventually they settled on this simple Doric column with a flaming urn. It is, nevertheless, the tallest free-standing masonry pillar in the world at 61.5m

(203ft). Inside are 311 steps to the viewing gallery which was caged in 1834 after six suicides. Apart from this monument Wren designed the new St Paul's Cathedral and 52 other churches.

The memorial to **Robert Hooke** (1635-1703) belatedly acknowledges the part he played in the design of The Monument; a true polymath, he was a pioneer in microscopy, gravity, and many other fields. There is supposed to be a bronze plaque depicting Old St Paul's in flames and with the date MDCLXVI (1666), though this may be covered by the stylish public bogs.

Returning to the river, pass the blue monstrosity on Dark House Walk, and you see **Old Billingsgate Market**. This was London's main fish market from the 11th century, the name becoming synonymous with fish and foul language. In time, other commodities including fresh fruit and grain were landed here; also salt from France, essential for preserving meat and fish. The present building dates from the 1850s, but the site was always inadequate for the volume of trade. It was eventually closed in 1982 and the business moved to the Isle of Dogs. A walkway subject to flooding leads to:

Old Custom House. The levying of customs duty on imports and exports goes back at least to the time of King Æthelred (978-1016), and a sequence of Custom Houses has been built on or near this site, the old Wool Quay. The one burned down in the Great Fire (1666) was replaced by a Wren design that succumbed to a gunpowder explosion in 1714. Ripley's replacement burned down in 1814, and Laing's fell down in 1825 due to jerry-built foundations. The building we see now (best from the other side of the river) was designed by Robert Smirke. The east wing was bomb-damaged in the Blitz and restored after the war. The building was used by Her Majesty's Revenue and Customs until recently. Plans are afoot for conversion to a hotel. Note the two old cranes at the end of the walk.

A broad pier projects from Sugar Quay Walk. Past the pods of the cafés you come to **Tower Millennium Pier** for Thames Clipper services. Time for a decision: either carry on along the riverfront to Tower Bridge or make a short detour around the Tower of London. To follow the riverfront, detour around Wharfinger's Cottage to reach the terrace in front of the Tower of London.

The central keep of the **Tower of London**, the White Tower, was built by William I (the Conqueror) shortly after he took London in 1066. Its purpose was to cow the defeated Saxons as much as to be a royal palace. The outer fortifications grew over the years and took pretty much their present form in the reign of Edward I (1239-1307). Despite brief use as a palace, the Tower has been mainly a place of imprisonment and execution for enemies of the state. Some executions were within the tower, more often in public on Tower Hill.

Traitors' Gate was the watergate through the outer fortification of Edward I. Few who entered the Tower this way exited alive. One exception was Princess Elizabeth, imprisoned by her half-sister Queen Mary I (1553-1558). It is said that after her coronation Queen Elizabeth I visited the Tower once – briefly.

To the right on the terrace is the **Gun Battery** where the King's Troop of the Royal Horse Artillery still fires salutes on royal occasions. We'd never noticed before the **Children's Beach** established by George V using 1500 barge loads of sand; must have been dreadfully polluted in those days. To the right of the archway through Tower Bridge is a memorial of Queen Victoria's Golden Jubilee in 1887.

Under the bridge is **Dead Man's Hole.** Steps lead down to the river, and bodies were recovered from the river here; note the half-steps to ease the process. The bodies were left in the white-tiled alcove for identification.

South bank

The **Pool of London** was where ships unloaded their cargoes before the building of the enclosed docks. The Pool was the stretch of river between London Bridge and Limekiln Creek, and it consisted of two sections. The **Upper Pool** was between London Bridge and Cherry Garden Pier, and the **Lower Pool** below that. Even after the docks were built, many ships unloaded in the Pool. If no wharf was available, they unloaded in mid-stream into lighters that were hauled away by tugs to warehouses and docks, often upstream of London Bridge. The system was very inefficient, plagued by constant labour problems, pilferage, and delay. No wonder containerisation caught on so fast.

André Derain captured the spirit of the Pool of London in 1906. The painting is not on display at present but can be seen at: https://www.tate.org.uk/art/artworks/derain-the-pool-of-london-n06030.

Pool of London (1951) is an atmospheric film that conveys a sense of how grim post-war London was: https://www.imdb.com/title/tt0042851/

Before you set off, walk out onto London Bridge to see the river front of **St Olaf House**, the Art Deco offices of the Hays Wharf Company built in 1931. Note the depiction of the exotic goods once landed there; binoculars are useful. There are panoramic views both up and downstream.

Access to the riverside walk from London Bridge is by precipitous and awkwardly angled stairs. If you do not like the look of them, walk downhill to Tooley Street, turn left and left again at St Olaf House. Tooley is a corruption of St Olaf, King of Norway in the early 11th century and ally of King Æthelred against Cnut's Danes. A succession of churches dedicated to St Olaf stood on the site until 1928.

The **London Bridge Experience** and **London Tombs** (opposite the Tooley Street exit from London Bridge tube station) are described as an 'immersive experience'. It gets mixed reviews and is not cheap.

Near the foot of the stairs is a **memorial plaque** to Old London Bridge. Looking straight across the river, you can see the tower of St Magnus Martyr and The Monument. To the right are Old Billingsgate Market and the Customs House. You are now on Hay's Wharf, still part of The Queen's Walk.

117

The pointy neo-Gothic building behind Custom House, as seen from London Bridge City Pier, is Minster Court, on Great Tower Street and Mincing Lane. Fun architecture.

Hay's Wharf was the oldest established (begun in 1651) and the largest in the Port of London, taking up the whole distance between London Bridge and Tower Bridge. Early investment in cold storage saw it handling the first imports of New Zealand butter and cheese in 1867.

The wharf closed in 1969 and was the first part of Docklands to be redeveloped. The warehouses became apartments, and the office block a part of London Bridge Hospital. The dock was covered (you can still see the lock gates at the river end) and became the base for **Hay's Galleria**, an upmarket shopping centre. Halfway down the galleria is **The Navigators,** a large kinetic sculpture by David Kemp (1987), great fun and a must if you have children with you.

Riverside Bookshop, Unit 15, 57 Tooley Street, Hay's Galleria, SE1 2QN. Tel: 020 7378 1824. It seems to be in the nature of things that there are few bookshops, new or second-hand, along the riverside, but this one is certainly worth a look.

The Horniman at Hays, Unit 26 Hays Galleria, SE1 2HD. Tel: 020 7407 1991. Nicholson's. Food and real ale. Outside seating by the river. An attractive pub created in an old tea warehouse, hence the name. In the 19th century, the Horniman company was the largest tea trader in the world. The family endowed a fascinating museum in South London, https://www.horniman.ac.uk/

Battle Bridge Lane may derive from Battle Abbey, site of the Battle of Hastings in 1066, as the abbot is known to have had an "inn" or house here.

Southwark Crown Court is a brick building of 1983, mercifully screened by plane and cherry trees. Crown courts are the second tier of the British criminal justice system, dealing with more serious crimes and appeals against decisions in the magistrates' courts.

HMS Belfast was laid down in the Harland & Wolff shipyard in Belfast in 1936 and completed in 1939, just before the Second World War broke out. She is a light cruiser (heavy cruisers were much the same size but had 8" guns), has a displacement of 11,500 tons and a speed of 32 knots (59 km/hr). Her main armament was twelve 6" guns plus twelve 4" mainly for anti-aircraft use. She escorted the convoys taking supplies to the Russian port of Murmansk and was part of the bombardment force on D-Day. HMS Belfast was much modified before the end of the war and again after, hence the enclosed bridge and twin Bofors guns. The camouflage scheme is that worn in 1942-44. Most of the ship is open to view, from bridge to boiler and engine rooms, four gun turrets & magazines. A new *HMS Belfast*, a type 26 frigate, is currently under construction.

We are lucky to have *HMS Belfast*, which narrowly avoided scrapping. But how much better if someone had had the wit to preserve one of the fourteen battleships (and a battlecruiser) that survived the Second World War? *HMS*

Warspite, for instance, had a career spanning the Battle of Jutland (1916) to the bombardment of the D-Day beaches in 1944.

Upper Deck Bar, over *HMS Belfast* ticket office. Tel: 020 7403 6246. Great views of the ship and the river.

Evergreen, opposite the stern of HMS Belfast, is a stainless steel and glass tree by David Batchelor, at its best when the real trees are bare of leaves.

More London, otherwise known as **London Bridge City**, is a 13-acre (5.3ha) high-rise development once listed for the Carbuncle Cup (see National Gallery). Moving into the open space, the five **Full Stop sculptures** (2004) by Fiona Banner may appear to be polished stone but are actually bronze. The black paint is the same as that used on London taxis. Each sculpture is named after the typeface that inspired it.

The Scoop is an open-air amphitheatre seating 800. Details of events at: https://londonbridgecity.co.uk/events

Over the years, London's local government (a council) has frequently been at odds with the national government in Westminster. So when one government closed down the existing council and sold off its head office by Westminster Bridge, it was inevitable that a later government of a different stripe would reconstitute the council and provide extravagant new premises. Hence, the **City Hall** (aka The Glass Gonad), which between 2002 and 2021 housed the assembly, the mayor's office, and space for yet more public servants. The glass construction by Foster was intended to symbolise transparency and, supposedly, to be energy efficient. The mayor and his minions have decamped to new premises in Newham, and the building is looking for a new tenant.

A grass strip beside the Norton Rose Fulbright building leads to the southern end of the **Tower Subway**. The subway, opened in 1869, was the first to be bored using a Greathead tunnelling shield and thus a precursor of the deep bored tube lines. Initially, the tunnel housed a 2' 6" gauge cable-hauled tramway, but the operating company went bust, and the tunnel became a foot subway. The subway was closed in 1896 when Tower Bridge opened, and then used for water mains and hydraulic power pipes, though the latter have been supplanted by fibre optic cables. The original building was demolished when this area was redeveloped in the 1990s, and a new entrance built behind the Unicorn Theatre. The other end is close to the entrance of the Tower of London.

Of more interest, **Potters Fields Park** is a welcome eco-friendly green space that extends to Tooley Street. The layout is by Dutch garden guru Piet Oudolf. Potteries were established here at least as early as the 17th century, and English Delftware was made here. 'Potters' Field' is a term of biblical origin, more used in North America, for a paupers' graveyard; there is no evidence for that use here.

St John's Churchyard is another, quieter, open green space on the other side of Tooley Street.

Tooley Street is the main road behind the river, and was the only thoroughfare when the riverfront was occupied by wharves. On the corner of Tooley Street and Bridge Yard is a fine bronze memorial plaque to **James Braidwood** (1800-1861). After establishing a proper fire brigade in Edinburgh, he was invited to do the same in London in 1833. Up to that time, the fire brigades were funded by individual insurance companies, and they would deal with fires only at properties covered by their sponsor. Buildings carried a plaque known as a "fire mark" of the insurance company as proof of cover.

On 22 June 1861, a major fire broke out, which eventually engulfed the whole riverfront from St Olaf's Church to Battle Bridge Lane. Leading his men from the front, as usual, Braidwood was killed by the collapse of a wall near this spot; he has a much more imposing memorial in Edinburgh.

Between the two green spaces is a statue of **Colonel Samuel Bourne Bevington**, first mayor of Bermondsey. A bronze bust commemorates **Ernest Bevin** (1881-1951), a trade unionist and Labour politician (remarkably) held in high regard by Churchill. From here, you can return through the gardens or simply walk up Tower Bridge Road to the bridge.

Following the river, before the riverside warehouses were knocked down, the approach to the passage under Tower Bridge was Pickle Herring Street. The Queen's Walk ends at Tower Bridge, so walk under the bridge onto Shad Thames.

Tower Bridge

By the late 19th century, it was obvious that a new river crossing was needed as London expanded to the east. The problem was that large ships had to be able to pass into the Upper Pool as far as London Bridge. The obvious answer was some form of opening bridge. The act of parliament authorising the bridge specified that the opening should be 200ft (61m) wide with 135ft (41m) headroom; it further demanded a design in Victorian Gothic style, a sort of throwback to the 14th century.

Construction work began on 22 April 1886 based on a design by the City of London architect Sir Horace Jones. 70,000 tons of concrete went into the two piers, and 12,000 tons of steel into the main structure; belying its appearance, this is a modern steel-framed structure concealed by a thin veneer of stone. Oddly enough, the planned cladding was brick; the change to Cornish granite and Portland stone to harmonise better with the Tower of London came later. A plan in 1945 would have seen the towers replaced by glass-clad office blocks, a Crystal Tower Bridge; fortunately, that came to nothing. Finance for construction came from the Bridge House Estates, a body founded in 1282 which also looks after London, Southwark, Blackfriars, and Millennium Bridges.

Two counterbalanced bascules weighing 1000 tons each form the crossing. Initially, steam provided the hydraulic power to raise them, modernised to electric operation in 1976. The outer sections are suspension bridges using lattice girders instead of chains. The bridge was opened to much celebration by the Prince (later

Edward VII) and Princess of Wales on 30 June 1894. The design is frankly whimsical, and many engineers at the time would have preferred a purely functional appearance. The result, however, is a building that has come to symbolise London in the same way as its contemporary, the Eiffel Tower, represents Paris.

There have been mishaps. At the time of writing, the bascules got stuck in the up position and created traffic chaos all over central London; normally, 40,000 vehicles cross the bridge daily. More spectacularly, in 1952, the bascules started to rise as a number 78 bus carrying 20 passengers was on the bridge. The driver boldly put the pedal to the metal and leapt the gap. In 1997, the rule that navigation takes precedence over road traffic resulted in Bill Clinton's motorcade being split in two to the chagrin of his security staff. And several aircraft, including a jet fighter, have been flown through the space under the walkway.

The two towers and the walkway are open to the public. Most of the operating machinery is visible, and the views are splendid. Access is from the south bank, and tickets can be bought online see: https://www.towerbridge.org.uk The website will also tell you when the bridge is due to be raised.

Getting there. Monument tube station to the north of London Bridge, and London Bridge tube and overground to the south.

Walking. Tower Bridge to Canary Wharf Pier is 2½ miles (4km) along the north bank. Tower Bridge to Doubletree Docklands Pier (opposite Canary Wharf Pier) is 3 miles (4.75km).

Jellied eels

Jellied eels is a classic East London dish dating back perhaps 200 years, an original fast food. Possibly of Italian origin, it consists of eels, plentiful in the Thames estuary, cooked in a spiced vegetable broth. Usually eaten cold, collagen in the eels causes the broth to jellify; the green colour comes from the parsley in the broth. Do note that the eels are not filleted and are very bony. Jellied eels were traditionally sold by street vendors and in pie and mash shops.

The nearest source of this epicurean delight to our route is the eel, pie and mash shop (established 1891) of M. Manze at 87 Tower Bridge Road SE1 4TW. Tel: 020 7407 2985. This is a bit over ½ mile, say 10-15 minutes walk from Tower Bridge or hop on a 42 bus. Details: www.manze.co.uk/ In Greenwich town centre, you can try Goddards of Greenwich at 22 King William Walk, SE10 9HU.

26. A STROLL AROUND THE TOWER

From **Tower Millennium Pier** the street leading up from the riverside is **Petty Wales**. The origin of the name is uncertain but very old; a Welsh community may have lived here, or it may have been the London home of the Princes of Wales. Prince of Wales is the title of the Crown Prince, a term not used in Britain. Petty is the French *Petit* for Little. In the same way, Petty France, near St James' Park, was a Huguenot settlement, and remembered by us of a certain age for the location of the Passport Office.

In front of the modern ticket office is the cylindrical entrance to the **Tower Subway** under the river. The subway, opened in 1869, was the first to be bored using a Greathead tunnelling shield and thus a precursor of the deep bored tube lines. The tunnel originally housed a 2' 6" (0.76m) gauge cable-hauled tramway, but the operating company went bust, and the tunnel became a foot subway. According to Charles Dickens Jr, this was not a place "for any but the very briefest of Her Majesty's lieges to attempt the passage in high-heeled boots, or with a hat to which he attaches any particular value". The subway was closed in 1896 when Tower Bridge opened; it once carried hydraulic power pipes and now telecom cables. The other end is in Vine Lane off Tooley Street.

The environs of the Tower have been much tidied up over the last twenty years. A broad terrace overlooks the tourist entrance to the Tower and the moat. The visitor entrance is through the **Middle Tower** and over what was once a drawbridge. Middle Tower because it was the central of three, the outer Lion Tower having been demolished in the mid-19th century. It had taken its name from two lions presented to Henry III in 1235; that was the foundation of the Royal Menagerie, eventually transferred to Regent's Park in the 1830s. The moat was drained in 1843 and once had tennis courts and football pitches.   In 2018, the centenary of the end of the First World War, 888,246 red ceramic poppies covered the banks to commemorate Britain's war dead. The battlements opposite you have been enlarged for artillery rather than bowmen, and Legge's Mount in the north-western corner has large gun ports installed after the Restoration in 1660.

Walk up past the Tower Vaults towards the looming presence of the Walkie-Talkie, and you come to **All Hallows by the Towe**r. A Saxon church was built in the seventh century AD on the foundations of a Roman house, making it the oldest church in the City of London. The church, much altered in the Norman period and later, survived the Great Fire in 1666 but was gutted by German bombing in 1940; all that remained were the outer walls and the tower. Samuel Pepys, who lived a stone's throw away, had watched the Fire from this tower. Rebuilt, the church is wonderfully light and seems much larger inside than out. In the west end is a Saxon arch incorporating Roman bricks. You can explore the **crypt** and **undercroft** with Roman tombstones and mosaic floors, a model of Roman London, and ancient chapels. A very old site indeed.

Seafarers have a long tradition of placing model ships in the churches where they worship. All Hallows has probably the largest collection in Britain ranging from a Thames sailing barge to a ferry that took part in the evacuation from Dunkirk in 1940. There are many other naval and maritime memorials. Behind the main altar is a mural of the Last Supper done during rebuilding. Unusually, there is no crucifix on the altar as that would obscure the face of Christ. The font, carved by an Italian prisoner of war, has a spectacular cover by Grinling Gibbons, providentially stored at St Paul's during the war.

William Penn, founder of Pennsylvania, was baptised here in 1644. In 1797, John Quincy Adams, sixth president of the United States, married Louisa Johnson here; she was the first First Lady to be born outside the United States, the second being Melania Trump. Note the full-length memorial to "Tubby" Clayton, vicar here from 1922-1962 and founder of the Toc H, an international Christian fellowship. In the sanctuary in the north aisle is what appears to be an elaborate reliquary topped by a cross of Lorraine, actually a housing of the ever-burning Toc H lamp.

The **Malta Siege Memorial** is just past the church. The stone has explanatory panels, headed by a Maltese cross, that are worth reading. The island of Malta, strategically placed between Sicily and North Africa, was a vital naval and air base for Great Britain during the Second World War. Despite overwhelming air attacks by Italian and German forces, it was kept alive at huge cost in both men and materiel. This great block of Malta limestone was donated by the Maltese government. This battle was, in effect, the second Great Siege of Malta, the first having been in 1565 when the Knights Hospitaller withstood the might of the Ottoman Empire for four months.

Up a flight of steps by the Tower Vaults is **Tower Hill Terrace**, a large and little-frequented open space with fine views. Within the nearest corner of the Tower is the **Chapel of St Peter ad Vincula**. This church, dating from 1520, stands on Tower Green, which was the more private place of execution. It was the burial place of many of those executed on Tower Hill; whether they were reunited with their heads is unclear. The name means St Peter in Chains and refers to St Peter's imprisonment by Herod II.

A short walk up Muscovy Street brings you to **Seething Lane Garden**. In the 17th century Seething Lane housed various Admiralty offices before they were moved to Somerset House. **Samuel Pepys**, whose diary (1660-69) tells us so much about the history and morals (or lack of them) of the time, worked and lived here. In the garden is a bronze bust of Pepys by Karin Janzen. Carved paving stones depict incidents in Pepys' life. At the end of Seething Lane is the **Church of St Olave** where Pepys and his wife worshipped and are buried. The churchyard, with a wonderful magnolia tree, is a little haven of peace and quiet. There is a memorial to Pepys on the wall of the church and also a mention of William Turner of Northumberland, 'the father of British botany'. It is debatable whether 'seething' derives from an old word for boiling food or means 'filled with chaff'; the Corn Exchange was nearby.

Return to Trinity Square (street) and enter **Trinity Square Gardens**. The first memorial is the place of execution on **Tower Hill**. Seventy-five enemies of the state, probably a few of whom just happened to be in the wrong place at the wrong time, were executed here, watched by a boisterous crowd of thousands. The first execution, of Sir Simon de Burley, was in 1388 and the last, of Lord Lovat, in 1746. The central plaque commemorates the Earl of Kilmarnock and Lord Balmarino, executed here in 1745. Both were victims, like Lovat, of being on the wrong side in the '45, the last Jacobite throw of the dice.

The **Mercantile Marine War Memorial** is a Lutyens classical pavilion in memory of the 12,000 men of the Merchant Navy and fishing fleet who were killed during the First World War and have no known grave. Note especially the plaques listing the 350 crew of the Lusitania, sunk by a U-boat in 1915. Lutyens' first design was for a massive arch on the banks of the Thames, but that was rejected. Lutyens also designed the Cenotaph in Whitehall, Britain's central war memorial of the 20th century, and many of the memorials for the military cemeteries in France and Belgium.

Losses in the Second World War were even worse, with 4700 British-flagged ships sunk and 24,000 men having no grave but the sea. Lutyens had died in 1944, and the 1939-1945 extension was entrusted to Sir Edward Maufe, who had succeeded Lutyens as principal architect of the Imperial War Graves Commission. Maufe proposed a similar colonnade, but that was rejected. The **Merchant Seamen's Memorial** eventually took the form of a sunken garden; it would have been deeper but for Underground tunnels beneath. Two figures, a master and a seaman, stand guard over the grassed area with its compass face. Maufe, incidentally, designed the quietly imposing Air Forces Memorial near Runnymede for the 20,000 airmen who have no known grave.

The **Falklands War Memorial** in the south-eastern corner of the gardens commemorates the seventeen men of the Merchant Navy and the Royal Fleet Auxiliary (the people who keep Royal Navy ships fuelled and victualled at sea) who died in the Falklands conflict in 1982.

The gardens are overlooked by the offices of the **Corporation of Trinity House**. This charity, founded in 1514, is responsible for the building and maintenance of all the lighthouses (66) and light vessels (8) in England, Wales, the Channel Islands, and Gibraltar. Scotland and Ireland have their own authorities. Its income comes mainly from a levy on all cargo ships entering British ports. The building dates from 1796; it was gutted by an incendiary bomb in 1940 and carefully restored with the help of old photos. The medallions of the coat of arms of George III and Queen Charlotte are of Coade Stone). Tours are available, see tours@trinityhouse.co.uk

The flamboyant Edwardian mass of the **Four Seasons Hotel** at 10 Trinity Square (built 1913-22) was formerly the head office of the **Port of London Authority**. The prominent statue, perhaps needless to say, is of Father Thames. The official architectural style is 'Beaux Arts', a term that brought back school memories of 'the torturer's horse/Scratches its innocent behind on a tree'. The magnificent interior was badly damaged in the Blitz and rebuilt more prosaically. The best view of the building is from the Falklands Memorial.

In front of Tower Hill tube station is a large **sundial** surrounded by a strip cartoon history of London from the Roman invasion in AD43 to the building of the Thames Barrier. This space tends to be crowded but offers fine views.

London's **Roman Wall** (begun in perhaps AD100) ran south from here, in what is now Tower Hill Garden, towards the river. A statue of the Roman Emperor Trajan fronts this fragment. You can follow the line of the wall to another fragment along the wooden walkway of the Citizen M Hotel. The stone inscribed "Dis manibus..." (To the gods of the departed) is a replica of a Roman tombstone found near here; the original is in the British Museum.

The statue of the Roman emperor **Trajan** (AD53-117, emperor from AD98) is something of a mish-mash. The body is a 1st century cast like one found near Naples; the head is from a different source, the whole apparently found in a scrapyard near Southampton. The statue is the bequest of "Tubby" Clayton, mentioned above. Trajan, one of the 'good' emperors, is not known to have visited Britain, but he had the idea of a northern wall between Roman Britannia and an unconquered Scotland. It was left to his adopted heir, Hadrian, to build it.

The underpass by Trajan's statue leads to the foundations of the **Tower Hill Postern**. Building the Tower of London required demolition of the section of the wall towards the river, and the Postern gate was built on the edge of the moat to provide pedestrian access to the city. A new path has been laid through the old moat, though the waterlogging of the ground has not helped. You can follow this path, and up the steps, to Tower Bridge Approach, though you would miss the **statue of a building worker** in Tower Bridge Piazza.

Over the road from here are the former buildings of the **Royal Mint**, now a mixed residential and office development. Walk down to Tower Bridge to regain the river.

Getting there. The nearest tube station is Tower Hill, from where you walk either way round the Tower of London down to the river. London Clipper to Tower Pier, and then a shorter walk.

27. TOWER BRIDGE TO CANARY WHARF PIER

North bank

The path passes in front of the **Tower Hotel**, an ugly brutalist 800-room job completed in 1973. Over to the right what appear to be two blue mosaic seats is a sculpture, *Through Blue* (2000) by Susan Goldblatt. From here you can see the steps leading up from Dead Man's Hole.

Girl with a Dolphin (1973) by David Wynne is one of London's best-loved statues; its similarly inspired (Wynne trained as a zoologist) *Boy with a Dolphin* stands at the north end of Albert Bridge in Chelsea. Dolphins and humans both seem to defy gravity. Wendy Taylor's *Timepiece* (1973) is equally attractive.

In 1749, the Dutch East Indiaman *Amsterdam* set out on her maiden voyage from Texel bound for Batavia (now Jakarta in Indonesia), but foundered in a storm in the English Channel. The wreck was discovered in 1969, and an **anchor** salvaged; it resides here in an unkempt flower bed. The wreck can still be seen near Hastings on a very low tide. The old **cannon** may be from the same source.

Cross the bridge over the entrance to **St Katharine's Dock**. The docks opened in 1828 following a land grab that made over 11,000 people homeless with no compensation. The dock closed in 1968, and the selling price was less than the construction cost. The dock is now a marina, known as St Katharine's Haven; this was home to a number of classic boats, mainly spritsail Thames barges, but now there are just expensive and little-used gin palaces. Some of the original warehouses have survived as apartments. Continuing to the dock and turning right, you find:

Dickens Inn, Marble Quay, Wapping, E1W 1UH. Tel: 020 7488 2208. Real ale and food. Attractive building that started life as a brewery on a site 70m away. Prices commensurate with the location but, we think, worth it.

Otherwise, go over the steps between Dockmaster's House and Devon House as a shortcut onto St Katharine's Way. Follow St Katharine's Way behind *HMS President* (a "stone frigate") Royal Naval Reserve centre. Then, out along the riverfront to Hermitage Entrance, which used to lead into Hermitage Basin, and thence to the actual **London Docks**, constructed from 1799 to 1815. These were the first enclosed docks in London as the wharves became overcrowded. Though mostly now filled in, it is still possible, to walk beside water from Hermitage Basin through to Shadwell Basin via Spirit Quay and Tobacco Dock.

St Katharine's Way becomes Wapping High Street. Walk through the **Hermitage Riverside Memorial Garden** and note the *Dove of Peace* (2008) by Wendy Taylor, a memorial to the civilian victims of the Blitz. The memorial has been encased in railings since yobboes defaced it. This area was devastated by bombing, and property developers destroyed what the Luftwaffe had missed. From here, you can see the prosaic HMS President and the more attractive cluster of houseboats, mostly Dutch barges with a few Thames spritsail sailing barges.

Continue along the riverside to **Cinnabar Wharf**. Cinnabar is mercuric sulphide (HgS), a toxic mineral mined mostly in Spain and from which mercury is refined. It is also the source of vermilion pigment and used as such since prehistoric times. The *Voyager* sculpture is by Wendy Taylor.

In the 17th and 18th centuries, Wapping was probably the roughest part of London, quite a distinction in a decidedly rough and ready city. This was a sailor's town and provided all the usual amenities: notably strong drink and prostitution. At one time, there were 140 inns in Wapping High Street alone. A few hardy survivors are worth a visit, though now outnumbered by posh estate agents. At Pierhead you cross the filled-in entrance to Wapping Basin, another access to London Docks.

The **Town of Ramsgate**, 62 Wapping High Street E1W 2PN. Tel: 020 7481 8000. Free house. Real ale and food. Named after the fishermen of Ramsgate who brought their catch to Wapping Old Stairs to avoid tax at Billingsgate. Judge Jeffreys was apprehended here, and convicts bound for Australia were kept in the cellars. Beside the pub an alleyway leads to Wapping Old Stairs, and this is the most likely location of **Execution Dock**.

Opposite the pub is the churchyard of **St John at Wapping**. Walk either through the churchyard or down Scandrett Street. The church was built in 1756 and destroyed by bombing in the Second World War. The tower has been restored, and what was left of the building converted to flats. Beside the church is **St John's Old School**. This was a 'bluecoat' school, as such charity schools were called, and the figures of boy and girl pupils are so dressed. The name apparently stems from blue being the cheapest dye. Behind the church is:

The Turk's Head, 1 Green Bank EC1W 2PA. Tel: 020 7709 0779. A former Taylor Walker pub, now a bistro. Opens early and does a full English breakfast as well as snails, moules, and the rest. Prisoners being taken from Newgate Prison to Execution Dock were allowed a last drink here.

Plod along Wapping High Street, some original buildings, some new, but all somehow rather sterile. The modern blue and white building is the Metropolitan Police boatyard, which incorporates the:

Thames Police Museum, 98 Wapping High Street, E1W 2NE. The Thames River Police was formed in 1798 which made it the first organised police unit in the country. At the time city merchants were losing over £50 million (at today's value) of merchandise annually. It merged with the newly formed Metropolitan Police in 1839. The museum shows uniforms, equipment, and memorabilia of the various forms the unit has taken over the years. Entry by appointment only; contact: curator@thamespolicemuseum.org

Waterside Gardens look across to the Angel pub and the 'leaning tower of Bermondsey'. You can also see the police pier. At the end of the gardens are Wapping New Stairs. **Wapping Rose Garden** is on the other side of the street.

The **Captain Kidde**, 108 Wapping High Street EC1W 2NE. Tel: 020 7480 5759. Samuel Smith. Real ale and food. Outdoor seating area and outstanding views. This characterful 19th century building, used as a coffee warehouse, only became a pub in the 1980s. Captain William Kidd (1655-1701) was a Scot who based himself initially in New York, where he was involved in the building of Trinity Church on Wall Street. His career in the Caribbean and Indian Ocean was less than successful, and he ended up being hanged at Execution Dock.

Samuel Smith is an idiosyncratic Yorkshire brewer founded in 1758 and still in family hands. They own a number of excellent pubs in London. All the beer they sell is made in their own brewery, and everything else comes from captive brands. Their real USP, however, is that you will never find muzak or television screens in any of their pubs. Oh, and producing a mobile phone or laptop is likely to get you thrown out. Excellent policy.

The exact location of **Execution Dock** is unknown, but sometimes said to be between Wapping New Stairs and King Henry's Stairs. Pirates were executed here. In the early days they were tied to stakes so they drowned as the tide came in; later they were hanged and left for the tide to submerge them three times. The bodies would hang in chains as a grisly warning to passing seafarers.

Wapping station marks the northern end of the Brunels' tunnel under the river, the first of its kind in the world. There is a full description in the South Bank section. After the station, take care not to miss an alleyway on the right back to the river. Follow the river as far as New Crane Stairs where you have to rejoin the road. Turn right into Wapping Wall and follow this along to:

The Prospect of Whitby, 57 Wapping Wall, E1W 3SH. Tel: 020 7481 1095. There has been a pub on this site since 1520. In those days, this was an extremely rough area, and the former name, The Devil's Tavern, reflects this. The present name comes from a ship, the *Prospect*, registered in Whitby in Yorkshire, once moored nearby. Why this ship, rather than the thousands of others should have been chosen is a mystery. As you enjoy your pint, you can reflect that Samuel Pepys, Charles Dickens, the artists Turner and Whistler, and various East End gangsters were here before you.

Beside The Prospect, **Pelican Stairs** lead to the river. Across the road from the pub are the red brick buildings of the **Wapping Hydraulic Power Station**. During the 19th century hydraulic power was a serious alternative to electricity. This station, built in 1890, provided the power for dock gates, factory machinery, lifts in buildings, and even the heavy fire curtains in theatres. Hydraulic power and surplus steam were carried all over central London and through the Tower Subway to the south bank. The tower conceals the accumulator cylinders that provide the pressure. The station continued in use until 1977.

Follow the path around modern developments to the entrance to **Shadwell Basin**. This was built in the 1850s to provide a wider entrance to London Docks and is the only part of those docks to maintain its original shape. After years of dereliction, the housing was put up in the late '80s. You can walk around the basin if you feel so inclined. Note the narrow channel leading to the footpath through Wapping Woods and back to Hermitage Basin via Tobacco Dock and Spirit Quay.

On the north side of the basin is the **Church of St Paul**. The present building replaced an older one, known as the Church of Sea Captains, in 1812. James Cook worshipped there, as did the father of Arthur Phillip, the first governor of New South Wales.

Otherwise, cross the bascule lift bridge and turn right into King Edward Memorial Park. Follow the diversion signs caused by Thames Tunnel works. The circular structure is a vent for the Rotherhithe traffic tunnel below your feet; on it is mounted the **Navigators Memorial** dedicated to the explorers of the Northern Seas, notably the search for a North-West Passage to the Orient.

Follow the riverfront along **Atlantic Wharf**; the central block here is named Mauretania Building, and others also bear the names of famous steamships. *Sirius*, for instance, was the first steamship to cross the Atlantic in 1838. You are forced inland at Keeper Wharf to join Narrow Street. Turn right before Old Sun Wharf to the riverside and follow that to the entrance to **Limehouse Basin**, originally called the **Regent's Canal Dock**. Its purpose was a transhipment point between seagoing ships and inland canal boats. Opened in 1820, the double locks on the north side connect with the Regent's Canal and thus the rest of Britain's inland waterway system.

The earlier **Limehouse Cut**, finished in 1770, connected the Lee Navigation with the River Thames here. The aim was to avoid the navigational hazards of Bow Creek, the mouth of the Lea at Trinity Buoy Wharf. The Cut now runs into the south-eastern corner of the dock.

Between 1852 and 1890, **Forrest's** built lifeboats here for the Royal National Lifeboat Institution and Scandinavian countries. They moved out to Wivenhoe on the River Colne in Essex; it was a Forrest boat that carried Conrad up the Congo, inspiring *The Heart of Darkness*.

Limehouse takes its name from the lime kilns first recorded in the 14th century. Chalk was brought from Kent to be burned for mortar. Many merchants and ship owners had fine houses here, and in the 17th century half of the population were seafarers. The prosperity of the area (for some, at least) is evidenced by the fine Hawksmoor Church of St Anne on Commercial Road.

Limehouse saw the first Chinese settling in London, mainly crew from the Blue Funnel Line. From 1857 to 1937 there was a **Stranger's Home** in West India Dock Road for Lascars. Lascars were seamen mainly from India but, by definition, anywhere east of the Cape of Good Hope. *Hindustani Without a Master*, a splendid little phrase book that accompanied John on many trips around India, usefully informs that *Gāvi istingi taiyār karo* is Laskar's Hindustani for "Stand by to clew up the topsails". The site of the Strangers' Home is now a block of flats. Continue along Narrow Street to:

The Grapes, 76 Narrow St, E14 8BP. Tel: 020 7987 4396. Free house. Real ale and food. No under-18s. View over the river. Ownership includes Sir Ian McKellen and Evgeny Lebedev. According to a blue plaque, its founding dates from 1583, but the present building is from the 1720s. Dickens used to visit his godfather in Limehouse and made The Grapes the model for the Six Jolly Fellowship Porters in *Our Mutual Friend*. Behind The Grapes, out in the river, is Anthony Gormley's *Another Time XVI* sculpture.

Opposite The Grapes is a sorry-looking little green with a **sculpture of a herring gull** by Jane Ackroyd. Beautiful on the wing maybe, but as attractive as a flying rat to its neighbours. From this side of the road you can appreciate the fine terrace of which The Grapes is part.

129

Past the entrance to Ropemakers Park turn down Dunbar Wharf. The path continues over the entrance to **Limekiln Dock** by a footbridge; this has to be a swing bridge to preserve the right of navigation. Limekiln Dock is a largely natural inlet, as suggested by its alternative name of Limekiln Creek; it takes its name from the lime kilns once situated on its south side. By 1900 the kilns had been replaced by two dry docks. Also, by this time, it was a serious health hazard due to sewage pollution. The fact that Black Ditch, another of London's underground rivers (for river read sewer), drained into it tells the story.

From here, it is a riverside walk to Canary Wharf Pier. You are now on the **Isle of Dogs**. The Isle of Dogs is usually taken to be the whole peninsula jutting south from Poplar down towards Greenwich. In 1800 the Isle of Dogs was a wind-swept and virtually unpopulated marshland. The need for more dock and industrial space saw rapid development in the 19th century.

The north of the peninsula enclosed the three large West India Docks; to the south were Millwall Docks, Millwall itself, and Cubitt Town. An old map (1703) shows the main part of the peninsula as the Hamlet of Popler (sic) and only the southernmost part as the Isle of Dogs. The **Isle of Dogs Canal** (or City Canal) was cut across the Isle of Dogs to provide a shortcut upriver. It never really worked and became part of the West India Docks as they expanded.

Closure of the docks and related businesses left the Isle pretty much derelict by 1980. A vigorous campaign by the government-backed London Docklands Development Corporation has seen Canary Wharf, centred on the West India Docks become a major business and financial centre. Similar residential development has made the Isle of Dogs a desirable place to live, not that this was achieved without much social turmoil. The origin of the Isle of Dogs name is obscure, sometimes said to derive from the royal kennels located there, otherwise derived from ducks or dykes.

Canary Riverside, the path, continues to Canary Wharf Pier. From there, it is a walk of roughly 300m to:

Museum of London Docklands, No 1, West India Quay, Hertsmere Road, E14 4AL. Tel: 020 7001 9844. Open every day, entry free. Does exactly what it says on the tin. First class.

South bank

Strictly speaking, the destination is Doubletree Docklands Pier; this is opposite Canary Wharf Pier on the north bank and connected by a ferry.

Bermondsey was first recorded as Vermundesei in AD708 and as Bermundesye in the Domesday Book. The name means Beormund's Island, the *-ei* or *-y* signifies island, as in the later *ait*. Bermondsey was probably not a true island, just an eminence in a marshy area. The land was drained and farmed by Cluniac monks from Bermondsey Abbey, which was founded in 1082.

From Tower Bridge, you enter an open space leading to **Shad Thames**; there is a lift from the downstream side of Tower Bridge. Shad Thames is a street that runs parallel to the Thames behind Butler's Wharf from Tower Bridge Road and bends around to meet Tooley Street. It gives its name to the area bounded by the river, Tower Bridge Road, Tooley Street, and St Saviour's Dock. This is a mixture of converted warehouses and newly built apartments. Pedestrian bridges cross between Butlers Wharf and the Cardamom Building; once for the transfer of goods, they now form balconies. The name may be a corruption of St John-at-Thames after a long-gone Templar church or may come from the shad, a fish once found in the Thames. Shad is the only member of the herring family to enter fresh water to spawn, and so rare now as to be protected.

Looking at the **Anchor Brewhouse** from Tower Bridge, you can see the chimney of the boiler house and, to the right, the hoist for barley and hops. This brewhouse, not to be confused with the larger Anchor Brewery, was bought in 1787 by John Courage. In 1955, Courage took over the Anchor Brewery to become probably the largest brewer in the country. This typified the mad sequences of company mergers and takeovers driven by egotists building empires too large to be managed effectively. The only real result was a lack of consumer choice and higher prices. Today, Courage is a mere brand; you may see a pump for Courage Director's Bitter in a pub, and that's it.

Horsleydown Lane runs south from Shad Thames, and on the left is:

Anchor Tap, 20a Horselydown Lane, SE1 2LN. Tel: 020 7403 4637. Sam Smith. Real ale and food. Originally the "tap" for the Anchor Brewery which once occupied the whole block behind it. Unspoiled traditional pub with many small rooms and an outside seating area.

Walking up Copper Row beside the Anchor Tap brings you to Tower Bridge Plaza. Note the reminder of the brewhouse's former ownership, the kind of wall painting now almost disappeared from London. Exiting by the fountain takes you back to Shad Thames.

Access to the river is through **Maggie Blake's Cause**, an alleyway named after the local activist who battled against the property interests that wanted to ban us plebs from the riverside.

The **Design Museum**, formerly based here in an old banana warehouse, has moved to (what is left of) the former Commonwealth Institution on Kensington High Street. Unfortunately, Paolozzi's remarkable *Head of Invention* sculpture went with it.

Butler's Wharf Chop House, 36e Shad Thames, SE1 2YE. Tel: 020 7403 3403. Chop houses were a Victorian phenomenon where the working man (and we mean men only) could get a good simple meal at a reasonable price, a bit like the French brasserie. The word chop implied any cut of meat suitable for grilling. This place has an enticing menu, but the prices will deter many.

Derek Jarman, the film director, stage designer, and gay activist, has a blue plaque awkwardly placed on the corner of Butlers Wharf and Curlew Street.

Down Maguire Street is the **Shad Thames Pumping Station**, built around 1905 to deal with stormwater surges. Before modernisation, this had six huge gas engines each driving a centrifugal pump capable of shifting 17,000 gallons (77,000 litres) per minute. All the machinery was made in Britain, see: www.glias.org.uk/glias/shad-thames-pumping-station. The station is being revamped as part of the Tideway Tunnel project to avoid raw sewage entering the river.

A stainless steel bridge crosses **St Saviour's Dock**, which takes its name from the patron saint of Bermondsey Abbey. The names of some of the wharves – China, Cinnamon, and Java – have a ring of the exotic East. Indeed, the sculpture *Exotic Cargo* just before the footbridge represents a split nutmeg.

Oliver Twist is set partly in this (then) poverty-stricken part of London. It was probably St Saviour's Dock that Bill Sykes fell into and drowned. The dock grew from the River Neckinger; Neckinger means neckerchief, and the Devil's Neckinger was the noose on the gallows here where river pirates were hanged. This is pretty much the point at which you escape tourist London for the next five miles to Greenwich.

The **Harpy Houseboat** on China Wharf Pier at the end of the footbridge sleeps ten in four cabins and is available for short lets. Contact: andrew@theharpy.com or on 07836 262222.

Downing Roads Pier is next with an interesting collection of old trading boats, Dutch botters, French peniches, and Thames sailing barges, all now in residential use. These moorings mirror the Hermitage Moorings over the river in Wapping. The 19th century **Reeds Wharf** warehouse at the end of the pier, was built to handle the grain trade with North America.

Thames sailing barges

Thames sailing barges were a common sight in the Thames estuary from the mid-17th century until around 1950. These maids of all work followed a similar pattern whilst varying considerably in size depending mainly on the nature of the cargo. A load of 40,000 Essex bricks weighing 120 tons could be brought right into central London.

The red treatment of the sails protects them from the sun's ultraviolet rays. The two foremost sails, the jib and staysail, were left in their natural colour as they were the only ones stowed below when not in use. The barges are flat-bottomed so they can take the ground for loading and unloading away from a wharf. To make up for the lack of a keel, they have a leeboard on either side, an idea borrowed from Dutch barges. Both masts can be lowered to clear bridges, though, unlike the Norfolk wherry, the mainmast is not counterbalanced, and this was no easy task. The barges can be handled by a crew of two, the largest vessels two can manage.

132

In the 1880s, it was reckoned that if (horse-drawn) traffic continued to grow at its present rate, London would soon be buried under many feet of horsh. The capital was saved by the barges carrying the horse dung out to the farms of Kent and Essex and returning with hay and root crops to continue the cycle. And then arrived the infernal combustion engine.

The first barge races took place in the 1860s and led to refinement of both the hull form and the rigging. Later, barges were fitted with an auxiliary engine, and a few were built with steel hulls rather than traditional timber. Either way, construction was heavy, which is why so many have survived, the oldest dating from 1887. Under sail alone, the barges were capable of 12 knots (14mph or 22km/hr). Their shallow draught, less than 3 feet (90cm), meant the barges could be taken up shallow rivers and estuaries.

Barges were regularly seen at St Katharine's Dock, but they seem to have been priced out. Regular races still take place, details at: https://sailingbargeassociation.co.uk/sailing-barge-championship/. You can organise a charter through the same site.

There is no riverside access here, so follow Bermondsey Wall West. Detour around the Chamber's Wharf construction site of the Tideway Tunnel on Chambers Street and pick up Bermondsey Wall East. The view when you regain the river is of Oliver's Wharf in Wapping; the prominent white building is the boatyard of the Metropolitan Police's Marine Policing Unit, formerly the River Division.

Cherry Garden Pier was a Port of London Authority lookout from where Tower Bridge could be warned of an approaching large ship. Pepys mentions in 1664 visiting the actual Cherry Garden, a cherry orchard and pleasure garden. The pier is thought to have been built around 1805, so it is quite possible that Turner painted the *The Fighting Temeraire tugged to her last Berth to be broken up* from here in 1838. *HMS Temeraire* was a 98-gun warship built at Chatham Dockyard and launched in 1798. Her name came from a French ship captured during the Battle of Lagos (1759) and means rash or imprudent. She achieved fame by coming to the aid of Nelson's beleaguered flagship H*MS Victory* at the Battle of Trafalgar in 1805 and capturing two French ships, hence the "Fighting" sobriquet. The painting was the favourite of both Turner himself and (by a poll in 2005) the British nation. It hangs in the National Gallery. Turner and his painting appear on the current Bank of England £20 note. More about *HMS Temeraire* when we get to Rotherhithe.

The sculpture group is **Dr Salter's Daydream**. Dr Alfred Salter (1873-1945) and his social reformer wife Ada rejected the opportunity of an easier life to live and work in one of the most deprived parts of London. They later moved into politics as well and, by all accounts, made a real difference. Their eight-year-old daughter Joyce died of scarlet fever (rubella) as a result of living in this unhealthy area. The cat on the river wall is Gorvin, Joyce's pet.

133

On the green opposite are the remains of **King Edward III's Manor House**. This moated building seems to have been more like a hunting lodge, used by the king mainly for hawking. The site was later used as a pottery and eventually incorporated into warehousing.

The Angel, 101 Bermondsey Wall East SE16 4NB. Tel: 020 7394 3214. Sam Smith. An ancient pub established in the 15th century by monks of Bermondsey Abbey. The pub was once frequented by Samuel Pepys and, one suspects, by smugglers who used a trapdoor in the floor. The notorious Judge Jeffreys is said to have watched pirates being executed at Execution Dock over the river from the terrace. Note that the address is sometimes given as 24 Rotherhithe Street. In the absence of real ale, try a Black and Tan, half and half stout and bitter. Before using that particular term, it is wise to ascertain whether the bartender is Irish.

Beside King's Stairs is what the locals refer to as **The Leaning Tower of Rotherhithe**. Standing alone, this was the end of a terrace of perhaps twelve rather shoddy tenements stretching downstream. It or its neighbours have been associated over the years with an arty crowd including Noel Coward, John Betjeman, the Mitford sisters, Anthony Armstrong-Jones, and Princess Margaret. The lean is less obvious here than from the other side of the river.

Over to the right is **King's Stairs Gardens**. Looking back you have a tremendous panorama from The Shard to the skyscrapers of the City. A stone pillar commemorating the Silver Jubilee of Queen Elizabeth II in 1977 was updated for the Diamond Jubilee in 2012. The Earl of Wessex (who has now succeeded his father as Duke of Edinburgh) is Edward, the late Queen's fourth and youngest child.

Around here, you cross the boundary between the ancient boroughs of Bermondsey and **Rotherhithe**, now amalgamated as Southwark. Like Bermondsey, Rotherhithe's riverside was lined by 19th century warehouses. The name is thought to derive from Anglo-Saxon, meaning 'landing place for cattle'. The alternative name, Redriff, is supposed to derive from an outcrop of red sandstone in the river, though this is disputed. Jonathan Swift (1667-1745) made Rotherhithe Lemuel Gulliver's birthplace. Rotherhithe has a Gulliver Street, not to mention a Defoe Close, but no acknowledgement of Swift. **Rotherhithe Street** is the longest in London, and, on and off, we follow it for all its 1½ miles (2.4km).

Hope (Sufferance) Wharf, Rotherhithe Street. In the 18th century, trade increased so much that the official wharves were overwhelmed. Hence, the growth of unofficial but tolerated wharves with "Sufferance" added to their names.

Christopher Jones, master and part-owner of the *Mayflower*, is buried in the churchyard of **St Mary the Virgin**, St Marychurch Street, off Rotherhithe Street. The memorial to Jones in the churchyard depicts him as St Christopher looking back to the Old World whilst the child looks forward to the New. Inside the church, one of the most unusual of all church memorial plaques is to Prince Le Boo of the Palau Islands in Oceania. Two bishop's chairs and the altar in the Lady Chapel are made from timbers from *HMS Temeraire*, and the four pillars are ship's masts. The church is normally locked; see the website https://www.stmary-rotherhithe.org/ for pictures of the fine interior.

The *Mayflower* itself was broken up after Jones's death. The process of shipbreaking and the recycling of materials was already well established by this time. Some of the timbers are said to have been used to build the Mayflower Barn in the Buckinghamshire village of Jordans.

Rotherhithe Picture Research Gallery, 82 St Marychurch Street, SE16 4HZ, is opposite the church. The gallery is in Grice's Granary, connected by an overhead gangway to Grice's Wharf on the riverside, still just visible. The interior is well worth seeing, constructed from old ship's timbers and knees (the parts joining the ship's frames to the deck beams). This is a free access resource; you can furkle around to your heart's content. A lot more goes on here, see www.sandsfilms.co.uk/

Rotherhithe Free School, 70 St Marychurch St, SE16 4HZ. The plaque between the two children in their bluecoat uniforms details the school's founding. The **Watch House** is the lower building to the right; it was used by a constable or watchman, especially on the alert for grave robbers supplying the nearby Guys Hospital. The Watch House was closed in 1829 when the Metropolitan Police was formed. It is now a little cafe, and you can take your refreshments into the quiet churchyard garden beside it.

The Mayflower, 117 Rotherhithe Street, SE16 4NF. Tel: 020 7237 4088. Black Dog Pub Company. Real ale and food. Claims to be the oldest pub on the river; it was first built in 1550 (as The Shippe) and much rebuilt since. The pub was known as the Spread Eagle and Crown until the last century when it was renamed as the Mayflower. Spectacular interior, and outside seating. Dog friendly. The *Mayflower*, which took the Pilgrim Fathers to America, was moored here before setting sail in July 1620 for Plymouth and the New World. Apart from everything else, ithe pub claims to be the only one in Britain licensed to sell postage stamps, a convenience for seamen as the nearest post office was a mile away. And then it trumped that by selling American ones as well! Note the milestone, you are two miles from London Bridge.

Brunel Museum, Railway Avenue, SE16 4LF. Sir Marc Isambard Brunel excavated the first tunnels under the Thames in 1843 with his son Isambard Kingdom Brunel as resident engineer. These were the first tunnels under a navigable river anywhere in the world. The work had been started earlier by a Cornish miner known as 'The Mole' and taken over by Richard Trevithick, the steam engine man. On both occasions, the river broke through. Despite the invention of a tunnelling shield, the Brunels suffered five inundations; the first nearly claimed Isambard's life, as evidenced by a plaque in the grounds. Work then stalled for seven years due to lack of funds. There were many casualties, as much from the already badly polluted river and bad air as from drowning.

The tunnels were used initially as footways but converted in 1871 for the Underground. A steam pumping engine was installed here to keep the tunnels dry.

This Engine House and the adjacent access shaft are now a museum dedicated to the two Brunels. The machinery has gone, but there is still a lot of interest. The shaft has been capped over the tunnels, and you can hear the trains rumbling beneath your feet. Water is still pumped up through the shaft, and it also provides ventilation for the tunnels. See https://thebrunelmuseum.com/ for opening hours.

The statue group in Cumberland Wharf Garden called **Sunshine Weekly – The Pilgrim's Pocket** depicts a Pilgrim and child, not to mention a bull terrier. It will repay close scrutiny; some nice little visual jokes.

The Ventilation Shaft No2 of the **Rotherhithe Road Tunnel**, which emerges nearby, was completed in 1908 and now hides behind horrible orange-painted railings. From the garden by the shaft, the small white building you see over the river is the Prospect of Whitby pub.

The red lift bridge crosses Albion Channel, which was the main entrance to the **Surrey Commercial Docks**, a complex of mainly small and interconnected docks and timber ponds. Except Greenland Dock, these were all built in the 19th century and covered 460 acres (1.9km²). The docks suited the smaller ships of the time but even so, getting a ship to its berth must have been a slow and laborious process. The docks closed in 1970 and have been largely filled in for redevelopment.

From the far side of the lift bridge, you have the choice of turning left to follow the river or right for a little **detour**. Right, and follow the channel to Surrey Water, formerly Surrey Basin. Bear left, and from the south-east corner, Dock Hill Avenue takes you straight to **Stave Hill Viewpoint**. This artificial hillock 30ft (9m) high was constructed in 1985 from surplus rubble after the docks had been filled in. This may not sound very high, but in a flat place like Rotherhithe, the views are surprisingly extensive. The orientation table on top by Michael Rizzello depicts Surrey Docks in their heyday. Stave Hill Ecology Park is to the north-east, and then east and south is Russia Dock Woodland, leading to Greenland Dock, a pleasantly quiet and bosky walk.

Returning to the riverside path, turn left from the end of the bridge and you come to:

Old Salt Quay, 163 Rotherhithe Street, SE16 5QU. Tel: 020 7394 7108. Greene King. Real ale and food. A modern building on the site of an old granary, its warehouse-style suits the setting. An extensive terrace overlooks Dinorwic Wharf, which took its name from the Dinorwic slate quarries in Wales.

Past the pub across the river, two large red and yellow cranes denote the Thames Tunnel site at King Edward Memorial Park in Wapping.

The irregularly shaped sheet of water you walk around at Bellamy's Wharf was once more extensive and included a dry dock. Also here was Beatson's Yard where the Temeraire was dismantled. Shipbreaking may be a dirty business, but "where there's muck, there's brass [money]". John Beatson paid £5530 (call that £250,000 today) for the Temeraire, and recycled much of the 5000 oak trees and other materials that went into making her. We can't find a profit figure, but the

136

family could afford to send Beatson's younger brother to Eton. John's brother William, a fine draughtsman, made a drawing of the ship as it arrived, now in the National Maritime Museum in Greenwich.

The only interruption to riverside walking from here is at **Globe Wharf**, a vast granary and rice warehouse dating from the 1880s and now apartments. The flats towards the end of Sovereign Crescent replace an oil refinery.

Cross the channel to **Lavender Pond Nature Park**, a 2½ acre (1.0ha) wildlife sanctuary. The 1920s building across the channel was a pump house to maintain the water level in the docks and timber ponds. It was at one time Rotherhithe Heritage Museum. The pond behind the pump house is all that is left of the large Lavender Pond, one of the main ponds for the wet storage of timber from the Baltic. The sanctuary is said to be open on Tuesday and Thursday. At other times, the woodland area is locked; the pond behind the pump house is accessible, but you may well wonder why you bothered. A sign in the pond informs that it is destocked regularly, the result of thoughtless behaviour by coarse fishermen.

Pageant stairs take their name from the old Pageant Wharf to the east, though the origin of the name is unknown. The **obelisk** to the east is modern and lines up with the central axis of the Canary Wharf development over the river.

You have to turn inland at **Horn Stairs**, just before Canada Wharf, and this marks **Cuckold's Point**. Horns were the mark of the cuckold, and for many years, a pair adorned a post just offshore. The story starts with King John (1199-1216) who, as you will know from the *Adventures of Robin Hood* or *1066 and All That,* was a "Bad King". He was also, by contemporary accounts, a lusty chap. One of his conquests was the pretty wife of a miller in Charlton (between Greenwich and Woolwich). To assuage the miller's feelings, the king made him a grant of land at the point and licenced an annual fair. A riotous rabble would assemble at Cuckold's Point and process to Charlton. Cross-dressing was the norm, and both men and women wore horns. The sight of ordinary people having a bit of licentious fun was too much for the authorities, and the fair was frequently banned for long periods. The axe finally fell in 1870, though a bowdlerised event still takes place in Charlton. Cuckold's Point, as it was ca1750, is the subject of a painting by Samuel Scott (1702-1772) in Tate Britain.

Blacksmith's Arms, 257 Rotherhithe St, SE16 5EJ. Tel: 020 7231 8838. Fuller's. Real ale and food. Pleasant patio (loomed over by Columbia Wharf) and pavement seating.

Just down Rotherhithe Street is **Nelson Dock House**, a fine Georgian house of 1730-40. This is the last remaining shipbuilders' house in Rotherhithe. It was not always lucky for its occupants, as in 1803 one committed suicide by self-defenestration. The house was used as offices and has recently been converted back to a dwelling house, recently on the market for a mere £4,750,000.

A little further brings you to the vehicle ramp and steps up to the Doubletree Hilton Hotel and the ferry to Canary Wharf pier. The hotel consists of the converted Columbia Wharf buildings plus two blocks originally built as flats, all surrounding the two **Nelson Docks**. To the left, as you approach the hotel, is the dry dock-cum-slipway; to the right, the permanently flooded dry dock. More details on the docks in the next section.

Getting there. The nearest tube station to Tower Bridge is Tower Hill. Tower Millennium Pier (Thames Clippers) is upstream of the bridge on the north bank.

Walking. Canary Wharf Pier to the Greenwich Foot Tunnel is 2½ miles (4km) on the north bank. Doubletree Docklands Pier to Greenwich Foot Tunnel is 2¾ miles (4.4km) on the south bank.

28. CANARY WHARF PIER TO THE GREENWICH TUNNEL

North bank

The progressive closure of London's docks from the 1960s onwards freed up a huge amount of space in previously unfashionable (and cheap) areas. This was also the part of London most badly damaged by German bombing during the Blitz. Advantage was taken to build a new, vibrant business area and all the necessary supporting services.

Canary Wharf takes its name from a warehouse in the West India Dock that used to handle fruit imported from the Canary Islands. That replaced an older warehouse where, in 1933, over three million litres of rum went up in smoke.

From Canary Wharf Pier head south with the river on your right. The riverside south of here became heavily industrialised in the 19th century with all sorts of chemical and metal-bashing plants. A footbridge takes you over the filled-in entrance to the **South Dock** of West India Docks. You then reach West India Pier, once used for landing goods and briefly as a river bus stop; this is at the end of Cuba Street. At Bullivant's Wharf look out for a plaque commemorating the casualties of a single bomb hit in 1941.

Sir John McDougall Gardens have been extensively revamped in recent years. They are named after a local politician (1844-1917) who was a member of the flour milling family. Part of the area was once a tank farm for storing paraffin and other oils.

At Arnhem Wharf turn inland to West Ferry Road; this was formerly known as the Deptford and Greenwich Ferry Road from the ferries that once connected the two banks of this long unbridged section of the river. Can't really complain about the detour as the riverside is blocked by one of the few companies still doing business there.

Millwall Slipway was the entrance, now filled in, to Millwall Outer Dock. On the south side is part of the mechanism for operating the lock gates. The Docklands Sailing and Watersports Centre is over the road and provides a good view of the docks. Two cranes remain. Millwall is the south-western part of the Isle of Dogs. The docks closed in 1980.

Walk on past a charming terrace of workers' cottages to **St Paul's Presbyterian Church**. This building of 1859 is often described as a pastiche of Pisa Cathedral, though the facade is composed of three colours of brick and white stone rather than marble. The roof is supported, not by iron girders as one might expect, but by laminated wood arches, quite in vogue at that time. The building cost £750 and was intended for the use of Scots attracted to the local shipyards. It is now an arts centre.

Trudge, trudge, trudge, until eventually you regain the river through Mast House Terrace and Ferguson Close (opposite St Edmund's School). You look across to the remains of Deptford Royal Dockyard and Convoys Wharf including the six arches of Payne's Paper Wharf.

By **Masthouse Pier** (Thames Clipper service) are the remains of John Scott Russell's shipbuilding yard. Brunel's huge steamship, the *SS Great Eastern*, was built here on a slipway parallel to the river. The ship was laid down in 1854 and completed four years later despite her reluctance to launch down the slipway. Intended for a non-stop trade run to Australia she used a combination of steam-powered paddles and screw propeller as well as sails. At 692ft (211m) long she remained the largest ship built for the next fifty years. After many financial tribulations she found her métier as a cable layer, notably the first transatlantic telegraph cable. She was broken up in 1889-90 at New Ferry on the Mersey. One of her topmasts still does duty as a flagpole on the Kop at Liverpool's football ground.

There is an interesting row of old buildings to the right as you face the slip. At 262 West Ferry Road, E14 3TR on an old gateway leading to Burrell's Wharf is a blue plaque to the *Great Eastern*. The adjacent building still bears the name of J. Scott Russell. It would make sense for the plaque to be on the riverside.

The path continues as Blasker Walk to **Burrell's Wharf Square**. The fine industrial buildings here, which succeeded shipbuilding, housed a dye works until the 1980s. The site has been converted for residential use. From here, you get your first sight of the masts of the Cutty Sark, then the Royal Hospital, and the four chimneys of Greenwich Power Station. This is hardly an exciting walk; no pubs, nowhere to sit, nowhere to pee. Just lots and lots of mediocre modern architecture.

The Ferry House, 26 Ferry Street, E14 3DT. Tel: 020 7537 7813. Real ale, food sometimes, best to check first. The present building dates from 1722 and claims to be the oldest pub on the Isle of Dogs. A traditional locals' pub, increasingly rare in this area.

Island Gardens was opened in 1895 as a much-needed open space. Wren reckoned that this was the best place to enjoy his work on the Royal Hospital and Queen's House. Canaletto, who spent ten years in England a little after Wren's time, painted the scene in ca1750. The painting, in Canaletto's photographic style, can be seen in Tate Britain. If you are heading to Greenwich by DLR, it is much better to leave the train at Island Gardens station, enjoy the view, and then take the foot tunnel under the river.

South bank

This walk starts at Doubletree Docklands Pier, opposite Canary Wharf Pier and connected by a ferry.

The two **Nelson Docks** are the only remnant of shipbuilding in Rotherhithe. A shipyard was probably in existence here towards the end of the 17th century and was used by different companies over the years. Forty-six warships and fifty-four East Indiamen (large armed merchant ships) were built here over the years. Around the 1820s, the docks were used by one Nelson Wake, though it is unclear why his name has become attached to them. From the mid-19th century, the docks were used mainly for ship repair. The last user was Mills and Knight (1890-1960), whose name is still visible on the entrance to the dry dock. Plans for modernisation failed, and the docks finally closed in 1968.

Assuming you have arrived on the ferry, exit through the hotel reception area, and bear right to see the northern of the two **docks**. This was converted in the 19th century to a slipway for ship repair. The ship was positioned in a cradle running on the rails and hauled out of the water by a hydraulic ram. The rack in the centre held the cradle while the ram was retracted for another pull. The machinery formed a short-lived museum; https://www.geograph.org.uk/-photo/2569484.

The two modern parts of the hotel (originally built as flats) are on either side of the southern dry dock. The dock was closed by a wrought iron caisson that could be pumped dry to float it out of the way. The caisson is now fixed and inaccessible, and the dock permanently flooded. The landward end of the dock collapsed in 1881 and had to be reinforced by massive wrought iron plates. Fountains aerate the water, and there is a floating duck house. Continue around the hotel block to reach the river.

The riverside is **Durand's Wharf**, originally a timber yard like most of the wharves along here, now a park. The concrete structure in the corner of the park is a ventilation shaft for the Jubilee Line.

Surrey Docks Farm is a working farm in miniature that has been running since 1975. The farm is a charity that gives city centre children a chance to see farming in action. The café is beside the riverside path, and the outdoor seating is by a small fragrant garden. Entry is free Monday to Saturday. If the gates are closed, you will have to detour down Rotherhithe Street.

The riverside path is currently blocked at New Caledonian Wharf (there is no sign to warn you that the way ahead is blocked), so turn inland at Imperial Wharf, down Commercial Pier Wharf [road], and turn left into Odessa Street. Where Odessa Street swings right, go straight ahead (unless you are aiming for the pub), then left into Randall Rents to regain the river. Hopefully, the council will get its act together and force the landowners to reopen the path.

Ship and Whale, 2 Gulliver St, SE16 7LT. Tel: 07 594 655 816. Shepherd Neame. Real ale and food (Sunday roast and daily specials). Beer garden. Pub dates from 1767, though rebuilt in 1880 (the year Ned Kelly was hanged in Melbourne).

140

King Frederick IX Tower is named for Frederick IX, King of Denmark (1947-1972). It overlooks Odessa Wharf, once a dock, with a new footbridge across its entrance.

The **Curlicue** sculpture by William Pye (b.1938) was installed here in 1989. Like *Zemran* on the South Bank, this is fun, but we still prefer his water sculptures.

Greenland Dock was initially known as Howland Great Wet Dock after John Howland, a local landowner. Work started in 1695, and until the late 19th century, it was London's largest dock. At the time, the surrounding area was a wind-swept marsh, and trees had to be planted down both sides as a wind-break. The dock covered 10 acres (4.0ha) and could hold 150 large merchantmen. The dock changed hands in 1763 and became a base for whaling ships, hence the later name of Greenland Dock.

North Dock, known as **Norway Dock**, and **South Dock** were later additions. A small part of the Norway Dock still exists and, whilst it never had direct access to the river, it used to connect with the rest of Surrey Docks. The South Dock was as long as Greenland Dock, but is now reduced to half its former size. Old maps and illustrations show dry docks on either side of the entrance to Greenland Dock.

Approaching the entrance of Greenland Dock, note the two hydraulic windlasses for warping ships into the dock. The slots in the top are for staves in case of power failure. Also here are the hydraulic rams to operate the lock gates, though this entrance is now permanently closed. The original **footbridge** was a swing bridge, and you can still see the gap in the middle. Walking down to the modern bridge will give you a better view of the dock. The buildings here are particularly awful, quite unworthy of the location.

From Greenland Pier (Thames Clipper), you look across to the southern entrance (now blocked) of Millwall Docks. Past the pier, you cross the entrance to the South Dock with the modernised lock gates, now the only access to the complex. Note how the lock gates point towards one another to cope with the tides, unlike the locks on a river or canal. Most of the boats here are residential rather than sea-going.

Continue down the river. The **boundary stone** between Rotherhithe and Deptford parishes, once the boundary between Surrey and Kent, is set in a section of old wall. A little further down, you get your first glimpse of the masts of the Cutty Sark, and then a row of old cannons indicates that you are entering the former Royal Navy dockyard.

Circumsphere, an artwork by Chris Marshall and Steve Lewis, was mounted on a disused dolphin (mooring point) in 1998. At that time, red discs on some of the rods traced the route of Sir Francis Drake's circumnavigation voyage in 1577-1580. Disguised as a voyage of exploration, this was a highly profitable raid on Spanish ships and territories in the Americas; it would lead indirectly to the launching of the Spanish Armada eight years later. To get to the point, Drake

141

sailed the *Golden Hinde* from Plymouth, his point of return, to Deptford and was knighted on board by Queen Elizabeth I.

Deptford, Chaucer's *Depeford*, takes its name from the ford near the mouth of the Ravensbourne River. After Aragon Gardens and the 29-floor Aragon Tower comes **Deptford Strand**. The two matching brick buildings were part of the victualling yard, rum stores to be precise. The Royal Navy continued to issue a daily rum ration to its crews until 1970. The ration was 1/8 pint (71ml) of 56.4 ABV rum diluted with water to prevent storage for a later binge. The ration was known as the *tot* or *grog* and replaced the gallon of beer they had previously been entitled to. The term *grog* came from Admiral Edward Vernon (1684-1757), known as Old Grog because of the grogram cloak he habitually wore. The first building carries a **plaque** about Drake's achievements, placed by the Drake Navigators Guild of California in 1981 on the 400th anniversary of his voyage. Both buildings were converted into flats around 1960 as part of the Pepys Estate project, a job made no easier by the 3ft (0.9m) thick walls.

A massive chunk of land here, now known as **Convoys Wharf** and mostly inaccessible at present, was once home to several establishments vital to Britain's security and wealth.

The **Royal Dockyard**, popularly known as the King's Yard, was established by Henry VIII in 1513. Queen Elizabeth I knighted Sir Francis Drake on the *Golden Hinde*, Captain Cook's ships were prepared here for his voyages of discovery in the Pacific, and Pepys was a regular visitor on navy business. The hangar-like building is **Olympia Warehouse**, constructed in 1845 over two slipways to provide undercover shipbuilding space. Altogether, at least 450 ships were built here before silting of the river, and the increasing size of vessels due to the move from wooden hulls to iron ones forced a move.

The dockyard closed in 1869, and in the same year, the movement inland of imported live cattle was banned to control disease. The Corporation of London bought the 23-acre (9.3ha) site to establish the **Foreign Cattle Market** and built slaughterhouses where the beasts were landed. The pens could hold 4000 cattle and 12,000 sheep. The business continued until 1914, when the War Department took it over to ship horses to the Western Front.

In 1650, part of the Sayes Court estate called the **Red House** was acquired to replace offices on Tower Hill controlling the provisioning of warships. Initially run by private contractors, in 1742 it was bought by the Admiralty to form the depot that supplied everything a Royal Navy warship needed before putting to sea. It became the **Royal Victoria Victualling Yard** in 1858 and closed in 1961. Much of its land was taken for the social housing of the Pepys Estate, a few old houses remaining.

The **East India Company**, established in 1600, was granted the monopoly of trade with India and the whole Orient. The company had a dockyard here between 1607 and 1644; after that date, it reverted to chartering speculatively built ships from other shipbuilders. There is a good picture here:

142

https://www.rmg.co.uk/collections/objects/rmgc-object-13352. **Trinity House**, the lighthouse authority for England and Wales, had its first base here, having been founded by Henry VIII in 1514.

In 1661, Deptford saw the first yacht race held in the British Isles, such events having originated a little earlier in the Netherlands. On this occasion, Charles II (1660-1685) in *Katherine* took on his brother James, Duke of York, in *Anne* for a race to Gravesend and back. These were pretty hefty boats, but within a century, yachts not unlike today's had evolved.

So much for history, development and conservation in the old dockyard now means a hefty detour away from the river. Follow the signposts through the two parts of Pepys Park. The first part of the park is better than the average city park, having a wildflower meadow and unregimented greenery. A National Cycle Network sign helpfully tells you that it is 110 miles to Oxford and 115 to Dover.

You reach Grove Street; a detour to the right for 400m or so will take you to the **Main Gate** (1788) of the Victualling Yard. The fine building inside, **The Colonnade**, was houses and offices. The cannon bollards here are the real thing.

To follow the path, turn left along Grove Street and left again into Sayes Court Park, all that remains of the **Sayes Court** house and estate of over 60 acres (25ha). John Evelyn (1620-1706), a polymath though best remembered these days as a diarist, came into possession of the estate by marriage and made many improvements. Pepys, a shrewd observer, was much impressed by the sophistication of both house and garden. When Evelyn moved to his estate in Surrey, he let the house to a naval officer. He, in turn, sublet to Peter the Great of Russia at the beginning of 1698 whilst Peter was learning about shipbuilding in the nearby dockyard. Peter and his entourage, a rough lot by all accounts, pretty well wrecked the place, and it never really recovered. Exit the park into the cobbled Sayes Court Street. Pass Dacca Street (now known as Dhaka), the capital of Bangladesh, and before that a major port for the East India Company, and turn left into Prince Street.

Dog and Bell, 116 Prince St, SE8 3JD. Tel: 020 8692 5664. Free house. Real ale and food. Dog-friendly, outdoor seating. A lifesaver on a warm day. Note the rather unPC wall advertisement for Guinness; the Irish brewer was famous for its clever advertising from the 1930s onwards.

Turn left into Watergate Street, and, as the name implies, this will return you to the river. The watergate here was for the **Master Shipwright's House**, a fine Queen Anne house dating from 1708, unfortunately all but invisible.

The six white arches, so prominent from the other bank, fronted **Payne's Paper Wharf** and, before that a boiler-making company. Parts for *HMS Warrior*, built by the Thames Ironworks and Shipbuilding Company on the other side of the river at Blackwall, were made here. *Warrior*, commissioned in 1861, was the Royal Navy's first iron-hulled warship; now restored, she is moored in Portsmouth. The building is now House of Phoenix, a China-funded creative and cultural centre. The terrace is a good viewpoint.

After a short distance, it's away from the river again down Wharf Street and then Borthwick Street until you can resume the river. The **Ahoy Centre** offers rowing, sailing, and powerboat training (https://ahoy.org.uk/). The extensive coal wharves in the river are a legacy of the Deptford power stations once situated here. They are long gone, but the four chimneys of Greenwich power station are visible from the viewpoint at the mouth of Ravensbourne River. Also visible is one of the domes of Greenwich Observatory with the red time ball that drops every day at 1300. Excavations at the power station site in 2022 revealed remains of the East India Company's dockyard and almshouses endowed by Trinity House.

The **Peter the Great Memorial** marks the tercentenary of Peter's visit. The sculptor is Chermiakin, who borrowed the out-of-scale small head from the style of Russian icons. The small figure, assumed to be one of the court dwarfs, has also been identified as a caricature of Evelyn. A gift of the Russian people, it was unveiled in 2001 by the Russian ambassador and the Duke of Kent (who is related to Nicholas II, the last tsar, murdered by the Bolsheviks). Vladimir Putin visited in 2003 in the company of Prince Andrew. Peter it was, surprised at the number of lawyers in London, who said, "Lawyers! I have but two in my dominions, and I believe that I shall hang one of them the moment I get home!"

The memorial was damaged when we passed, apparently attempted robbery rather than a political statement. Notwithstanding that, the hoarding was well decorated with Ukrainian flags.

Away from the river, Deptford boasts two interesting churches:

St Paul's Church, Mary Ann Gardens, SE8 3DP is a baroque masterpiece (1730) by Thomas Archer, who did St John's, Smith Square. It is considered by many the finest parish church in London. Amongst the memorials inside is one to Margaret Hawtrees, a midwife who "brought into this world more than three thousand lives".

Church of St Nicholas, Deptford Green/Stowage, SE8 3DQ. The tower is medieval, though the church was rebuilt in 1697 and again after bomb damage. The skull and crossbones on the gateposts are repeated at the top of the pillars inside. Grinling Gibbons, who lived locally and was promoted by Evelyn, did the wood carvings of the valley of the dry bones. There is a memorial to Christopher Marlowe and, somewhere outside, his unmarked grave. Most unusually for an English church, the graveyard also has a charnel house.

The **Ravensbourne River** rises at Caesar's Well in Kent and flows 11 miles (17km) to join the Thames, this lower part known as Deptford Creek. Crossing Deptford Creek swing bridge, the promontory here was previously occupied by a gasworks. Turn left to follow the riverside into Greenwich passing:

Marryat Gardens are named after Captain Frederick Marryat RN (1792-1848). A naval officer of distinction, he pioneered the naval fiction genre later taken up so well by C.S. Forester and Patrick O'Brien. Latterly, he wrote mainly for children; his two best-known titles are *Mr Midshipman Easy* and *Children of* *the New Forest*. His connection with Greenwich was through the navy, and he also set his book *Poor Jack* here.

The Oystercatcher, 7 Victoria Parade, SE10 9FR. Tel: 0208 161 8225. Restaurant with interesting menus. Pub prices downstairs and on the riverside terrace, more expensive upstairs.

The Sail Loft, 11 Victoria Parade, SE10 9FR . Tel: 020 8222 9310. Fullers. Real ale and food. Modern place right on the river. Outdoor seating and fine views along the river.

Greenwich Foot Tunnel

The entrance to the Greenwich Foot Tunnel that connects the Isle of Dogs to Greenwich is a glass-topped rotunda. The tunnel was built in 1897-1902 to replace the old ferry and mainly for the convenience of dockers who lived in Greenwich. In 1940 a bomb hit above the Isle of Dogs end caused the tunnel to collapse and flood. A temporary repair using iron collars was soon effected. Eighty years later they are still there, and why this part of the tunnel is smaller than the rest. Blue plaques, presumably the only ones under the river, tell the story.

If you are not going to walk the North Bank, it is well worth taking the tunnel to Island Gardens for the view of Greenwich. Canaletto's take on this view can be seen here: https://www.tate.org.uk/art/artworks/canaletto-a-view-of-greenwich-from-the-river-l01926. Be warned that there are many steps at each end of the tunnel, and that the lifts are unreliable; latest info:

https://www.royalgreenwich.gov.uk/info/200259/transport_and_travel/693/foot_tunnel

Getting there. The easiest (and most scenic) way to Canary Wharf Pier. is by Thames Clipper. Otherwise DLR, Jubilee, and Elizabeth Line Canary Wharf stations are a 10-minute walk from Canary Wharf Pier. A regular ferry (Thames Clipper RB4) runs between Canary Wharf Pier and Doubletree Docklands Pier.

Walking. Greenwich Foot Tunnel to Trinity Buoy Wharf is 2¾ miles (4.5km) on the north bank. Greenwich Foot Tunnel to the Thames Barrier is 4¼ miles (7km) on the south bank; you can break this stage at North Greenwich Underground station, where the London Cable Car crosses the path.

29. GREENWICH

Greenwich appears in the Domesday Book as Greenuiz. Opinions vary as to the origin of the name; the *wich* part may come from the Latin *vicus*, a word with many meanings, including dwelling, dairy farm, or village. Alternatively, it may be Anglo-Saxon for Green Port. It is known that the Danish fleet moored here in 1011 during a raid in which Alphege, Archbishop of Canterbury, was murdered.

The first palace was built here in 1426, and Greenwich subsequently became a royal residence, a particular favourite of Henry VIII (1509-1547).

The riverfront

The obvious attraction here is **The Cutty Sark Clipper Ship**, King William Walk, Greenwich, SE10 9HT. Tel: 020 8858 4422. Full details of advance booking and so on: www.rmg.co.uk/cuttysark

The *Cutty Sark* was built in 1869 by Scott & Linton of Dumbarton on the River Clyde west of Glasgow. Interestingly, despite her Scottish origin and ownership, she never returned to Scotland. She is of composite construction with iron frames and wood planking, American rock elm below the waterline and Indian teak above. The underwater section was protected by a sheathing of Muntz metal, an alloy of copper and zinc that was more durable than plain copper. The lean lines and light weight were designed for speed as the intended cargo was China tea, a seasonal cargo that had to be brought to Europe as fast as possible. Her load was 600t (590 tons) of tea worth over £270,000, pushing £20 million today. She could carry 32,000 square feet (near enough 3000m²) of sail, giving her a speed of 17.5 knots (32.4km/h; 20.1mph). For comparison, a modern container ship travels at 20-25 knots. The *Cutty Sark* was one of the last of her kind; improvements in steam power and the opening of the Suez Canal meant that she had a short career in the tea trade.

By 1895, the *Cutty Sark* was engaged in the Australian wool trade. She was recorded as getting from London Docks to Sydney (via the Cape of Good Hope) in 80 days and back (via the formidable Cape Horn) in 73 days. Remember that this is with nothing but the wind as a source of power. She continued as a cargo ship, under the Portuguese flag, until 1922, and then returned to Britain as a cadet training ship. She was restored in 1954 and brought to this specially constructed dry berth.

Ships are designed to have their weight supported by water. Keeping wooden and other old ships in dry dock results in their weight gradually deforming the hull. Rebuilding after the otherwise disastrous fire in 2007 allowed steel reinforcement of the keel and ribs to be inserted.

The modern enclosure, put up after restoration, won the Carbuncle Cup in 2012. You can visit the whole ship and even climb the rigging (on Saturdays only; book on the website). Apart from the ship's history, there is a fabulous collection of figureheads from merchant vessels.

Have a look at the Cutty Sark's own figurehead. The witch Nannie's slightly immodest dress is a cutty sark, a short shirt or nightdress in old Scots dialect. In her left hand, she grasps the tail of a fleeing horse and rider. Read Burns' poem *Tam O'Shanter* for the full story.

At one time, *Gipsy Moth IV* was on display on the waterfront; this is a traditionally built Camper & Nicholson yacht used by Sir Francis Chichester for his single-handed circumnavigation of the world in 1966/67. Queen Elizabeth II knighted Chichester on his return using the same sword Elizabeth I had used to knight Sir Francis Drake after his circumnavigation. Before the Second World War, Chichester had specialised in air navigation and named his yachts after his de Havilland Gipsy Moth light aircraft. After restoration in 2004, *Gipsy Moth IV* was owned by a charity that provided sailing experience to youngsters; now, in private hands, she is a regular on the classic sail scene. Dire Straits sang *Single Handed Sailor*, and Gypsy Moth IV was, for a time, illustrated inside the back cover of British passports.

At weekends, there is a good selection of street food stalls alongside the Cutty Sark. Now, we have the choice of heading into town or to the old naval college.

Greenwich Palace and the Old Royal Naval College

Entrance to the palace campus is past the bow of the Cutty Sark and opposite the Thames Clipper ticket office.

To the right is an **obelisk** to men and officers of the Royal Navy who lost their lives in New Zealand during 1863/64. A series of unrelated campaigns between the Maoris and settlers dragged on between 1845 and 1872 (following wars between the Maoris themselves) and are sometimes referred to as the New Zealand Wars. This memorial seems to relate to the Tauranga Campaign. Among those commemorated is Captain J.F.C. Hamilton after whom the city in North island is named. Hamilton's statue was removed from the city in 2020.

Sir Walter Raleigh (ca1552-1618), whose statue is here, was an adventurer, poet, scholar, and herbalist. The story of his laying his cloak over a puddle to protect the queen's shoes may or may not be true, but he was a favourite of Elizabeth I and named his colony in America, Virginia, after her. Implicated, fairly or not, in an early plot against James I, he was sentenced to death and locked up in the Tower of London. Released for one last adventure, he failed to bring home the promised gold and was executed in 1618.

The **Visitor Centre** (entry free) has a lot of information about Greenwich and the old palace. A black and gold plaque in the gallery on Tudor Greenwich commemorates **John Blanke**, a trumpeter who arrived in England in 1501 in the entourage of Catherine of Aragon, the first wife of Henry VIII. His name seems to have been a rather witless play on his skin colour. Mentions of black musicians at the royal courts of Europe go back to the 12th century. Tickets for the Painted Hall are sold here, £15 but valid for a year. Outside the side door here is:

The Old Brewery, The Pepys Building, Greenwich SE10 9LW. Tel: 020 3437 2222. Youngs. Real ale and food. Charming old building with outside seating area.

The first **Greenwich Palace** was built in 1426 by the Duke of Gloucester, brother of Henry V. It became a favourite of the Tudor monarchs, and many of the significant events of their reigns took place here. Anne Boleyn came unstuck, Raleigh laid his cloak over a puddle for Elizabeth I, and that monarch signed the death warrant of Mary, Queen of Scots. The Parliamentarians used the palace as a biscuit factory and held Dutch prisoners of war there. Charles II, after the Restoration, had great plans and made a start on what is now King William Court, then the money ran out.

The only remaining part of the old palace is the **Queen's House**. James I had Inigo Jones design this in 1616 for his wife, Queen Anne of Denmark, though it was not finished properly until later in the century. Only the central pavilion is original. The two wings and the connecting colonnades were added in 1809 to commemorate the Battle of Trafalgar. A few years earlier, the Hospital had bought the house as a school for sailors' orphans, all 950 of them. The school moved out to Suffolk in 1933, and the buildings were restored to house the National Maritime Museum, which opened in 1937.

The Queen's House represents a great step forward in British domestic architecture. After recent restoration, it displays a fine art collection; well worth a visit even if the Maritime Museum is of no interest to you.

The Chelsea Hospital (hospital in this sense means retirement home) had been founded for old and disabled soldiers in 1689; a similar need existed for sailors, especially following the Dutch Wars. The moving force was Queen Mary II (1689-1694), and she saw to it that the view from Queen's House to the river was left open. Wren was the lead architect, giving his work for free; Hawksmoor, Vanbrugh, and others played major roles. Much of the finance came from fines on smugglers and the expropriated estates of pirates like Captain Kidd and aristos who had picked the wrong side in the two Jacobite Rebellions.

The **Royal Hospital for Seamen at Greenwich** took the form of four "courts", actually quadrangles around open courtyards. In King William Court, the south-western block, is the Great Hall (Thornhill's "Painted Hall"). Nelson's body lay in state here before being taken upriver for interment at St Paul's Cathedral. A replica of the statue on the column about a quarter in size is in a side room. Sir James Thornhill (1675-1734) spent 20 years painting the ceilings. The main painting is not, as one may expect, of a great naval victory; it is an allegory of Protestantism's permanent triumph over Catholicism, hence a united Britain's stability and prosperity. It is worth remembering that this period includes the Act of Union of 1707, bringing England (and Wales) and Scotland under one crown. Thornhill also painted the dome of St Paul's Cathedral and worked at Chatsworth House in Derbyshire.

The hospital opened to its first 42 inmates in 1705 and, at its peak, accommodated 3000 men. In later years, the behaviour of the pensioners left something to be desired, and an 1865 Act of Parliament offered them generous terms to move elsewhere. A further Act in 1869 disestablished the hospital altogether.

In the undercroft (fancy word for basement) under the Painted Hall is the **Painted Hall Cafe**. Tel: 020 8269 4747. Email: boxoffice@ornc.org in advance for their special afternoon tea. This undercroft is older than the building above, and also houses a Victorian skittles alley.

The **Chapel of St Peter & St Paul** occupies part of the Queen Mary Court, the south-eastern block. It was designed by Wren but not completed until 1742. Its present appearance is later as the result of a major fire. The memorials in the porch include one to Franklin and the crews of his two ships *Erebus* and *Terror* (see Ballot Memorial below). The wrecks of the two ships were found in 2014 and 2016.

The two courts nearer the river are occupied by Greenwich University, including part of the Trinity Laban Conservatoire of Music and Dance. They are not open to the public, though you often catch interesting snatches of music. As mentioned elsewhere, the best view of the palace, as captured by Canaletto, is from across the river. Walk through the tunnel, as described in the previous section. The southern side is closed by the Queen's House, now the National Maritime Museum.

The town centre

From the open space by the Cutty Sark, head to the right of:

The Gipsy Moth, 60 Greenwich Church Street, SE10 9BL. Tel: 020 8858 0786. Mitchells & Butlers. Real ale and food. Pleasant covered patio.

The historic centre of Greenwich town is a block bounded by Greenwich Church Street, Nelson Road, King William Walk, and College Approach. Despite the awful traffic, it is worth walking around to enjoy the fine Georgian and Victorian architecture. Go anti-clockwise to see:

Church of St Alfege, Greenwich High Road, SE10 9BJ, is named after an Archbishop of Canterbury murdered here by marauding Danes in 1012. The present church, by Hawksmoor, dates from 1712-18, with the tower added in 1730. The church had to be rebuilt after bomb damage in the Second World War and has been renovated lately. The west end of the church overlooks a quiet close with seating. The coat of arms on the organ loft is that of Queen Anne (1714-1727), and the extra lion and unicorn on the corners of the loft have fishtails, a tribute to maritime Greenwich. Note the little carved panel on the steps to the pulpit, one of the few surviving pieces of Grinling Gibbons' work.

General Wolfe (see below) is buried in the family vault; there is a painting of his death and the entry in the burials register. Windows commemorate Henry VIII and 'Chinese' Gordon, who were both christened here; Tallis was once the organist. There are frequent music events, often drawing on the talent at Trinity-Laban Conservatoire.

Goddards at Greenwich, 22 King William Walk SE10 9HU. Tel: 020 8305 9612. A traditional London pie and mash shop; a nourishing meal and a cuppa char for under a fiver! Jellied eels too! The business was established in 1890, though this Johnny-come-lately shop has been running for only 50 years.

149

Admiral Hardy, 7 College Approach, SE10 9HY. Tel: 020 8293 9535. Mosaic Pubs. Real ale and food (and Sunday lunch). Access also from market and seating there. Hotel rooms. Sir Thomas Hardy (1769-1839) was flag captain to Nelson at the Battle of Trafalgar in 1805, commanding *HMS Victory*.

This brings you to the **covered market** entrance. Greenwich's evolution as a tourist venue has seen the demise of many small interesting shops; to an extent the covered market in the centre of the block makes up for this. The market is open every day 1000-1730, and offers crafts, street food, antiques, fashion, and bric-a-brac, though sellers and merchandise vary from day to day.

Coach & Horses, Greenwich Market, SE10 9HZ. Tel: 020 8293 0880. Young's. Real ale and food. Traditional pub within the market.

Naval & Maritime Books, 66 Royal Hill, SE10 8RT. Tel: 020 8692 1794. Open 1000-1700 Thursday to Saturday. Traditional specialist bookshop. More details: info@navalandmaritimebooks.com

The **Monument for a Dead Parrot** stands in the garden in front of Devonport House. Though not immediately identifiable as a Norwegian Blue, it has, beyond all doubt, shuffled off this mortal coil and gone to meet its Maker.

From here, walk up King William Walk to the entrance to the:

National Maritime Museum, Romney Road, Greenwich, SE10 9NF. Tel: 020 8858 4422. Website www.rmg.co.uk for all information. The Museum is housed in the wings of the Queen's House, as already described. The Museum is open daily 1000-1700, last entry 1615. Entry is free though a charge is made for special exhibitions.

Britain's power and prosperity were always based on the sea, and the Museum tells that story. The Royal Navy's ability to project that power enabled it to close down the slave trade between West Africa and the Americas during the early 19th century. Later, in two World Wars, it defeated the German submarines that tried to starve Britain into submission. Highlights of the Museum include the coat Nelson wore at Trafalgar and Turner's huge *Battle of Trafalgar*, a later work than that in Tate Britain on the same subject.

The Museum has a library, photo archive, and research facilities, much of which can now be accessed online. The Prince Philip Maritime Collections Centre at Kidbroke (SE3 9QS) houses a vast reserve collection. See the website for information on visits.

The park and observatory

Entrance to the park is just past that to the Museum. From the gate head left over to the double line of trees and follow the path up to the **statue of Wolfe**. General James Wolfe (1727-1759) was a British hero of the Seven Years War (1756-1763) that was fought in Europe, the Americas, and in India and The Philippines. Wolfe's part in this was the capture of Quebec and other French possessions in Canada, though at the cost of his own life and that of the French commander Montcalm.

The immediate results of this war, among others, were a British Canada and gains in the Caribbean. Longer term, it laid the foundations of a British Raj in India (rather than a French one) and worldwide British naval and colonial dominance. More ominously, it saw the rise of Prussian power in Europe.

The statue, a gift of the Canadian people, is relatively recent (1930) and was unveiled by the Marquis de Montcalm whilst descendants of Wolfe were also present. The statue is at the highest point of Greenwich Park, and there are **stunning views** of the city from the terrace around it.

The **Royal Observatory, Greenwich** stands on the site of Greenwich Castle, a hunting lodge favoured by Henry VIII for his many dalliances. The observatory was commissioned by Charles II in 1676 and designed by Sir Christopher Wren, himself an astronomer among his other talents. The main building is known as Flamsteed House after the first Astronomer Royal, John Flamsteed (1646-1719). The main purpose of the observatory was to devise means for accurate maritime navigation. The two main aspects of this were to establish a universal meridian and a standard mean time. A meridian is an imaginary line on a map or globe joining the North and South Poles. The Greenwich Meridian at 0° is the baseline from which the others are numbered: 180° east and 180° west.

In the same way, Greenwich Mean Time (GMT) is the standard by which other time zones around the world are set. One might assume that the sun would be over the meridian at midday, but not exactly. Because of the erratic spin of Earth, it in fact varies by up to 16 minutes either way; the *Mean* in GMT averages this out.

On one of the domes is the **red time ball** that is raised to the top of its mast and then released at precisely 1300hrs. 1300hrs because at mid-day the staff were preoccupied with important observations. When the ball was installed in 1833, it was the first visual time signal for mariners. In pre-radio days, and long before radio beam or GPS navigation, you needed to know the time accurately to work out your position by the sun and stars.

The **clock** by the entrance with a twenty-four-hour face was installed in 1852; it is a slave originally worked by electrical impulses from the master clock within. One of the first systems of its kind, it also controls the time ball. The signal was distributed to London Bridge and other major cities in the United Kingdom, and in 1866, the first Atlantic telegraph cable allowed Harvard University to be connected. A modern quartz system has replaced the earlier mechanism; note that the clock always shows Greenwich Mean Time regardless of daylight saving during the summer.

The main work of the observatory was gradually moved to Herstmonceux Castle in Sussex from 1946 because the air pollution in London was so bad at the time. Since 1990 it has been located in Cambridge. Some work is still done here, but the site is mainly a museum and a successful tourist attraction. The planetarium was added in 2007.

Head south from the Wolfe statue and, past the Pavilion Cafe, turn right towards the wall of the park. A small gate gives access to:

Macartney House, Chesterfield Walk, SE10 8HJ, the home of James Wolfe. Despite its blue plaque the house is now flats and of no other interest.

Continuing south inside the park, the **Rose Garden** has more than 100 varieties and quiet seating. This is overlooked by the **Ranger's House** (SE10 8QX), English Heritage, 1100-1600 April-October, free for members otherwise £10. Fine Georgian house with 700 works of art ranging from Renaissance paintings to the porcelain of the Wernher Collection.

Follow the perimeter wall as it turns to the east. Somewhere here (we missed it) is **Queen Caroline's Bath**. She was the estranged wife of George IV (1820-1830), and this is all that remains of her home, Montague House. Pass Blackheath Gate (toilets here and bus service) and continue through **The Wilderness** to the gate on Maze Hill road. Outside here to the south are the **Greenwich Park War Memorial** and the **Andrew Gibb Memorial**. The latter is a shelter and clock tower over a (non-working) drinking fountain endowed by a local alderman. The open space is Blackheath, once notorious for its highwaymen.

Adjoining this gate is the **Flower Garden**. From the gate, you can either head back towards The Observatory or follow inside the wall downhill. At the bottom are a children's play area, a boating lake, the **Millennium Sundial**, and easy access to Maze Hill mainline station.

Some way out is **East Greenwich Pleasaunce**, a quiet public park. Construction in 1875 of an extension of the London and Greenwich Railway (first built in 1836) disturbed the Royal Hospital's burial ground. The remains of 3,000 people, some of them Trafalgar veterans, were reburied here. There are some interesting memorials, but probably of interest only to naval historians. The park is a short walk from Westcombe station on the Greenwich-Woolwich railway line.

Getting there. Thames Clippers run to Greenwich Pier, easily the nicest way to get there. Island Gardens station on the DLR is near the far end of the foot tunnel; get off here for the fine view of Greenwich Palace and then walk through the tunnel. Cutty Sark DLR station is nearest the riverfront and town centre. Greenwich DLR is combined with Greenwich overground station (trains from Cannon Street and London Bridge) but a bit further out.

If the DLR and Clippers are impossible (as they can be late on summer weekends), walk up Creek Road past the Cutty Sark DLR station; the 188 bus runs into central London via Waterloo mainline and tube stations to Holborn and Russell Square.

30. GREENWICH FOOT TUNNEL TO TRINITY BUOY WHARF

The northern end of the **Greenwich Foot Tunnel** marks the end of the official Thames Path with its familiar acorn waymarks. The local authority, Tower Hamlets, has waymarked (with a Thames sailing barge motif) a path for another 2½ miles (4km) along the river to East India Dock, and then we can walk a little further to Trinity Buoy Wharf.

Island Gardens. From here, you look across to the Greenwich Hospital buildings. To the left is the Power Station with its four chimneys and a disused coal unloading stage in the river. Just to the right of the power station are the Trinity Hospital almshouses. Leave the gardens on the riverside path.

Newcastle Public Draw Dock dates from 1840; a plaque on the north side of the dock records its being re-erected in 1882. This area was developed in the 1840s by Thomas Cubitt (1788-1855) and became known as Cubitt Town. His brothers William and Lewis collaborated with him in developing large swathes of London and many of its public buildings.

Waterman's Arms, 1 Glenaffric Avenue E14 3BW. Built in 1853 by Cubitt as part of their development of this bleak area. This pub was once owned by Daniel Farson an early and provocative presenter for Associated-Rediffusion when commercial television started in Britain in 1955. He intended here to recreate the days of music hall, but the venture failed, and he retreated to Devon to pursue his career as a prolific and outspoken writer, including a biography of his friend Francis Bacon, the artist. Farson's recreation of a Victorian pub seems to have disappeared in recent modernisation, presumably to suit the new locals.

Turn inland at **Cubitt's Wharf**, a warehouse now restored as apartments, and take a shortcut through the car park to regain the river. Back on the riverside look across to the few remaining industrial buildings and working yards, and your first sight of the O2 arena.

Dudgeon's Wharf is named after two Scottish brothers who built ships here, including blockade runners for the Confederates during the American Civil War. They went bust when an ironclad they had built for the Brazilian Navy refused to progress down the launching slip. The site was later occupied by a tank farm, and that went bust, too. Demolition of the derelict site in 1969 caused one of the tanks to explode killing five London firemen and a demolition worker. Two plaques on the riverside obelisks remember the casualties.

Sextant Avenue appears to delineate the dock that existed here. Noise along here is from the aggregates plant across the river. The long pier at what is now called **Millennium Wharf** once carried a travelling crane.

Rather a surprise is a neat sandy beach overlooked by apartments named after the Dutch painters Vermeer, Van Gogh, and Frans Hals. The gardens and modern buildings behind here are called London Yards, another reminder of shipbuilding.

A little further along and to the left is the 25-storey Kelson House, built in the 1960s as part of the **Samuda Estate.** The Samuda brothers, Sephardic Jews, started building marine engines in 1843 at a site on the River Lea. Needing more space they moved to the Isle of Dogs in 1852 and branched out into shipbuilding, mercantile and naval, and atmospheric railways. Apart from the Royal Navy, they built ships for the navies of Peru, Egypt, Prussia, Ottoman Turkey, Argentina, and Brazil. The royal yacht that Samuda built in 1865 for the Khedive of Egypt, variously *El Mahrousa* or *El Horreya*, is still in service as the president's yacht, though much altered.

Jacob lost his life in 1844 in an explosion on a ship he was testing; he is described on his tombstone as "the first Jewish engineer". Noted for his command of detail, his brother Joseph was instrumental in forming the Institute of Naval Architects and went on to a distinguished political career. The business was wound up after Joseph's death in 1885.

Samuda built the ironclad battleship *Fuso* for the Imperial Japanese Navy in the 1870s. Admiral Togo, the victor of the Battle of Tsushima (1905), spent time here as part of his seven years studying in Britain as a naval cadet. Yarrow Shipbuilders, still building warships for the Royal Navy, was also established here before moving to Clydeside for extra space.

The **Isle of Dogs Pumping Station** is a fun bit of PoMo (postmodern) architecture put up in 1988. With hints at Egyptian and Tibetan temples it was described by the Prince of Wales (now King Charles III) as 'witty and amusing'. Better appreciated from the other bank, its function is to pump excess stormwater into the river.

Pierhead Lock apartments, in startling white, hint at a cross between Bauhaus and a 30s ocean liner. **Pierhead Lock** itself and the lifting bridge mark the entrance to the South Dock of the West India Dock complex, now mostly taken over by the Canary Wharf development. Until the building of South Dock, opened in 1860 sixty years after the two to the north, this was the entrance to the City Canal, the unsuccessful shortcut across the Isle of Dogs.

Two historic vessels, the *Massey Shaw* fireboat (1935) and the steam tug *Portwey* (1927), are moored a short distance inside the dock; a bit outside the scope of this book, but they can be visited. Cross the lifting bridge and look out for Coldharbour (a lane) on the right.

The Gun, 27 Coldharbour, E14 9NS. Tel: 020 7519 0075. Fullers. Real ale and food. Famous old pub with a cosy sitting room and outdoor terrace overlooking the river. Probably takes its name from the local foundries that produced guns for the Royal Navy. Frequented in its time by Nelson (who met Lady Hamilton in an upper room) and smugglers.

Further down Coldharbour, a nice mix of old and new, is Nelson House, though there is no real evidence that Nelson lived or even stayed here. Rejoin the main road and you come to **Blackwall Basin Entrance Lock**. This was the entrance to the two northern West India Docks and also Poplar Dock. Walk down towards the river past the windlasses for hauling ships through, and you get a panoramic 270° view of the river, not to mention a sweet whiff of garbage from the transshipment dock. Cross the lock gates, a couple of dispirited ducks were becalmed in the pondweed, and rejoin the main road. The really keen can cross the road and walk along the south side of the lock to see the graving dock.

Blackwall Yard was a complex of docks, dry docks, and shipbuilding slipways. Occupied by different companies over the years, the yard was founded sometime in the 16th century, and was sometimes described as the oldest private business in Britain. It was particularly famous in the days of sail for its 'Blackwall frigates', faster and handier than competing ships. Building major ships became more difficult as sizes increased in the 19th century, and the emphasis shifted to repairing. Many smaller vessels, such as Thames barges and lighters, and minesweepers during the First World War, continued to be built here. During the Second World War warships were repaired and landing craft built. Latterly, work switched to oil rigs and so on. The yard finally closed in 1987.

And this is where walking gets a bit confusing because of the huge amount of redevelopment going on. Turn off the main road (Prestons Road) into Yabsley Street; note the PLA's radar watching the river. At the roundabout, you may be able to go straight on into Fairmount Avenue and regain the river, but this was all closed off when we visited. Instead walk down Blackwall Way/Baffin Way (confusing) past a Majestic Wine Warehouse and the ventilation tower of the Blackwall Tunnel until you reach East India DLR station. The area behind hoardings on your right is the actual Blackwall Yard with what is left of its dock.

At last, turn right into John Smith Mews, then Newport Avenue, and down **Prime Meridian Walk**, an avenue of trees, to **The Compass** and the riverside.

Virginia Quay was formerly Brunswick Wharf; the street behind is Jamestown Way, and the area behind that was a dock and, after 1945, a power station. In 1606, fourteen years before the *Mayflower* and the Pilgrim fathers, three tiny sailing ships left this wharf bound for America. After a hard four-month voyage they arrived at Cape Henry, then sailed up the James River to found Jamestown and the Commonwealth of Virginia, a title in use to this day. This was the first permanent British settlement in the Americas. The Virginia General Assembly, founded in 1619, is the oldest representative legislature in North America.

The **Settlers' Memorial** commemorates those pioneers – and has a tale of its own to tell. The main plaque was installed on a now demolished building and transferred to a new memorial, topped by a bronze mermaid in 1951. This was vandalised, and the mermaid stolen. Barratts, the developers, built this new memorial in 1999 and commissioned the astrolabe, a navigational device, to replace the mermaid. Flagstaffs carry the Union Flag, the Stars and Stripes, and the flag of the Commonwealth of Virginia.

The **East India Docks** had their origin in Brunswick Dock, excavated in the 18th century and used for shipbuilding and repairs. The East India Company took it over in 1803 and constructed two major docks to handle their trade with India, the East Indies, and China. These were low-bulk/high-value goods, and the docks had to be protected by high walls. Pilferage was a major problem in all docks around the world, and was one of the major drivers towards containerisation.

Brunswick Dock became the Dock Basin which led to two new docks. The smaller (Export) dock was behind the Settlers' Memorial, and the larger (Import) dock to the north of that. The docks were severely damaged in the Second World War. Import Dock was pumped dry and used to construct the concrete caissons for the Mulberry prefabricated harbour that supplied the Allied armies after D-Day. Some can still be seen at Arromanches in Normandy. Import Dock had limited use after the war before being closed in 1967. The Export Dock was so badly damaged that it was filled in and built over. A fragment of the Import Dock remains and is visible from East India DLR station.

Cross the lock gates and walk up to the **Millennium Beacon**. What you see now is the remnant of the **Dock Basin** (the old Brunswick Dock). Funny to think that one of the busiest docks in the world is now a nature reserve and reed bed with moorhens paddling over the mud. Even, if you are very lucky, a kingfisher. Bear right to follow the path to Orchard Place.

This is the end of the official North Bank paths. So, let's do a little exploring off our own bat, though it's a shame we didn't do it twenty years ago. The writer of the official guide describes **Trinity Buoy Wharf** as "one of London's best-kept secrets" and "a little oasis of calm". Not any more, it ain't. It is a huge building site and, for the moment at least, it is hard to find anything. It is, however, a lively and constantly changing arts centre, well worth the short walk, so turn right into Orchard Place.

Before the builders moved in, the remoteness of this area made it a dumping ground for smelly and noisy industries, and its isolation led to a remarkable degree of inbreeding. The wall painting 'Mather's Whale Oil Extraction' indicates one of these businesses, founded by James Mather in 1784. Much as one may disapprove of whaling, it has to be remembered that whale oil kept everybody's oil lamps (and the street lights in London) alight until the development of refined mineral oil. Paint and varnish were also based on whale oil, and soap base was supplied to Lever. Mather's eventually evolved into the processing of vegetable oils which continued into the 21st century.

Walking down Orchard Place, the **dry dock** on the right has been filled in and a long wooden seat constructed. New trees have been planted, and you may even catch a game of *boules*.

Trinity House's buoy-making works was based at the end of Orchard Place from 1803 to 1988, and light vessels were also maintained here. The miniature **Lighthouse** (open weekends only) was used for testing new equipment and training lighthouse keepers. The glass was made locally by the Thames Plate Glass Company. Within the lighthouse is **Long Player,** an electronic music installation initiated at the Millennium and designed to play without repetition for the next 1000 years. The lighthouse was used by **Faraday** for his experiments into the effect of electromagnetism on light transmission. The wooden hut by the lighthouse is a memorial to his work, but don't disturb the cat!

Container City, a seemingly higgledy-plggledy pile of brightly coloured shipping containers, provides workspace for artists and other creative people.

Trinity Buoy Quay is home to three historic vessels: ***Knocker White*** (ex-*Cairnrock*) (Tug 1924). Built by T. van Duivendijk in Lekkerkerk, Netherlands for Harrison Lighterage in London Docks. Originally steam-powered, she now has diesel engines. She was bought in 1960 by W. E. White & Sons of Rotherhithe and given the nickname of one of the family. She was rescued from scrapping in 1982.

Suncrest (ex-Sun XXIII). This tug, visibly more modern than *Knocker White*, was built by Philip & Sons of Dartmouth in Devon in 1961. Her 1000hp Mirrlees diesel engine made her too expensive to run for the lighter loads as Thames traffic declined, and she was retired in 1968.

Light vessel №95 was built, like *Suncrest* and most other light vessels, by Philip & Sons. Light vessels or light ships were used to warn mariners of a hazard where it was either impossible to build a lighthouse or where the hazard moved around, like a sandbank. The first lightship was placed in the Thames estuary in 1734, and the first radioed SOS was sent by a light vessel in 1899. Manned lightships like this were replaced by unmanned floats in the 1970s and 80s. №95 was moored at different times off the coasts of Kent and Norfolk; she is now a recording studio.

As an alternative to returning along Orchard Place, follow the River Lea by going down the alley between Curtis House and Faraday School. The land over the river was home to the Thames Ironworks & Shipbuilding Company between 1857 and 1912. *HMS Warrior* (restored and afloat in Portsmouth), the world's first iron warship was launched there in 1860. The peninsula across the Lea from there (to the left as you look at it) is the part originally known as Goodluck Hope, a name dating from the 14th century.

Getting there. East India station on the DLR is a short walk past East India Dock. The ferry that ran on weekdays between North Greenwich Pier (O2) and Trinity Buoy Wharf is suspended; see https://www.trinitybuoywharf.com/visit. Alternatively, take the DLR from East India round to Royal Victoria and then the cable car to North Greenwich for the Jubilee Line. On the way the DLR passes over a peninsula in the River Lea that is now the Bow Creek Ecology Park.

31. GREENWICH TO THE THAMES BARRIER

We resume the riverside walk at the foot tunnel rotunda. The red granite obelisk is a memorial to **Joseph-René Bellot** (1826-1853), an officer in the French navy who disappeared in the Canadian Arctic while part of a search party for Sir John Franklin. Franklin (1786-1847) had died, with all 134 of his men, while trying to force a way through the North-West Passage, a supposed link between the Atlantic and Pacific Oceans. The wrecks of Franklin's two ships were found recently, *HMS Erebus* in 2014 and *HMS Terror* in 2016; both well preserved in the icy water.

Walk through the splendid wrought iron gates to the statue of **George II** (1727-1760) by J.M. Rysbrack, the Flemish sculptor; this was installed in the central vista in 1737. The Queen's House, now part of the National Maritime Museum, is directly behind it. The 11 ton block of marble was liberated from a French ship captured in the Mediterranean. The Latin puffs for George, which include quotations from the Roman poets Horace and Virgil, evoked unpleasant memories of double Latin lessons sixty years ago. George II, incidentally, was the man who described an English summer as "three fine days and a thunderstorm". A plaque in the pavement in front of the statue was unveiled in 1983 on the 450th anniversary of the birth of Queen Elizabeth I.

The beach along here looks suitable for a try at mudlarking, but read the warning in the back of this book before venturing onto any Thames beach. The statue of **Admiral Lord Nelson** by Lesley Pover (b.1950) was installed on the bicentenary of his death at the Battle of Trafalgar in 1805.

Trafalgar Tavern, Park Row SE19 9NW. Built in 1837 (the year of Queen Victoria's accession) on the site of the George Inn. Grand interior. Frequented by Dickens – he set the wedding breakfast in *Our Mutual Friend* here – and purveyor of political whitebait dinners. And whitebait (tiddlers to the uninitiated) is still on the menu. Turn left into Crane Street and look up as you pass the Trafalgar; there are the badges of many Royal Navy ships and an impressive display of flower baskets.

The Yacht, 5 Crane Street SE10 9NP. Tel: 020 8858 0175. Greene King. Real ale and food. Ancient pub, formerly the Waterman's Arms and, before that, the Barley Mow. Rebuilt after being destroyed by bombing in the Second World War. Prints and charts inside. The meridian runs through the building.

The walk becomes Highbridge Wharf and leads to **Trinity Hospital**, a group of almshouses first built in 1614 and rebuilt in its present Gothic style in 1812. Managed by the Mercers' Company, the two buildings provide 41 retirement apartments for established Greenwich residents. Opposite the entrance to the hospital is a plaque and high tide markers.

Greenwich Power Station was built between 1902 and 1910 to burn coal brought up the river to the jetty standing on cast iron Doric pillars. Its main function was to provide power for London Transport trolleybuses, trams, and the Underground. Steam turbines replaced the reciprocating compound steam engines in 1922. A further update to a Rolls-Royce Avon gas turbine (same as in the Hawker Hunter jet fighter) saw it able to run on either oil or natural gas; the elegant chimneys were much reduced at the same time. Controlled from Lots Road, it is still a standby for the tube network and can be up to full output in three minutes. **Plaques** on the wall, the work of Amanda Hinge, tell the tale of a lad who takes his dog for a riverside walk.

The path leads into the pleasant open space of Anchor Iron Wharf. **The Anchor** sculpture by Wendy Taylor (b.1945) was installed in 2000 to mark the area's regeneration. Beside it is the **C.A. Robinson & Co. foundation stone**. Robinson's was a scrap metal company founded in 1835 and operating here from 1905 until their lease expired in 1985. Their main line of business was breaking old barges and lighters and loading the scrap onto ships moored alongside. The alleyway between mountains of scrap metal was the setting for a murder in the 1961 novel *The Worm of Death* (Day-Lewis as Nicholas Blake) and for a Bananarama pop video. Also here is the spoof **blue plaque** "Gordon of Greenwich loved here". Good views across to the Isle of Dogs and Canary Wharf.

Cutty Sark Tavern, Ballast Quay SE10 9PD. Tel: 020 8858 3146. Young's. Real ale and food. There has been an inn on this site for over 500 years. The present building dates from 1804 and was known as the Union until 1954, when the *Cutty Sark* was installed in Greenwich. Well worth the walk.

A private garden on the left has a **foot and mouth memorial** in the form of a goat, suggesting that the cure may have been worse than the disease. This refers to the 2001 outbreak in England that led to the slaughter of more than six million farm animals; the cause was probably the illegal importation of infected meat.

Manilla Walk takes its name from a rope walk (a long shed for twining rope) on Enderby Wharf, as confirmed by old maps. The names of some of the apartment blocks – Bowline, Lariat, and Gordian – reflect this.

Enderby House, Enderby House, 23 Telegraph Avenue, SE10 0TH. Tel: 0208 897 6755. Young's. Real ale and food. Combination of a modern building and a 19th century house. Riverside terrace, many different rooms and rooftop terrace. Dog friendly. General "Chinese" Gordon spent his last night in England here.

The narrow and rather grubby path after the Enderby is made miserable by cyclists, though pleasantly shaded by self-seeded willows, buddleia, and even pampas grass.

Brew by Numbers Taproom, Southern Warehouse, Morden Wharf Rd, London SE10 0NU. A modern brewery in a Victorian warehouse that is part of a local regeneration project. The brewery tap is open Wed 1700-2200, Thur & Fri 1500-2200, Sat 1200-2200, Sun 1200-2000. There is an adjacent pizzeria.

Walk around the back of **Thames Craft Dry Docking Services**, a ship repair yard with what appears to be a floating dock. Continue along the bleak Hanson's deep water terminal aggregate plant. Just past the golf driving range, you look across to the temple-like pumping station, followed by a pleasing range of small-scale buildings, some old, some new. The Greenwich Meridian clips the riverside along here, and it is planned to build the futuristic **Aluna**, the world's largest moon and tide clock here. See https://alunatime.org/

And so to the **Millennium Dome** or **O2 Arena**, as it is now known. The Dome was a government vanity project paid for, needless to say, by taxpayers. It was supposed to showcase the brave New Britain that their New political party wanted us to believe they were creating. Amazingly, it was under budget, and not so amazingly, it was mentally unchallenging (at least, compared with its predecessor, the Dome of Discovery) and attracted half the predicted audience. The big black hole in the west side is due to an existing ventilation shaft for the Blackwall Road Tunnel and seems to symbolise the whole thing.

Eventually, it was sold for far less than it was worth and has now become a successful music venue. You can walk over the top, all 52m (170ft) of it. Details at: up-at-the-o2.london-tickets.co.uk Hardly Sydney Harbour Bridge, but a bit of fun all the same.

When you come to a drawdock or slipway, make a short detour down Drawdock Road for a view of what appears to be an electricity pylon speared into the ground; *A Bullet from a Shooting Star* is by Alex Chinneck (b.1984). This is the last item in **The Line**, a sculpture trail that starts on the other side of the river in the former Olympic Park.

The *Millennium Milepost (Here 24,859)* stands on the Greenwich meridian and indicates the distance (in miles) around the earth and back here. Devised by Jon Thomson and Alison Craighead. See https://theminimuseum.tumblr.com

A Slice of Reality is a section of the former sand dredger *Arco Trent*. The ship was built in Appledore in Devon (like the *Golden Hinde* replica); she was 60m (200ft) long, weighed 800 tons, and could lift 480m³ of sand or gravel. You see a section through the bridge, crew accommodation, and engine room created by Richard Wilson (b.1953) and installed here in 2000.

From the tip of the peninsula you look across to the Virginia Memorial. This is about as close as you get to the O2 and the walkway over it.

Tribe and Tribulation is a sound installation made mainly from the recovered timbers of Ghanaian fishing boats by Serge Attukwei Clottey. The wave sounds, which some will like more than others, were recorded at four points on the coast of Ghana, one of them Tema, a city on the same meridian but only 5° north of the Equator.

As you round the corner here, you get your first view of the IFS Cloud cable car, still often referred to as the Emirates cable car after its original sponsor. On the other side is Trinity Buoy Wharf and its miniature lighthouse.

The next sculpture is *Liberty Grip* by Garry Hume, part of The Line, said to be London's first dedicated public art walk. John (dirty mind) found this rather suggestive and called it the Singapore Grip.

And back to apartment blocks, the first relieved by Damien Hirst's *The Mermaid*. **North Greenwich Pier** is served by Thames Clipper. Just after the pier is Antony Gormley's *Quantum Cloud;* a celebration of the millennium, the sculpture grew from a conversation with a physicist and explores the relationship between the body, its composition, and the world around it. This is the last item in The Line south of the river.

The **IFS Cloud Cable Car** that you pass under here is described below in the section *Woolwich Free Ferry to the London Cable Car*. Near the cable car terminal on this bank is North Greenwich Underground station. Below your feet, as the cable cars pass over, are the two bores being excavated for the Silvertown traffic tunnel. The verges along here are eco-friendly, planted with marram grass and other things attractive to wildlife.

You are now walking on Mudlarks Boulevard. Over on the pier is Damien Hirst's **Hydra and Kali** sculpture, an odd mixture of Hindu and Greek iconography. Originally shown at the Venice Biennale in 2017, the theme was an ancient hoard of statuary recovered from a shipwreck. The Hydra, in Greek mythology, was a nine-headed snake-like water monster. Kali is a destructive aspect of the god Shiva, properly depicted with four or ten arms rather than the six here. Kali, in particular, was a lot more attractive in its original bronze form before the marine accretions were splattered all over it. The next pier is Mudlarks Pier.

The **Polar Sundial** was created by the Royal Engineers ("The Sappers") of the British Army to celebrate the Millennium. It has two scales to show both Greenwich Mean Time and British Summer Time.

The **Greenwich Peninsula Ecology Park** is a freshwater wetland, a recreation of the marshes that once occurred naturally along much of the Thames estuary. Boardwalks give access to viewpoints and hides for bird watching. Entry free, no dogs.

Walk around the back of Greenwich Yacht Club past uglier than usual apartments. Regain the river and pass under two lofty conveyors that carry ballast from ships at the deep water moorings. There is now some fairly grim road walking along Riverside (road) – which isn't – and this brings you to:

Anchor & Hope, Riverside, SE7 7SS. Tel: 020 8858 0382. Real ale and food. Riverside seating area, best enjoyed at high tide. A shellfish stall is just past here. Where Riverside turns right, keep straight on and follow the river to the Barrier.

The Thames Barrier. The North Sea is funnel-shaped going south, leading into the Thames Estuary, which is similarly shaped. The combination of an Atlantic low pressure with its strong north wind and a high spring tide can cause a tidal surge and the potential for severe flooding. Planning for flood defences after the 1953 disaster estimated that a severe flood could submerge 45 acres (18ha) of the city and put the London Underground out of action for months.

The *Anglo-Saxon Chronicle* records a major flood in 1099, and Westminster Hall was flooded regularly until Bazalgette embanked the river in the 1870s. Defences were raised on an ad hoc basis until the 1953 storm surge killed over 300 people in England (and many times that number in The Netherlands) and concentrated minds. The result, 30 years and £634 million (more like £1.75 billion today) later, was the Thames Barrier.

The river is 520m wide at this point, and the barrier consists of ten huge steel gates. Four of the six central gates between the stainless steel-clad caissons provide navigable channels 61m (200ft) wide. These gates are 20m (66ft) high and weigh 3700 tonnes each with their counterweights. They are flanked by two smaller gates 30m (100ft) wide. All six gates, curved one side and flat the other, normally lie in a concrete housing on the riverbed. Machinery in the caissons rotates the gates to a vertical position when needed. They can also be turned through 180° clear of the water for maintenance. The four non-navigable gates by the banks are parked horizontally above the water and lowered into place. A tunnel links the caissons. Apart from maintenance and annual testing, the gates are closed only as needed, not at all some years and up to a maximum of 24 times in 2000-01.

Getting there. The 177 bus runs from Greenwich town centre (Nelson Road) to the Greenwich Trust School stop, backtrack a few yards, and follow the strip park or Eastmoor Street to the Barrier. The same bus continues to Woolwich Arsenal stations (DLR and Elizabeth Line). Woolwich is also served by Thames Clipper, and many bus routes.

Walking. Thames Barrier to the Woolwich Free Ferry is 1¼ miles (2.0km) along the river bank.

32. THAMES BARRIER TO THE WOOLWICH FREE FERRY

The riverside path goes through a tunnel beside the barrier; if this is closed, you have to walk around the control building and back to the river. Odd bits of machinery are scattered about artfully. Climb the steps to regain the riverside. At the end of the lower riverside walk, there is a memorial to 2100 people who lost their lives in the floods of 1953. The **Visitor Centre** and **café** here were closed at the time of writing. A notice on the door says that they were funded by the conference rooms and that revenue had dried up as a result of Covid.

From here, you walk away from the river until you see a ramp leading up to the left into Bowater Road. The building on the left was the Faraday cable works, scheduled for renovation as a school. Cables made here formed the first undersea telegraphic connection to North America; cables remain more important than satellites for internet connection. At the end of Bowater Road, turn left into Warspite Road towards the river. On the left is **New Trinity Wharf**, which replaced the one at Trinity Buoy Wharf over the river. To the left is an industrial estate containing :

Trinity Wharf Arts Cafe, Harrington Way, SE18 5NR. Open weekdays only until 1700. Terrace overlooking the river. Apparently, an Ethiopian restaurant is open Saturdays (we missed it).

The *Royal Iris* was a Mersey ferry built by Denny of Dumbarton on the Clyde in 1950. It was fitted out for day excursions with proper kitchens, a dance floor, and so on. The Beatles and Gerry and the Pacemakers played aboard, and Queen Elizabeth II and the Duke of Edinburgh were passengers. Taken out of service in 1991, it briefly became a floating nightclub in Liverpool. Despite grand plans, it has ended up here in its present sorry state.

Over the river is the huge Tate and Lyle sugar refinery. Two muzzle loading cannons on traversing mounts indicate arrival at the old **Royal Naval Dockyard**, now completely redeveloped. You cross two graving or dry docks, and then, at a slipway, construction work forces you to detour to the main road and follow that to the ferry.

The **Woolwich Free Ferry** opened in 1889. Modern vehicle ferries built in Poland have replaced the old paddle steamers, but it's still free! One of the two ferries is named *Dame Vera Lynn* (1917-2020) after the songstress who came from nearby East Ham. She achieved fame during the Second World War as the "Forces' Sweetheart" for her efforts in entertaining troops all over the war zones. Her signature tune was the nostalgic *We'll Meet Again* – a promise unfulfilled for all too many of her audience.

When the ferry is closed, as it may be for a very high tide or fog, the alternative is the **Woolwich Foot Tunnel**. Opened in 1912, the tunnel provided access for dock workers at the Royal Docks from their homes in Woolwich. Like the Greenwich Foot Tunnel, the termini are two red brick rotundas with copper roofs.

Woolwich itself is an ancient town, probably established by the Romans, traces of one of their cemeteries having been found. Well before the time of the Domesday Book, it was known as Uuluuich. Henry VIII took advantage of its Thames-side position to establish one of his many **Royal Dockyards** in 1512. One of the first ships built here was the *Henry Grâce à Dieu*, popularly known as the *Great Harry*, the flagship of his new Royal Navy. Later, in the reign of Queen Elizabeth, ships were built for Sir Francis Drake and Sir Walter Raleigh. Woolwich remained a major dockyard for the Royal Navy throughout the age of wooden-built sailing warships. The introduction of iron shipbuilding saw the dockyard closed in 1869.

Various military establishments sited in **Woolwich Warren** in the 17th and 18th centuries became known as the **Royal Arsenal** from 1805. The Royal Military Academy, begun in 1721 in the arsenal, was moved to Woolwich Common in 1806 into a building designed by the architect James Wyatt. Many famous soldiers, including Field Marshal Lord Kitchener, Major-General Charles George Gordon, and Major-General Orde Wingate received their training in this building,. The academy at Woolwich closed when it was amalgamated with the Royal Military College at Sandhurst in 1947 to form the new Royal Military Academy, Sandhurst.

During the Second World War, the Royal Arsenal employed around 40,000 workers on munitions production. It was considerably reduced in size in the late 20th century, much of its land being turned over to housing development.

The Royal Artillery Barracks on Woolwich Common, together with a nearby building known as the Rotunda (long used as a gun museum), became the home of the **Royal Artillery Institution Museum**. The museum was closed in 2016, apparently because Greenwich Council wanted to create a taxpayer-funded "cultural centre". There are currently no plans for its re-establishment. Similarly, the Royal Artillery's **Afghan and Zulu War Memorial w**as moved from Repository Road to Larkhill Garrison in Wiltshire, a place inaccessible by public transport.

There is thus very little to see in Woolwich away from the river. There is, however, the ruin of **St George's Garrison Church**. This large church, built in 1862-63, is interesting architecturally as it combines Romanesque and Byzantine elements. It was pretty much destroyed by a V-1 flying bomb in 1944, though parts of the Venetian mosaic work survive.

Woolwich Cemetery, King's Highway, has a memorial to victims of the *SS Princess Alice* disaster (see Southend) in the Thames in 1878, but this is a long way from the river.

Getting there. Woolwich Ferry stop on the 177 bus route between Greenwich and Woolwich. Woolwich station (Elizabeth Line) and North Woolwich DLR station; from either station follow №1 Street from opposite the Woolwich Arsenal Gatehouse to the river and the Thames Clipper Woolwich Arsenal Pier. Turn left and follow the riverside path for roughly 600yds (550m) to the Woolwich Free Ferry.

33. WOOLWICH FREE FERRY TO THE LONDON CABLE CAR

This section, on the north bank of the river, makes a circular walk back to the London Cable Car.

There is no riverside path between the north bank ferry terminus and the Thames Barrier Park. As you walk from the ferry, note the flood barriers that slide across the road. Follow Pier Road as it turns north. The building on the corner is **North Woolwich Old Station**, once a railway museum. It was planned to be one terminus of a heritage steam railway, but the Elizabeth Line (formerly Crossrail) took over its tracks. On your right are the **Royal Victoria Gardens**, opened in 1851, the year of the Great Exhibition. One William Holland, who operated a funfair here, escaped his creditors in style – by balloon. Continue on Pier Road, not an exciting walk, until you reach King George V DLR station and take the train west to Pontoon Dock DLR station.

From Pontoon Dock, walk to **Thames Barrier Park**. The park is pleasant enough but scarcely merits a visit as the views of the barrier are better from the southern bank. The café is closed, and the toilets seem unlikely to last much longer. From the park, walk west along North Woolwich Road to Mill Road and follow that and Rayleigh Road past an old chimney until you reach the Royal Victoria Dock.

The Royal Docks were the last built and largest of London's docks. The Victoria Dock was built by the St Katharine's Dock company to replace their eponymous dock and opened by Prince Albert in 1855. This was extended to the east in 1880 by the Royal Albert Dock. Finally, in the early part of the 20th century, came the King George V Dock. Although smaller than its predecessors, it could take the largest liners of the day, up to 35,000 tons in the case of the *Mauretania*. At the western end was a large graving dock and ship repair workshops operated by Harland and Wolff, the Belfast shipbuilders. This was filled in, and the space occupied by the terminal of City Airport. Altogether, the docks covered 240 acres (97ha) of water and had well over 8 miles (13km) of quays. The Royal Docks were the largest of their kind in the world. They lasted longer than the other London docks but finally closed in 1981.

Over to the right are two historic ships. **SS Robin** (ex-*Maria*) is a steam coaster (1890) built by Mackenzie MacAlpine & Company on the Thames at Blackwall. She is the only surviving British 19th century steam coaster of thousands built. She worked, latterly under the Spanish flag, right up to the 1960s when she was brought back to Britain and restored. A more recent survey proved her hull to be too fragile for restoration; almost complete replacement would have been needed, so she now sits on a pontoon. Not open when we visited, but see: http://ssrobin.com/

Lightship 93 was built in Dartmouth (in Devon) in 1938 for Trinity House. She was in service until 2003 in and around the Thames estuary, notably guarding the Galloper and East Goodwin sandbanks. The ship is currently the studio of photographer Michele Turriani.

Visible here is the huge **Spillers Millennium Mill**. Several flour mills in this area processed grain directly from the ships; at the time, British-grown wheat was good for cakes, but bread needed strong flour from imported grain. The original building, dating from 1900, was badly damaged in a huge munitions explosion in 1917; it was replaced by an Art Deco one in 1933. Rebuilding after further damage in the Second World War resulted in the present building. Restoration of the whole area should see the mills restored as space for business start-ups. In the meantime, the mills have been a popular, not to mention hazardous, target for urban explorers.

Royal Victoria Bridge is 50ft (15m) over the water: the design included an as-yet unrealised glass cabin to travel under the span. The lifts probably will not work, but the tremendous views are worth the effort. Beyond Victoria Dock is the Royal Albert Dock. The centre of the bridge aligns with the runway of London City Airport. On the south side of the runway, which looks as exciting as the old Hong Kong one, is the King George V Dock. To the right as you cross the bridge is the vast **ExCel London** exhibition and conference centre constructed on the site of old warehouses.

You can walk along either side of the dock; both still have cranes in place. Let's take the south side. Towards the end of the dock, **Wakeup Docklands** offers paddle boarding and wakeboarding during the spring and summer. Tuition available if needed; see https://www.wakeupdocklands.com/

The Oiler Bar, Royal Victoria Beach E16 1AG. Tel: 07 588 247 500. Beer and pizza on an old Royal Navy refuelling lighter. Closed Mon/Tues, generally opens 1500. Great location.

Love Open Water, Dock Rd, London E16 1AH. Swimming is banned in the tidal Thames, but you can do it here. Wet suits for hire, full details: https://loveopenwater.co.uk/

The Crystal, a futuristic glass-clad building, is currently used as **City Hall** for the Greater London Assembly. When built in 2012, it was reckoned to be the most sustainable building in the world. The heating bill is reputed to be zero. The GLA moved here from near Tower Bridge in 2019.

On a small pontoon in the dock is *Bird Boy* by Laura Ford. It represents a lost boy with the head of a bird, hoping not to be noticed. Like other of the sculptor's works, it shows vulnerability and menace.

The **IFS Cloud Cable Car**, still known as the Emirates Cable Car from an earlier sponsor, was completed in 2012 in time for the London Olympics. Planning permission had been granted in 1998, but politicking prevented an earlier opening. Intended as part of London's transport system, it is usually regarded as a tourist attraction that requires constant subsidy. It uses a single cable system to support 34 cars, each capable of carrying ten passengers, though it rarely reaches that capacity. The tallest of the towers is 285ft (87m), and the crossing takes 10 minutes, less if busy, as the system can be run faster.

The ride is well worth it for the views. On the horizon heading south is the 719ft (219m) Crystal Palace television mast, built on the site where John Logie Baird operated the first TV transmitter in 1933. The area now known as Crystal Palace comes from the huge glass and cast iron building created in Hyde Park for the 1851 Great Exhibition. It was moved to South London after the exhibition but burned down in 1936. Apart from the mast, Crystal Palace is also home to concrete dinosaurs and the thinking man's football team. The works on the north bank below the cable car are for the two Silvertown road tunnels.

Behind the cable car station are prints of **artworks by Madge Gill** (1882-1961). She was a local woman who, despite a very hard life, produced complicated art works well ahead of their time.

The two blue cylinders on the way to the DLR station are the **Tidal Basin Pumping Station (**1988), designed by Richard Rogers.

Getting there. Royal Victoria DLR station is a short walk from Victoria Dock cable car terminus. North Greenwich underground station (Jubilee Line), adjacent to the O2 Arena, is near the other terminus of the cable car.

Walking. From Pontoon Dock DLR station to the cable car terminus is roughly 1½ miles (2km).

34. FURTHER AFIELD (NORTH BANK)

The Thames Estuary offers much of interest further out from London.

River Lea

The River Lea (or Lee) rises at Leagrave near Luton in Bedfordshire and flows 50 miles (80km) to join the River Thames beside Trinity Buoy Wharf. As the River Lea Navigation it is navigable all the way to the centre of Hertford. There is/was a nice pub at the end of the Navigation, remembered from many years ago. It is possible to walk the whole course of the Lea, though the lower stretches are a bit dour. A branch along the River Stort, as the Stort Navigation, runs to Bishops Stortford. Past plans to link the Lea-Stort Navigations to the Fens never came to anything, but the popularity of leisure boating may yet see the connection made. Once badly polluted, the river is now cleaned up and provides a substantial part of London's water supply.

Tilbury

The first docks at Tilbury were opened in the 1880s by the East and West India Dock Company as they suffered competition from the new Royal Docks. Being downstream offered space to expand and easier access for ever-larger ships. The docks were taken over by the PLA in 1909 and expanded rapidly to include a large dry dock and passenger terminal. Now known as the Port of Tilbury, the business was privatised in 1992.

Tilbury Fort, Tilbury, Essex, RM18 7NR. Tel: 01 375 858 489. English Heritage. Open daily. As the range of artillery increased, London's defences could be moved further down the estuary. Henry VIII built an artillery blockhouse here in 1539-40, and a matching one in Gravesend provided fire right across the river. The present fort was built on the same site in the late 17th century as a result of war with Holland. This is a fine river fort with complex landward fortifications and twin moats. There is an interesting collection of artillery of all ages, and the fort is (usually) a pleasantly quiet place to visit. Simple refreshments and good views. The fort is 1½ miles (2.4km) from Tilbury Town rail station.

World's End, Fort Road, Tilbury, RM18 7NR. Tel: 01 375 840 827. Food but don't rely on real ale. Ancient weatherboarded riverside pub.

The **Tilbury-Gravesend Ferry** is an inexpensive ferry service across the river for foot passengers. It runs every 30 minutes or so from early morning up to 1900 in the evening. The terminal is Tilbury Riverside Pontoon. No service on Sunday. Gravesend is described below.

Getting there. Train from London Fenchurch Street to Tilbury Town (40 mins). Ensignbus service 99 half-hourly from station to ferry and fort.

Thames Estuary Path

This roughly 30-mile (48km) walk runs from Tilbury to Southend-on-Sea. It takes in Tilbury and Coalhouse Forts, several historic churches, and Leigh-on-Sea, famous for its seafood. The path follows the shoreline through wild salt marsh country. The whole route is close to the London-Southend railway line, so is easily split up into manageable sections. Full details here: http://thamesestuarypath.-co.uk/pdfs/TEP

Southend-on-Sea

Sarfend is London's Blackpool, a brash holiday resort to escape the big city – though there are quieter places to do that. Southend is notable for having the longest **pleasure pier** in the world, all 1⅓ miles (2.14km) of it; so long, in fact, that it has its own railway. Looking due south from the end of the pier and about five miles (8km) away is the wreck of the ***SS Richard Montgomery***. This was a Liberty ship (a mass-produced freighter) that went aground and broke its back in 1944. That made her just one of the over 5000 Allied merchant ships lost during the Second World War. The difference is that the *Richard Montgomery* was loaded with over 6000 tons of munitions, mostly aircraft bombs. Much was salvaged at the time, but it is reckoned that if the remainder exploded, it would create a 3.000m (10,000ft) waterspout and a 5m (17ft) tidal wave.

    Southend Central Museum, housed in the former Carnegie Library, has a lot of interesting stuff, including an Anglo-Saxon burial hoard.

    Getting there. Trains from London Liverpool Street to Southend Victoria (1hr) or London Fenchurch Street to Southend Central (50mins); the line to Southend Central should provide views of the salt marshes.

    Walking. See Thames Estuary Walk above.

35. FURTHER AFIELD (SOUTH BANK)

We finish our guide to the south bank walk at the Woolwich Free Ferry, though the path is waymarked for a further 10 miles (16km) or so to the River Darent. God willing, we'll get round to that sometime; meanwhile these notes may be of interest.

Plumstead Marshes

Whilst there is still a lot of industry to come, it is here that you start to get an idea of the wide open spaces of the Thames Estuary. The first promontory, on a right hand bend as you walk from Woolwich is Tripcock Ness, also known as Margaret Ness.

SS *Princess Alice* disaster

On 3 September 1878 an excursion steamer, the *SS Princess Alice,* was returning from Sheerness to a pier near London Bridge. She had on board around 900 passengers. For reasons unknown her captain took the wrong line at Tripcock Point and collided with the collier *Bywell Castle.* The *Princess Alice* broke up and sank immediately. To compound the disaster, 75 million gallons (340.000m³) of raw sewage had just been released from the Beckton works on the north shore. Between 600 and 700 died on the spot, and more in following years from effects of the effluent. This remains Britain's worst peacetime disaster. Monuments to the disaster stand at Creekmouth Open Space, itself the site of a village devastated by the floods of 1953, and in the churchyard of St Mary Magdalene in Woolwich.

Looking across the river you can see the two 40m (131ft) high towers of the **Barking Creek Tidal Barrier**. These support a 300 tonne barrier to close the creek to high tides; at low tide you'll see the barrier raised to the top of the towers. This, and the main Thames Barrier, are the result of a disastrous storm surge in 1953 that breached many of the Thames estuary sea defences and killed 300 people. The village of Creekmouth beside the barrier was wiped out.

Barking Creek itself is where the River Roding flows into the Thames. The river was once the base of the largest fishing fleet in England. Commercial use has mainly given way to houseboat moorings. Just upstream of barking Creek is the Beckton Sewage Works, mentioned above

The **Battle of Barking Creek** took place on 6 September 1939, three days after war was declared between Britain (and France) and Germany. This brief air battle marked the first victories for the Supermarine Spitfire. Unfortunately, due to air control confusion (no IFF in those days) the victims were two RAF Hawker Hurricanes. One pilot was killed and the other parachuted to safety.

Erith

Bazalgette's sewage system certainly cleaned up the river as it flowed through central London. The trouble was that the sewage was pumped to two holding points, Beckton on the north bank (by Barking Creek) and Crossness on the south bank, and dumped into the river on a falling tide in its raw state. **Crossness Pumping Station** is one of the glories of the Victorian steam era. Four huge beam engines survive from its opening in 1864, and one has gradually been restored to working order. Full details: https://crossness.org.uk/

Also here is the **RANG (Royal Arsenal Narrow Gauge) Railway**. This is a new 2 foot (610mm) gauge line close to the contractor's line used during the building of the pumping station.

River Darent

The River Darent is a chalk stream that flows 21 miles (34km) from near Westerham in Kent to the Thames. It is joined by the River Cray shortly before the junction. Its flow has been much reduced by extraction; previously it powered many mills grinding corn and supplied paper mills, the latter needing clean water. A large floodgate at its mouth prevents flooding at high tide.

Gravesend

Gravesend is a port and riverside town of great antiquity. Situated opposite the entrance to Tilbury Docks and the Ocean Terminal for cruise ships there is always plenty of shipping on the river.

Gravesend has two piers. The **Royal Terrace Pier** (built 1844) is the base for the Port of London's Thames Navigation Service which provides pilotage to Tilbury Docks and further upstream on the rare occasions it is still needed. The PLA's operations centre is here and controls all commercial traffic on the river. This is a working pier and rarely open to the public.

The **Town Pier** was built in 1834 and is the oldest surviving cast iron pier anywhere in the world. A pontoon has been added recently, and this is now the boarding point for the ferry, traditionally known as the 'Short Ferry', to Tilbury. The 'Long ferry' used to run to Central London but that is long gone. The Town Quay which preceded it was often the base for emigrant ships to the British colonies in North America.

Gordon Promenade, named after 'Chinese' Gordon, gives a good view of the river and shipping. Nearby is the canal basin, which marked this end of the Thames and Medway Canal.

The **Church of St George**, Church Street, DA11 0DJ. The church is the last resting place of Pocahontas, the daughter of a chief of the Powhatan tribe. She married John Rolfe in 1614 and travelled to London where she became quite a celebrity. Sadly, she died in Gravesend at the start of her return journey and was buried in the church. The exact place is unknown due to a later fire. The statue in the churchyard is a replica of one by Partridge in Jamestown, Virginia.

Gravesend Blockhouse was built by Henry VIII to match Tilbury Fort and provide fire cover over the river. The Blockhouse was superseded by **New Tavern Fort** built in 1778. This was modified in 1868 and again in the 20th century. Open summer weekends.

The Three Daws, Town Pier, Gravesend, DA11 0BJ. Possibly the oldest pub in Kent dating from around 1450. A proper boozer with an interesting menu. In 1873 Tissot painted *L'Auberge des Trois-Corbeaux*, daw being an old word for a crow. Tissot obviously liked The Three Daws, using the same background for several artworks.

Getting there. Fast train from St Pancras International (22 mins) but expensive. Also from London Bridge station (55 mins), the only option on Sundays. Monday to Saturday it is more fun to take a train to Tilbury, visit the fort, and then take the ferry, full details in the section on Tilbury on the North Bank.

3. PRACTICAL STUFF

PLANNING YOUR WALKS

The walks along the two banks are split up according to crossings and public transport. Sections are rarely more than three miles (5km). This means you can easily plan a point-to-point walk along one bank or return to your starting point via the other bank.

The walks

The riverside paths are, by their nature, reasonably level and involve no steep gradients. They are mostly suitable for wheelchair users. The notable exceptions are in Brentford (Richmond Bridge to Kew Bridge on the north bank) and in Mortlake (Chiswick Bridge to Barnes Bridge on the south side) where the path is very broken up. Detours avoid both.

The weather

Forecasting is more reliable than in the authors' youth, but the weather is not for nothing a topic of conversation in Britain. Always check before setting out; www.bbc.co.uk/weather is a useful source.

Clothing and footwear

This is not mountain trekking; dress according to the season and the weather. Comfortable footwear suitable for hard and sometimes lumpy surfaces is essential. Mud is likely in the stages up to Putney Bridge.

Diversions

London is an ever-changing city. Building can cause footpaths to be closed, often for long periods. Detour routes are always marked. Check for updates on our website: www.thamesbook.com

GETTING AROUND

The river

What better way to get around other than the river itself? London's **water bus** service is Thames Clippers, currently branded as Uber Boat. The service runs between Putney and Woolwich Arsenal piers, though services vary at weekends and at different times of the day; always check times at https://www.thamesclippers.com/ before using the service. River Roamer all-day tickets are available. Bikes and dogs travel free, and refreshments are available. The boats are wheelchair accessible from most piers. Apart from their usefulness, you get a good view of the river. Use a contactless debit card or Oyster card.

Other operators run services; some are tourist-orientated and can have a running commentary.

A few **ferries** still provide crossings. **Hammerton's Ferry** runs in the summer months between Twickenham and Ham House. The **Thames Clipper RB4** connects Canary Wharf and Doubletree Docklands on the south bank. The Woolwich Free Ferry connects North and South Woolwich. The Tilbury ferry runs from Tilbury to Gravesend. All but the Woolwich are foot ferries.

Not sure if you would call a cable car a ferry, but the **IFS Cloud Cable Car** (still often called the Emirates Cable Car) crosses the river between the O2 Arena on the south bank and Victoria Dock. The ride is well worth it for the view even if of no practical use.

Overground trains

To the west, Hampton Court, Kingston, Richmond, Teddington, and Barnes Bridge are reached from Waterloo, which is on the tube network.

To the east, you only need an overground train to visit Tilbury Fort, Southend-on-Sea, or Gravesend, details in the text.

Underground

London's **Tube** or **Underground** is an extensive underground railway system, albeit better to the north of the river than south of it. This is the most convenient way of getting around London outside rush hours. Integrated with this are two other networks. The **Elizabeth Line** (formerly known as Crossrail) is a high-speed east-west link; for our purposes, it runs (from Heathrow Airport) through Central London to Canary Wharf and Woolwich. The **Docklands Light Railway** (DLR) is a driverless, often elevated, system serving the former docklands of East London and running out to Greenwich.

Wheelchair access is being improved on the Underground network; see https://content.tfl.gov.uk/step-free-tube-guide-map.pdf. Elizabeth Line trains are fully step-free between Paddington and Woolwich (and at Heathrow); ramps are available at other stops.

Pedants may tell you that the term Underground applies to the shallow cut-and-cover sections of the system, and Tube refers only to the deep-bored parts. In fact, most people use the two terms quite indiscriminately.

Buses

London's extensive bus services are covered at: https://tfl.gov.uk/modes/buses/. Most buses are now wheelchair and mobility scooter accessible.

Payment

Most people now use a contactless debit card, credit card, or linked payment device for all these services. Tickets can usually be bought for cash, but the bus system is card only. Other than on a bus, always remember to "tap out" when ending a journey. Always use the same card; fares are capped daily and weekly, which can save a lot if you travel intensively.

The London **Oyster card** is a pre-paid debit card that can be used on all these services and Thames Clipper water buses. It costs £7 and can be topped up at any station through the ticket vending machines. Its real value is that if lost or stolen, your loss is limited to the amount of credit on the card. There is no effective difference in price unless you are travelling with children, in which case Oyster provides a discount.

Foreign visitors need an Oyster Card if their card simply does not work, and they will save money if the card issuer charges a fee on every transaction.

Senior citizen discounts apply only if you are a London resident.

Cycling

I used to cycle in London forty years ago but would not do it now. There may be more cycle lanes, but driving standards and behaviour have declined, and other cyclists, especially despatch and delivery riders, can be a menace.

London's cycle hire system is currently branded as Santander. Twelve thousand bicycles, both pedal and electric, are available from around 800 docking stations. Full details: https://tfl.gov.uk/modes/cycling/santander-cycles.

Cycling is permitted on the parts of the Thames Path that are bridleways; check before you set out.

EATING AND DRINKING

Pubs, cafes, and restaurants are mentioned because of their location or historical interest. We do not make recommendations; management and staff turn over too often. You can try the various rating sites, but our experience as catering professionals is that far too many people writing reviews either have an axe to grind or no understanding of the subject. Some are clearly unhinged. We have avoided, on the whole, places that do not serve real ale or have obtrusive television screens or loud music. All serve food unless otherwise stated. You will find that most of the chain pubs have standardised menus, usually of the 'chip and ping' variety.

In theory, at least, licensed premises (i.e. those that serve alcohol) are obliged to provide tap water for drinking when asked. The law is less than straightforward, and you should remember that hospitality businesses need to make a profit to stay in business.

TOILETS

Provision of toilets along the banks is erratic, to say the least. Pubs, cafes, shops, and so on are under no obligation to provide facilities to non-customers, though a polite request usually produces a result.

For a long time, "spend a penny" was a polite euphemism for using a women's public toilet. The expression dates from around 1850, when you had to put a penny (1/240 of a pound in pre-decimal days) in the door lock to gain access. Allowing for inflation, that would be about 50 pence today. A useful negotiating point, perhaps.

SPORT

Angling. The Thames may look murky but is clean enough to support a wide variety of fish, including salmon and sea trout. As anywhere else in England, you need a rod licence before fishing on the Thames, and you must take it with you when fishing. Fishing in the river is free between Hampton Court Bridge and Teddington Lock; no day ticket or club membership is needed.

Sailing, rowing, and kayaking are all popular on the river, and some information on joining in is given in the text.

Swimming. The best advice is not to swim anywhere in the tidal Thames. The Port of London Authority bans swimming downstream of Putney Bridge. Whilst it is allowed between Putney Bridge and Teddington Lock, you must be aware of the dangers. The water is cold and full of silt. The tide can run at 5mph (8km/h), and there are dangerous currents and undertows, especially around moored boats and

175

bridge abutments. River traffic, whether powered or oared, is a further risk. If you really want to try it, see: https://loveopenwater.co.uk/tidal-thames/

SAFETY

Personal safety is unlikely to be a problem. However, parts of the walk east of Tower Bridge can be very lonely after dark and are probably better avoided.

Two dangers are worth mentioning. Too many London cyclists, not just courier and delivery ones, are a menace. They think traffic laws do not apply to them, and the police do nothing to impose discipline. Only rely on a green pedestrian light if checked; many cyclists take no notice of traffic lights. The same applies to one-way streets; always look both ways before crossing.

Beware of Thames beaches at low tide. They may look inviting, but the tide changes and rises very quickly (more so than on a sea coast), and egress can be difficult. The surface, whilst looking solid, can be dangerous cloying mud. The Thames RNLI rescue boats often have to deal with people trapped by the rising tide.

4. Sources

We acknowledge the help these books have been and recommend them all as good reading. The same goes for the websites.

BIBLIOGRAPHY

Ackroyd, Peter. *Thames: Sacred River*. Vintage. London, 2008.

Ashley, Peter. *London Peculiars*. ACC Art Books, 2019.

Barker, Felix & Hyde, Ralph. *London as it might have been*. John Murray, 1982.

Bloom, Clive. *Violent London: 2000 Years of Riots, Rebels and Revolts*. Sidgwick & Jackson, 2003.

Chambers, Michael. *Chambers' Guide to London: The Secret City*. Millington, 1979.

Clapham, Phoebe. *Thames Path in London*. Aurum. London, 2018.

Corbeau-Parsons, Caroline. *Impressionists in London: French Artists in Exile 1870-1904*. Tate Trustees, 2017.

Davies, Hunter (ed). *The New London Spy: A Discreet Guide to the City's Pleasures*. Anthony Blond, 1966.

Dickens (Jr), Charles. *Dickens's Dictionary of London 1888: An Unconventional Handbook*. Old House Books, 1993.

Dickens (Jr), Charles. *Dickens's Dictionary of the Thames 1887 from it's* (sic) *Source to The Nore: An Unconventional Handbook*. Old House Books, 1994.

Ekwall, Eilert. *The Concise Oxford Dictionary of English Place-names*. Oxford, 1960.

Fathers, David. *The London Thames Path*. Frances Lincoln. London, 2015.

Hardyment, Christina. *Writing the Thames*. Bodleian Library. 2016.

Harvey, Jacky Colliss. *Walking Pepys's London*. Haus Publishing, 2021.

Hollis, Leo. *The Stones of London: A History in Twelve Buildings*. Phoenix, 2011.

Howard, Rachel & Nash, Bill. *Secret London: An Unusual Guide*. Jonglez. Versailles, 2020.

Inwood, Stephen. *A History of London*. Macmillan, 1998.

Jenkins, Simon. *England's Thousand Best Churches*. Allen Lane, 1999.

Maiklem, Lara. *Mudlarking: Lost and Found on the River Thames*. Bloomsbury. London, 2020.

de Maré, Eric. *Wren's London*. Folio, 1975.

Parker, Philip. *The A to Z History of London*. Collins, 2019.

Piper, David. *The Companion Guide to London*. Collins, 1964.

Schneer, Jonathan. *The Thames: England's River*. Little, Brown, 2005.

Smith, Stephen. *Underground London: Travels beneath the city streets*. Abacus, 2004.

Trench, Richard & Hillman, Ellis. *London Under London: A subterranean guide*. John Murray, 1993.

Vallance, Rosalind (ed.). *Dickens' London*. Folio Society, 1966.

Various. *The Royal River: The Thames from Source to Sea*. Bloomsbury, 1985. [Reprint of work first published in 1885.]

Weinreb, Ben & Hibbert, Christopher (eds). *The London Encyclopaedia*. Macmillan, 1993.

Weinreb, Ben; Hibbert, Christopher; Keay, Julia; Keay, John (eds). *The London Encyclopaedia*. Macmillan, 2008.

Wilson, A.N. *London; A Short History*. Weidenfeld & Nicolson, 2004.

Winn, Christopher. *I Never Knew that about London*. Ebury Press, 2007.

Winn, Christopher. *I Never Knew that about the River Thames*. Ebury Press, 2010.

Plus, fiction readers will probably enjoy Ben Aaronovitch's *Rivers of London* (Gollancz/Orion); it will certainly impart a very different significance to many of the places you walk past.

PERIOD PIECES

These books were published in the 50s and 60s, just as London became a major tourist destination. If you see a copy at a sensible price, buy it.

Anon. *London from the River*. British Travel Association. 1968.

Deighton, Len (ed.). *London Dossier*. Penguin, 1967.

Fletcher, Geoffrey. *Offbeat in London*. Daily Telegraph, 1966. (The author also wrote *Offbeat in the City of London*).

James, Betty. *London on a Pound a Day*. Batsford, 1965.

Lambert, Sam. *London Night and Day*. Architectural Press, 1951 (Reprint 2014).

Nairn, Ian. *Nairn's London*. Penguin, 1966 (and later reprints).

Norman, Frank & Bernard, Jeffrey. *Soho Night and Day.* Secker & Warburg, 1966.
    Corgi, 1968.

WEBSITES

http://www.beerintheevening.com
https://www.derelictlondon.com/boats.html
https://exploring-london.com
www.geograph.org.uk/
https://historicengland.org.uk
www.knowyourlondon.wordpress.com
https://londonist.com
https://www.londonremembers.com
http://mapco.net/
https://www.openstreetmap.org
http://www.panoramaofthethames.com
https://www.streetsigns.co.il
https://thames.me.uk/
http://www.thamespathway.com
https://www.theundergroundmap.com
https://whatpub.com

5. And finally...

THE AUTHORS

John Leak was born in Westminster in 1943, Colette in Manchester some years later. Their previous travel writing included guides to India and Sri Lanka.

They were prompted to write this book by the rapid and ongoing changes to London, especially its riverside. It is interesting to reflect that many of the paths described did not exist in their younger days.

John and Colette have a wide range of interests including history, the arts, architecture, wildlife, and engineering, and you will find all in here. Both are in their seventies and have walked every inch of the two routes.

ACKNOWLEDGMENTS

Special thanks to David and Janella for providing a pied-à-terre in Central London. And to Simon and Sandy, Ken and Shirley, and all our other relatives and friends who have read proofs and otherwise contributed help and encouragement.

UPDATES

We've put a lot of effort into this book, but we don't claim to be infallible! If you spot an error or note changes, please let us know. Email us at thamesbook@outlook.com. We will publish this information on our website www.thamesbook.com. Remember to tell us your name or nom de plume if you would like an acknowledgement on the website.

Printed in Great Britain
by Amazon

45859315R00106